DEEP EDDY

(See Page 243)

TEXAS

THE MARVELLOUS

THE STATE OF THE SIX FLAGS

By
NEVIN O. WINTER

TEXAS CENTENNIAL EDITION

With fifty-three plates, of which five are in colour

GARDEN CITY PUBLISHING CO., INC.

Garden City, New York

Printed in U. S. A.

Texas Centennial Edition
Revised June, 1936

TO

HON. CHARLES M. MILROY
MAYOR OF TOLEDO

FOREWORD TO CENTENARY EDITION

———◆———

The year 1936 will always be a memorable year in Texas, for it marks the completion of the first one hundred years of freedom from political oppression. Although there never has been any regret manifested at yielding the absolute independence of the Republic for the restrictions imposed by the Federal Constitution upon each one of the United States, the name Texan is still cherished. It is not difficult for an orator to arouse an audience to a high degree of enthusiasm by recounting the heroic deeds of the pioneers and the memory of the brave leaders who led the small armies of patriots to victory and honoured death.

During the last score of years much water has run over the dam and many changes have taken place in the Lone Star State. Cities have grown until five municipalities now exceed one hundred thousand inhabitants. Thousands of small farms have been established where powerful ranchers once ruled like feudal barons. Drills have penetrated the earth to a depth of several thousand feet and tapped enormous reservoirs of oil in every direction, until Texas has become the greatest producer of this "liquid gold." More than a million and a half of citizens have been added to the population.

I have visited Texas many times during the past third of a century and for months at a time. Within the last few years it has been my good fortune to motor over several thousand of the one hundred and sixty thousand miles of public roads now in use. Placed end to end these roads would encircle the earth half a dozen times. All of the roads are not good, but one can reach almost any section by an excellent hard-surfaced thoroughfare. Two splendid coast to coast highways cross the state from east to west: the Bankhead Highway from Texarkana to El Paso, and the Old Spanish Trail following the route of the Spanish padres and officials from St. Augustine to the missions of California.

The transcontinental tourist is thus enabled to vary his route and visit many places of historical interest. The Pan American Highway runs south through Fort Worth and crosses the Rio Grande at Laredo, thus offering an inviting trip by improved highway to the City of Mexico and eventually to Panama and the west coast of South America.

"Hurry back!" said the garage owner as I settled my bill in a Texas town. The words sounded strange, and I did not fully grasp the meaning the first time I heard them. "Hurry back!" was the parting valediction of the genial hotel clerk when I liquidated my account. "Hurry back!" repeated the smiling coloured porter as he placed my baggage in the car.

"Hurry back!" It is a friendly expression, which has recurred to me many times since I last crossed the border. I had enjoyed the long journey across the state as on previous occasions. Now I have visited places and countries in extensive travels to which I would not return, if any other promising highway led in the general direction I wished to go. But Texas? Well, they treat you mighty fine down there and, after your first visit, you will be glad to go back.

NEVIN O. WINTER.

TOLEDO, OHIO

PREFACE

WHETHER one is in search of alluring and romantic history, is interested in great natural resources, or is attracted by its mere "bigness," Texas offers an inviting field. The Spanish conquest, with its early missions, has left a deep imprint. The great explorer, La Salle, whose adventures surpass the chimeras of the most imaginative novelist, ended his earthly career on the plains of the Tejas. After a couple of centuries of the rule of Spain, during which the booted and mailed cavaliers of that kingdom misruled the country, followed by a few years as a province of Mexico, there came the Republic of Texas. This Republic is one of the most unique examples of national sovereignty that the world has ever witnessed, for a province of thirty thousand people won independence from a nation of several millions. But these thirty thousand were, for the most part, men of sturdy Anglo-American stock.

Interesting and fascinating as is the history of the Republic of Texas, a nation in an almost undeveloped wilderness, that of the succeeding State of Texas is no less worthy of our consideration. After almost ten years of independence, the Texans voluntarily gave up their sovereignty to become one of the galaxy of States under the glorious banner of the United States. This action is also almost without precedent; but the change from independence to interdependence was accomplished with little friction. Then came the sanguinary struggle to wrest the soil from the aborigines, as well as from the lawless whites and Mexicans, who made it their home.

All of these changes and struggles, and their accompanying influences, have developed the Texans into a people differing somewhat from those of the other States; and these characteristics make the study of Texas and the Texans still more fascinating.

Few persons, unless they have had a visual demonstration, fully appreciate the almost unprecedented development that is now taking place in Texas. The primeval sword is disappearing before the onslaughts of the tractor, with its dozen ploughs. The million-acre ranch is still there, but these princely domains are disintegrating into smaller holdings, a change which is followed by a more intensive cultivation. The semi-arid prairie is in many places yielding to the influence of irrigation. Furthermore, this marvellous State of illimitable distances, which is primarily an agricultural domain, is becoming a commonwealth with great and progressive cities. There seems to be no limits to the Texas of the future. But while we look forward to the possibilities of the years to come, we should also look backwards to the romance of the past.

This State, which has been under six flags, representing as many different sovereignties, is worthy our study and attention. There is scarcely a grove, a canyon, a river, or a valley that has not been the scene of some romantic or daring incident. In fact, we will not thoroughly comprehend the United States, and especially the great Southwest, until we know and understand Texas—the greatest State in the greatest republic of the whole world.

NEVIN O. WINTER.

TOLEDO, OHIO.

CONTENTS

LIST OF ILLUSTRATIONS

———◆———

TEXAS,
THE MARVELLOUS

———•———

CHAPTER I

THE LAND AND THE PEOPLE

MY COVENANT: I agree to STUDY Texas, to TALK
Texas, and to WORK for the upbuilding of my State.

This is a characteristic motto that one will stumble upon
in many places in the great Lone Star State. It is indicative likewise of the character of the average Texan.
He is a natural born, dyed-in-the-wool, unblushing, and
indefatigable booster for his State. And well may he be.
The man who lives in a State whose area equals all New
England and New York and Pennsylvania and New
Jersey and Virginia and Delaware and North Carolina—
nearly as many square miles as the original Thirteen
Colonies—has something to boast about. It is greater
in expansion than Germany and the British Isles together.

I mention these comparisons because every Texan does.
On my first visit to that State, several years ago, in the
course of a conversation, a great burly citizen, the brim
of whose hat spread from shoulder to shoulder, abruptly
said:

"So you have never been in Texas before?"

1

The answer was in the affirmative.

"Well, stranger, it is a great country," said he. "Do you know that it is six times as big as New York, and——"

"Oh, yes, I know all that, but size is not everything."

"Well, sir," he continued, in the drawl peculiar to that State, "it is filled with a great people, and you'll like Texas."

He was right. I did like Texas, and several subsequent visits have only deepened the impression. The descendants of those who died in the Alamo, of those who followed Houston in his retreat before the Mexicans, and finally turned on their pursuers with destructive energy at San Jacinto, the traditions of the revolution and the independence that followed, the indomitable determination of those colonists and pioneers who wrested this land from the savages, has left an imprint of courage, self-assertion, virility, and hatred of subservience that characterizes the Texans of to-day in spite of the intermixture of races and nationalities that has followed.

Texas, indeed, is a land of illimitable distances. In journeying from Texline, on the northwestern corner of the Panhandle, to the mouth of the Rio Grande in a direct line, one travels farther than from Chicago to New York. From El Paso to the Sabine River, on the border of Louisiana, the distance is barely a hundred miles shorter. Just turn the State completely over and Brownsville would almost obliterate Winnipeg, Canada. A Texas editor puts it in this epigrammatic way: "If you tipped the State up and dropped it north like a tossed pancake, it would knock down the skyscrapers of St. Paul; and east, El Paso would drop into the Atlantic; and south, the State would blot out most of Mexico. Of course Texas is big; children in school learn that it is big." The

A GRAZING SCENE

rest of us, who live in smaller States, must also admit that Texas is big, for it possesses an area of a quarter of a million square miles and several thousand more besides.

To travel across Texas by the fastest train now running requires one full day and several hours over. The Rio Grande forms its boundary for nearly eight hundred miles, and the Gulf of Mexico washes four hundred miles of its border. Hence it is that one's discursions throughout Texas are measured not by hours but by days. But it is not unending monotony. There is as much divergence in Texas climate as there is between Florida and Connecticut. In the southern counties the orange, the lemon, and other citrus fruits grow luxuriantly; in the Panhandle, a precipitation of two feet of snow is not uncommon. While the cattle out on the Staked Plains, at the top of the Panhandle, are suffering from a driving blizzard, the bananas are ripening in the warm sunshine near Brownsville. In the east there is a broad timber belt which, while only an inconsiderable portion of the State, is in itself larger than any one of a dozen of our commonwealths. There is a black waxy prairie, on which cotton grows to perfection, which is vaster than the great State of Ohio. It possesses more wheat land than the Dakotas, and is vested with more corn land than Illinois.

Proceeding from the east to the west the rainfall continuously decreases. The splendid pines and oaks of East Texas gradually give way to less pretentious growths until even the sturdy and stubby mesquite succumbs to the insignificant sage brush. Thus it is that one finds a wonderful diversity of physical features in Texas. This unconformity is caused by the variety of climate and geological conditions. The Gulf Coast region is uplifted

but little above sea level. This district is from fifty to
one hundred miles in width. The greater part of it presents many features of a subtropical province. Though
it is low, most of the coast land is well drained, and
only a small portion of it is under cultivation.

The eastern portion of Texas presents almost identical
conditions with Louisiana. Texas is one of our largest
producers of pine lumber, and there is also a liberal supply of hardwood timber. The forest conditions are very
diverse, comprising the swamp and bayou growths, the
wide territory of long-leaf pine, and the broad region of
oaks to the north. Central Texas is a region of plateaus
and rolling lands, much of it at an altitude of from one
to two thousand feet above sea level. General farming
and stock raising are the principal industries here, alter-
nated with extensive cotton fields. It has large areas of
fertile soil and a temperate climate.

Away out in Northwestern Texas is found the great
Panhandle section. This consists generally of high plateaus at an altitude of from three thousand to four thousand feet. It comprises forty-four counties, with an area
about equal to Pennsylvania. For a long time the Panhandle was almost exclusively a thinly settled stock country, but in recent years its settlement has been advancing
rapidly. The rainfall varies from fifteen to twenty-five
inches annually, but the fertile soil yields good .returns
under proper cultivation. Western Texas is still more
arid. Here is a region of broad valleys and many ridges,
interspersed with some lofty mountains that loom up nine
thousand feet above the level of the sea. Very little
of this section, with a rainfall of from ten to fifteen
inches, is desert, for thousands of cattle graze in the
valleys and on the slopes of the mountains. Two great
rivers, the Rio Grande and the Pecos, traverse this belt,

and a number of local irrigation projects have grown up along them.

Texas is, and probably always will be, pre-eminently an agricultural State. Notwithstanding that the climate is extremely varied, it is generally mild, and the soil is fertile. Only a small portion of the state is as yet under cultivation, and yet the total of products produced is enormous. It already produces one-third of the aggregate amount of cotton grown in this country. Nevertheless, it is claimed that not more than one-tenth of the land suitable for cotton is under cultivation. If that statement is true, Texas could market forty or fifty million bales of cotton yearly.

Although the greater part of Texas is watered, the question of water is all important. The more water there is, the more cattle that can be owned. The grass may become short, and the rancher looks upon it philosophically. Cattle will eat almost anything under the compulsion of hunger. If the wells or rivers are failing, however, great excitement results. Hence a story is related which illustrates this characteristic. A wild-catter bored a well on a ranch with the hope that he might discover another Spindle Top pocket. He handed over to the rancher the tidy sum of five thousand dollars for the privilege of sinking the well. When the well was completed, no oil appeared—but a great overflowing well of pure water gleefully bubbled forth. The well driller was disgusted, but the rancher danced with joy. He was far happier than if oil had been found, for water added thousands upon thousands of dollars to his land. He repaid the money to the driller with a handsome bonus besides. The artesian wells found in several sections of Texas have opened up to farming and gardening immense tracts aggregating millions of acres.

"It will be a sad day for the country when the ranches disappear," said a big rancher to me. I felt like agreeing with him. To watch the day die over one of the distant plains is a rare privilege. To look out across miles and miles and then more miles of grass, fringed with mesquite, and in places dotted with sage brush or prickly pear, to where sky meets earth, is an experience worth seeking for; to close in the view with a fringe of blue hills standing clearly outlined against a cloudless sky in which the stars are beginning to appear is wonderful.

"There's a hundred-dollar fine against carryin' a shootin'-iron in Texas these days," explained a rancher to me. Some of the picturesqueness of the ranch life has gone. The cowboys do not stand around wearing the "chappies," and with revolvers stuck in their belts as suggested by moving pictures. The cowboy is not extinct, but he is a changed creature. He is a part of a business establishment, and he generally conducts himself as such. The boss and the superintendent are far more likely to ride in a six-cylinder automobile than on the back of a horse.

"*Tempus fugit*," said the Roman writer, and the expression is just as true to-day. The days of the million-acre ranch have already ended. In a few years the one-hundred-thousand-acre ranch is likely to be infrequent, and farms of a thousand acres will supplant it.

Were Texas peopled to-day as thickly as is Holland, it would contain more than one hundred millions of human beings, almost as many as are found in the entire Union. Just step into the crowded east side district of our metropolis and you will discover thousands of people, men, women and helpless little children, huddled together in a cluster of rookeries extending over a few city blocks only. There is scarcely sufficient breathing room for all, and it makes you sigh. Here on these bound-

DAVID CROCKETT

less plains of Texas is elbow room and breathing space and distant vision for as many millions as there are thousands now on a single ranch. There is soil as splendid as any in these United States, with rain enough for ordinary farming, and water in abundance not far beneath the surface. If the entire population of our land was put into Texas, that State would not be as crowded as are some of the New England States to-day.

Will they come out where unpolluted air and freedom await them? Not voluntarily, perhaps. Forcible dissemination of these gregarious city dwellers, from which the flotsam and jetsam of humanity arise, would accomplish wonders in the upbuilding of the race and the solution of many vexatious problems. Each year scores of thousands of real Americans emigrate from between the Atlantic and Mississippi, and disappear like the turgid flood of the Red River sinks from sight in the desert sands. They are absorbed by the level-horizoned lands which lie under the haze of the Southwest. A large percentage of these settle in Texas.

It is the race for cheaper lands—the unconscious effort of the nation to maintain its balance. The Poles, Hungarians, Lithuanians, Jews, and Italians take their places back East. The American-born demand greater freedom—less subjection to industrial conditions. Not many of the foreigners—excepting Mexicans, of course —reach Texas. Ninety per cent of them never cross the Father of Waters. The men who are developing Texas hail from the Middle Western States, and from Iowa, Kansas and Nebraska. Oklahoma developed as much in fifteen years as did Kansas in forty years. The same progress is now being made in many parts of Texas.

There is an originality about the Texan that thrusts itself out in many ways. It is amusing to study the names of the counties. There are several Davis counties in the South, but in order to avoid confusion as to identity, Texas has a Jeff (not Jefferson) Davis county. Then Tom Greene has a large block of land named after him, a Tom Greene County. And Tom Greene well merits such a distinction. Way up in the Panhandle it rather startled me to see on an imposing courthouse the name "Deaf Smith County." Now there are many Smiths in Texas, but there can be no confusion about the hero bearing that name. His full name was Erasmus Smith, but his infirmity induced the nickname. He was a splendid example of the hardy frontiersman, thoroughly at home in the wilderness, with a passion for the loneliness of the prairie and forest. The county named is a memorial to this Texan pioneer.

Not many years ago down in southeastern Texas they wished to honor a local political leader, so a generous section was carved out of another county and named Jim Wells County. Jim Wells has since passed to his reward. Governor James S. Hogg likewise had the distinction of giving his name to Jim Hogg County. Your map may not reveal all the counties, since they make a new one every now and then, so a map of Texas becomes obsolete after a time. It would not be surprising to find a "Ma Ferguson County" established some day, for former Governor Miriam Ferguson, one of two women thus far honored by election to the highest office in the gift of a state, is almost universally referred to in this way. The only constitutional restriction is that a new county shall have an area of not less than seven hundred square miles, and it must not be nearer than twelve miles to the county seat of the county from which it is taken.

They now have two hundred and fifty-four of these subdivisions in Texas. The names of the counties contain quite a complete roster of the noted men in the history of the State. None are diminutive in area, but some are exceedingly meagre in population. In one of them, after thoroughly searching around among the mesquite and prickly pear, some thirty-two voters were discovered at a general election not very long ago. Hidalgo and Cameron Counties in southernmost Texas would hold two and a half Delawares, or one Connecticut. In the viewpoint of some old-time cattlemen this would constitute a sizable cow-lot. These two counties are dwarfed by the side of Brewster or El Paso.

The population of Texas is as diversified as her landscape. There is a discernible disparity in the men from the rice fields and the cotton fields, the piny woods and the *Llano Estacado,* the bustling cities, and the mesquite-covered ranges. The early settlers were generally Southerners with their slow drawl. Yankees followed up with their nasal twang. Settlers from the Middle West entered in with a burr on their tongues. The life on the plains developed a class of free-stepping men who had a picturesque language of their own.

There are counties in the eastern part of the State where the negroes are as numerous as in the "black belt" of Alabama; in others, they are not permitted to reside. As some one has put it: "Texans hate the negro, are fond of the negro, consign him to perdition, and declare they cannot get along without him." It all depends on which section of Texas you have in mind. In Houston, there are "Jim Crow" cars; in Galveston, a couple of hours distant, such a thing is unknown. Down in Hidalgo and Cameron Counties, more than half the inhabitants are Mexicans; in Bowie or Red River Counties a Mexican is unknown unless he happens to be a track employé along the railroad.

The population of Texas has increased from about thirty thousand in 1836 to six million in time to celebrate the first centennial of the establishment of the Republic in 1936. The cities everywhere are growing in numbers and inhabitants. Many little cities have increased from one hundred to one hundred and fifty per cent in ten years. The boom is not confined to any one section but spreads all over the State, from Texarkana to El Paso, from the remotest corner of the Panhandle to Brownsville. If one compares the Texas of today with the Texas of a quarter of a century ago, the transformation is almost unbelievable. Counties, which had difficulty in finding enough voters to conduct the elections at the beginning of this century, now enumerate several thousand contented folks.

Houston has passed all her rivals in the competitive race and now has a population exceeding three hundred thousand. Its enterprising citizens brought the Gulf of Mexico to its very doors, which resulted in making it the premier city. Dallas has more than a quarter of a million inhabitants and is still hopeful of regaining first place. San Antonio follows along as a close third. Each of these cities is the metropolis of a large and prosperous area. Only thirty miles from Dallas is the hustling rival city of Fort Worth, which has gathered one hundred and sixty thousand people within its corporation boundaries.

Galveston is a record of achievement almost unparalleled. Six thousand of her inhabitants perished and twenty million dollars worth of property was destroyed in 1900 by hurricane and devastating flood, but today the city is greater than ever, and it has provided against the recurrence of such a disaster. It is a good example of Texas pluck. Amarillo, Port Arthur and Wichita Falls have entered the growing cities of fifty thousand or more. It is a long, long journey from Houston to El Paso, with many changes of scene. In many ways El Paso is an isolated city, for it is hundreds of miles east or west or north to an important city. Although in a sparsely inhabited region, it is for that reason a most important business centre, exceeding one hundred thousand. Situated as it is, on our Southern frontier, with only the river separating it from our neighbouring republic, El Paso handles a large proportion of our Mexican trade.

Half a century ago Waco was an Indian village; now it is a progressive city of fifty thousand inhabitants. It is situated on the banks of the Brazos River, in the central part of the State, and is the metropolis of one of the most productive cotton-growing districts. Austin is the capital and, while not increasing so rapidly as some other Texas towns, is an important centre of civic and educational interests. Beaumont is another of the important towns of Texas. The discovery of phenomenal deposits of oil here in 1901 gave wide fame to this city of the coastal plain.

No State of the Union has enjoyed a more remarkable history than Texas. It was two hundred years after the discovery of America before the State had even an official designation. In fact, its boundaries were scarcely definite enough to claim such a distinction. The present appellation is explained in several different ways. Some say that it referred to the covering of the tents or wigwams of the Indians, the plural of which was Tejas. In that event this State would be "The Land of Tents." Another exegesis is that the Spaniards were greeted with the cry of "Tejas! Tejas!," which meant paradise. There are many Texans who aver that they are very well satisfied with this interpretation. The origin of the name is generally accredited to that of a tribe of Indians, or confederation of tribes, who dwelt on the shores of the Gulf. The name of these savages was generally spelled Tejas, and many of the earlier Spanish manuscripts adopt this spelling, but in either case the pronunciation would be the same. They could not have been very numerous, for the early explorers would frequently journey for days without seeing one red man. The name Nuevas Filipinas was tried for a while by the authorities, but Tejas, or Texas, finally prevailed.

Six flags have flown over Texas, including the banners of three foreign powers—France, Spain and Mexico. First came the French flag, which was carried down the Mississippi River to the Gulf of Mexico by the intrepid La Salle; following this was the Spanish emblem, first thrown to the breeze under the direction of the Franciscan priests; then came in succession the Mexican flag, and the Lone Star emblem of the Republic of Texas; the Stars and Stripes followed the Lone Star, but was supplanted for a time by the Stars and Bars of the Confederacy. In the struggle for ascendency among these various groups it is needless to say that much blood has been spilled, and countless tragedies have taken their places on the pages of history. For almost ten years Texas was an independent republic, with ministers at foreign courts as well as at Washington.

In 1895, when the Texans celebrated their first semi-centennial of statehood, there were people still living over whose heads had flown the Spanish flag, the Mexican flag, the Lone Star emblem, the Confederate flag, and the glorious starred and striped banner of the United States. It is only a little over a hundred years since Captain Zebulon Pike returned from his exploration of the Spanish province of Texas, and presented his report to President Jefferson about this almost unknown land.

Much history has been made since the long hike of old Zeb Pike, but it is a glorious record that vitalizes the spirit of every Texan to-day. The Texas child is required to study the history of the State—and he never forgets it. The tradition of Texas thus becomes a part of the daily life and thought of the State. One cannot do otherwise than admire this pride of the Texans. Few States afford such heroes as Stephen Austin, Sam Houston, David Crockett, and Ben Milam for a background.

The Spaniards sailed along the Gulf Coast in 1519, and were the first Caucasians to visit here. No effort at colonization was made at this time. Chevalier La Salle skirted the shore of Texas on New Year's Day, 1685, and sailed into Matagorda Bay. He believed it was one of the mouths of the Mississippi, which he had discovered three years previous. He established a colony there, which was short-lived, however, because of the assassination of the leader. A quarter of a century later the Spaniards planted a mission at San Antonio. This settlement was chartered by Ferdinand III, in 1731, with the name of San Fernando. It was subsequently known as Bexar, and finally as San Antonio.

It cannot be asserted that the Spanish *Conquistadores* were successful, for they were not followed by genuine settlers, as was the case with both French and English colonies on the Atlantic Coast. The Spaniards were audacious, venturesome and courageous, and their accomplishments fire the imagination. But the wanderings of De Soto, Coronado, and Cabeza de Vaca stand out as conspicuously for their fruitlessness as their prowess and fortitude. English colonists were satisfied with the New World, in spite of its newness and hardships, because of their dissatisfaction with the tyranny of the home government. Spanish colonists preferred the old home; they

sought America only to secure an easy existence without
labour. The mission establishments introduced priests,
and occasionally lay religious brothers, who endeavoured
to Christianize the natives. Twenty-five of these missions, with the accompanying presidios (garrisons), were
founded on Texas soil during Spanish occupation. And
yet at the time the Americans began their incoming, there
were only a few centres of Spanish settlement. The
Spanish policy had failed as completely at Christianizing
the Indians as it had in peopling the country.

Mexico accomplished little more in Texas. Whereas
the Spanish yoke had been endured for a hundred years
and more, the Mexican was overthrown in fifteen. The
Mexican leaders had enjoyed an unfortunate political
schooling. The republic was only nominal. Of genuine
republicanism there was scarcely a trace. There was no
peace or agreement among the leaders. Finally came the
arch traitor, Santa Anna. In 1836 the Mexican yoke was
subverted by the brave Texans, and in 1845 Texas entered the Union.

"If it had not been for the almost unparalleled bravery
of the early Texans, this land on which we now travel
would have been covered with cactus, mesquite and jack
rabbits," said a San Antonian to me. And who can deny
it? It is always fascinating to speculate concerning "what
might have been." But here we have something to measure by. Compare the Mexico of to-day, as it exists across
the Rio Grande, undeveloped, unprogressive and revolution torn. Could Texas have expected a better fate had
she remained under Mexican rule? Would not the Mexican civilization have produced here just what it has developed across the river? It does not seem at all un-
reasonable so to believe.

The reminders of the Spaniards are many. The most

STEPHEN F. AUSTIN, FROM AN OLD ETCHING

noticeable are in the names of cities and counties and rivers. The Nueces means nuts. Trinidad (Trinity) was the Spanish name given to the Ar-ko-ki-sa, as it was designated among the Indians. San Jacinto signifies Saint Hyacinth. Colorado is the Spanish for red, but the Indian name was Pash-o-ho-no. Brazos was probably Brazos de Dios, the arm of God. Then we have San Marcos (Saint Mark), Rio Grande (Grand River), Angelina, Pecos, etc. Among the counties there are Llano, meaning a plain; Bandera, a flag; Blanco, signifying white; Concho, a shell; Frio (cold), Presidio (fortress), and many others. Under the Spanish custom municipalities took the place of counties with us. The Spanish municipalities covered immense territories, and the former names are still preserved in the appellations of many of the counties. The lands were originally measured by leagues and labours, after the Spanish custom, but sections have generally taken their place. Likewise an abstract of title to Texas lands will show many transfers by varas, instead of by our more common designations by acres.

Texas has always maintained her own individuality. The United States has never exercised control over her government. She never was a territory. When Texas entered the Union, she came in under her own terms. The act provided that the State reserved the ownership and control of her own public domain, and that her territory should not at any time be subdivided except by the consent of her own people. This was a unique condition which no other State has enjoyed. At that time Texas claimed a territory greater by one hundred thousand square miles than to-day. Some of her extensions to the north and west were transferred to the United States for ten million dollars, and now constitute the eastern half of New Mexico and parts of other States. It is still a sizable commonwealth, however, with one hundred and seventy million acres of land.

Texas possesses a public land policy of her own which is materially different from that of all other commonwealths, the main feature being that it grants larger areas to the settler. The Republic of Texas possessed little cash, had no credit, but owned much land, and hence there were liberal grants of land. The new State was confronted with identical conditions. A few years ago several million acres were given to a syndicate as payment for a new capitol. Half of the public domain was set apart for educational purposes. As this land is sold, the principal is invested, and only the income is used for educational purposes. Thus the education of the future youth is assured.

This liberal provision for education began back in the time of the republic. The Constitution of 1836 says: "It is the axiom of political science that unless a people are educated and enlightened, it is idle to expect the continuance of civil liberty, or the capacity of self-government." President Lamar, in his first message to Congress, urged appropriations of four leagues of land for school purposes to each county, and this recommendation was enacted into law. A number of years after statehood two million dollars in cash were set aside as a permanent school fund. This fund has been accumulating until to-day it has almost doubled. Subsequent legislation also reserved to the schools each alternate section of land which had been retained by the State in the grants made to railroads or other public improvements. By this legislation it is estimated an area larger than all New England was added to the public school endowment.

Will there ever be more than one Texas? Like a glass

snake it may sometime break apart into several parts.
The contract entered into between Texas and Uncle Sam,
when the republic consented to become one of the United
States, provided that it could be separated into five parts
without any act of Congress. Whether that compact was
abrogated or affected at all by the later purchase of a large
portion has never been decided. Quite recently the people of West Texas have strongly agitated the creation
of that section of the State into a new commonwealth
to be called Jefferson. They allege that the policy of the
entire State is dictated by the more populous eastern portion, and their own needs and desires are entirely overlooked or ignored. Only the future will answer this question, for a prediction is valueless. It is safe to say, however, that this dissatisfaction represents a condition which
may grow and become formidable.

CHAPTER II

BEHOLD the great province of Texas, after a century or more of Spanish attempts at colonizing, with only three centres of Spanish population between the Sabine and the Rio Grande. These nuclei were at San Antonio, or Bexar, as the Spanish generally called it; at Nacogdoches, and at Goliad, which was also known as La Bahia. Goliad at that time contained probably a couple of thousand Mexicans. It is situated on the San Antonio River, about ninety-five miles below the city of San Antonio and forty miles from its mouth. After the defeat of Santa Anna most of the Mexicans abandoned the place. The dilapidated walls of the old mission and a few other ruins are all that remain to mark the old city. The new town of the same name is situated almost opposite the old town on the north bank of the river. San Patricio, the Irish colony, might almost be termed a fourth, for it possessed six hundred souls. The ancient town of Anahuac contained only fifty inhabitants.

The failure of the Spanish method of colonization lay in the aversion of the Spanish creoles to agriculture, and the dangers to which the settlers were exposed. In Mexico the enterprise of Spain was chiefly directed to the development of mines, while the cultivation of the soil was left to the passive natives. In Texas there were no mines to be developed, and the savage natives could

18

GENERAL SANTA ANNA, FROM AN OLD ETCHING

not be made to till the ground. Thus it was that the colonization of Texas was confined to the establishment of a few settlers in the immediate vicinity of the military posts.

Among those who had been drawn to Texas were murderers and manslayers, bandits, and robbers, who had escaped the hands of justice in the States and Territories of the United States. Others were members of outlaw gangs that had been banished from their country, while many were convicted criminals of Mexico who had come here to serve in the army. Fraudulent debtors in the United States skipped away from their creditors during the night, and chalked on their shutters the three cabalistic letters "G. T. T."—"Gone to Texas." To some of these elements all law or restraint was an absolute mockery. These were the scouts and flying columns who preceded the advancing hosts of the Anglo-Saxons.

With the opening of the nineteenth century, Texas began to emerge from that slough of stagnation in which she had been so long imbedded. Henceforth she became an object of attention and a field of strife, until she finally rose to the dignity of an independent republic. It was not an internal development, however, but was due to the advent of another race. At the beginning of the nineteenth century, when American settlers and expeditions began to pour into Texas, the borders of that province on at least three sides were in a constant state of irritation. Along the Gulf Coast, pirates had established themselves at various places and preyed upon commerce of all kinds. The Comanches and the Apaches, in spite of all the efforts made to Christianize them, were a perpetual source of trouble. Although at least twenty-five missions had been established on Texas soil, nearly all of these had been destroyed, and in this work of destruction the Comanches had taken the leading part. The efforts to Christianize the Indians had been just as pronounced a failure as the attempts at colonization, even though the mission establishments had been multiplied. In 1834, a Spanish official, after a complete tour of inspection, estimated its white population at twenty-one thousand. There was but one school in the entire department of Bexar, and that was so poorly supported that it amounted to little.

"What," says this official, "is to be the fate of those unhappy Mexicans, who dwell in the midst of savages without hope of civilization? In the whole department there is but one curate; the vicar died of cholera morbus in September last." He also says: "Money is scarce in Texas; not one in ten sales is made for cash. Purchases are made on credit, or by barter, which gives the country, in its trading relations, the appearance of a continual fair." The Spanish garrisons were filled with the inmates of all the jails of Mexico, who had been turned loose as soldiers. They were about the most wretched and abandoned set of cutthroats and evildoers that ever made an indentation on the soil of any country. Their influence was almost wholly for evil. Many of the people were but slightly removed from barbarism. There was but little foreign export except in skins and furs. The purely Mexican settlements had degenerated rather than advanced in the preceding half century.

When the Americans first set foot in Texas is a matter that history does not make clear. Aaron Burr had evolved a far-reaching scheme to overthrow the government of Mexico in Texas, and, perhaps, some adjacent territory, and set up an independent government with himself at the head. At that time war with Spain seemed imminent, and this might have made possible the ambitious plan of the man who almost became our third president. The failure of war, and the arrest of Burr for treason, made abortive his plans. It is undoubtedly true that adventurers set out into this little known land, singly and in companies, to prospect its riches. Following these came a steadily flowing stream of pioneers, who sought new homes under better conditions than they had heretofore enjoyed. There is proof of instances of isolated settlers before the close of the eighteenth century, but when they came, or from whence they came, is not a matter of known record.

The first real invasion of Texas by Americans was led by a man named Nolan. The real reason for his expedition is not known, and all kinds of conjectures have been made concerning it. It has even been said that the incursion was begun with the connivance of President Jefferson, who had an eye to future expansion. It is definitely known that Nolan was backed almost openly by General Wilkinson, who was commander-in-chief of the United States Army in the Southwest. The avowed purpose of the expedition was to purchase horses for the army. In a previous expedition under a passport, Nolan had proceeded as far as San Antonio, and did actually purchase several hundred head of horses, which he took back with him to Louisiana. The Nolan expedition left Natchez, Mississippi, late in 1800. Three of the party deserted, but with the remainder Nolan continued his journey into the interior of Texas.

The expressed object of the second expedition into Texas was to capture wild horses. Nolan and his men penetrated the province as far as the Brazos River, where they camped and gathered about three hundred wild horses. He undoubtedly had some ulterior object, and the Spaniards were very suspicious. One of his party deserted, and made statements of what he claimed to be the real purpose of the expedition to the Spanish authorities. On the 21st of March, 1801, this party was attacked by a much superior force of Spanish troops somewhere near the site of Waco, and after a fight of three hours, in which the leader himself was killed and three men wounded, the little band was captured. There were in the party at this time only fourteen Americans, the others being Spaniards, or Mexicans and negroes. A trial of these men was held and the judge ordered their release, but the commandant objected, and the matter was referred to Spain. The final decision was that one out of each five of those actually engaged in fighting was to be hanged, and these were to be chosen by lot. Because of the death of one, which left only nine surviving, the commandant decided that the execution of one would suffice. The others were sentenced to hard labour, and only one of them is heard of afterwards.

A decade and a little more passed before any noteworthy American expedition was made into Texas. This incursion was headed by a Mexican refugee by the name of Gutierrez, and a former Lieutenant in the United States Army, whose patronymic was Magee. The filibustering expedition led by Gutierrez numbered one hundred and fifty-eight men when it crossed the border in August, 1811. The Spanish forces were not taken unawares, but they were unprepared and so abandoned Nacogdoches, which was the first Spanish outpost. The Spanish commander notified his government that the people appeared to welcome this invasion rather than assist him in resisting. There seems to be some truth in this, for the little force was swelled to five hundred before it left for

MIRABEAU B. LAMAR, FROM AN OLD ETCHING

the interior and, at its maximum, numbered one thousand.

The avowed object of Gutierrez was to win Texas for the revolution then proceeding in Mexico. The fact that the leader himself was a Mexican undoubtedly attracted many of his own nationality to his command. He won a notable victory at La Bahia, where his army was besieged by the Spanish general for a number of months. Hence it was that, in 1813, they marched to Bexar, or San Antonio, and were victorious over Spanish forces which greatly outnumbered them, and entered that city as victors. Because of the treachery of Gutierrez in murdering in cold blood the Spanish General Salcedo, and his staff, many of the Americans deserted him. Reverses afterwards overtook Gutierrez, and only a little more than half of the Americans with him reached American soil at Natchitoches.

Another noted incursion of Americans into Texas was under the leadership of James Long, who had been an officer in the United States Army and later a merchant in Natchez, in which city the expedition was organized. The avowed purpose was to aid the Mexicans in Texas, but the prospect of material reward undoubtedly was the real animus. Seventy-five men marched out of Natchez, but their number continually swelled until there were four times as many by the time they reached Nacogdoches. At a meeting gathered together here, Texas was declared to be an independent republic, and an administrative system was organized. The new Republic was short-lived, for the Spanish troops broke up the forces of the alien invaders, which had been separated into several bodies. Long himself escaped to Louisiana, but came back, collecting together the remnants of his forces, together with new recruits, and actually penetrated as far as La Bahia, which he captured in 1821. A short time afterward Long was killed by a Mexican soldier while being held as a prisoner, but his men were released.

The expedition led by Long was the last of the filibustering expeditions by Americans into Texas. In a sense, Nolan, Magee and Long, with the men under them, were but the advance couriers of American expansion. The United States had gradually pushed its settled frontier westward to the Mississippi, and had crossed that line when Louisiana became a State in 1812, and Missouri in 1820. The natural line of further expansion was toward the southwest. The filibusterers served the purpose of spying out the country, and of paving the way for the peaceful invasion that was to follow. The opportune attainment of independence by Mexico in 1821 undoubtedly favoured the colonization of Texas by Americans, for it created a glow of friendship for Americans, whose liberal institutions the Mexicans dreamed of emulating. Texas had been laid waste, however, so that nearly all signs of civilization between San Antonio and the Sabine River had been swept away. It is said that in 1820 the total population of Texas, exclusive of Indians, did not exceed four thousand.

Early in the nineteenth century, the United States began to appear as a factor in the troubles of Texas. Before that the French were the immediate neighbours of Spain on the Texas border, and the border had never been definitely settled between the two countries. Nacogdoches was the easternmost outpost of Spanish settlement, while Natchitoches marked the westernmost station of the French advance. In 1762 the French monarch, Louis XV, ceded all of Louisiana to Spain, and the Spanish border was then extended to the Mississippi. In 1800, however, "the Colony or Province of Louisiana with the same extent that it now has in the hands of Spain, and that it had when France possessed it," was re-ceded to France. Three years later France sold Louisiana, with the same indefinite limits, to the United States. The border, so indefinitely described, immediately caused trouble.

As Napoleon had instructed his representative to take possession of the Rio Grande, President Jefferson and other prominent statesmen were inclined to claim the Gulf coast of Texas. But Florida was still more desired, and especially West Florida, a narrow strip along the coast reaching to the Mississippi. The United States, immediately after the purchase of Louisiana, set up claim to a considerable section of the eastern portion of Texas, but this border was finally adjusted in the bargain that was made for Florida in 1819. By this treaty the United States surrendered all claims to territory west of the Sabine River. But many patriotic citizens believed that the government exceeded its constitutional power in alienating national territory, and it was this belief that made possible the demand for the re-annexation of Texas in the Democratic platform of 1844.

One fruitful source of trouble in Texas was the so-called Neutral Ground. As finally concluded by informal agreement, the strip of Neutral Ground extended from the Sabine River to Arroyo Hondo, which was the original western limit of French actual occupation. Although fixed in boundaries on the east and west, the limits were never defined on the north and the south. Neither the United States nor Spain exercised actual sovereignty over this Neutral Ground, and it therefore became the refuge of all sorts of lawless and desperate men who lived by depredating upon caravans. These land pirates formed buccaneer expeditions, robbed traders, and did many other unlawful acts. They had their rules and regulations, their headquarters and their outposts. Their bravery and audacity were unsurpassed, and their fidelity to each other was inflexible. Both the Spanish and United States authorities took measures to stop this lawlessness, but it was impossible to exterminate them wholly. This Neutral Ground finally fell within the boundaries of Louisiana, and therefore of the United States, in 1819, and the outlaws were driven out.

At some time in the future it may be that the real significance of the pioneer, and the debt we owe to him, will be fully appreciated. We are more inclined to worship military heroes than the man who strikes out into the primeval wilderness, and who forms the vanguard for the civilization that is to follow.

Our gifted writer and diplomatist, Henry Van Dyke, has given expression to this in these words from his poem, *Texas: A Democratic Ode:*

"Men of mark from old Missouri,
Men of daring from Kentucky,
Tennessee, Louisiana,
Men of many States and races,
Bringing wives and children with them,
Followed up the wooded valleys,
Spread across the rolling prairies,
Raising homes and reaping harvests,
Rude the toil that tried their patience,
Fierce the fights that proved their courage,
Rough the stone and tough the timber
Out of which they built their order!
Yet they never failed nor faltered,
And the instinct of their swarming
Made them one and kept them working,
Till their toil was crowned with triumph,
And the country of the Tejas
Was the fertile land of Texas."

The man who was the first American pioneer in Texas, who went there with a truly legitimate purpose and in a peaceable manner, was Moses Austin. He was a native of Connecticut, and had been trained for the mercantile profession. After becoming a partner in a large Philadelphia importing house, he removed to Richmond, Virginia, and then to Southwestern Virginia, where he became a manager of some lead mines. A little later he secured a grant of land in Missouri, on which there were some lead mines. To this wilderness he moved with his family and slaves in 1797, and built up a pioneer settlement which grew and flourished in spite of many attacks from the Indians. Missouri was then a Spanish colony, and Austin thus became a Spanish citizen. With the Louisiana Purchase, he again became an American citizen. Failing in business, he again struck out to lands unknown.

Although in his fifty-fifth year, Moses Austin refused to bow beneath the stroke of misfortune, but retained a firm mind and a resolute heart. With his son, Stephen F. Austin, who was then a young man of promise, he proposed to establish a colony in Texas. It was in the autumn of 1820 that Moses Austin journeyed to San Antonio to open negotiations for the proposed colony, while his son busied himself in gathering together the immigrants. The father made the long journey of more than eight hundred miles to San Antonio on horseback. The Spanish Governor, instead of welcoming the proposition, peremptorily ordered Austin to leave without delay. As he crossed the plaza, however, he accidentally met a man, a German, with whom he had spent a night at a country tavern in one of the Southern States. Through the influence of this German, who was then in the Spanish service, the governor finally approved the petition of Austin that he be allowed to bring into Texas three hundred settlers from the United States.[1]

The meeting with Baron de Bastrop was a chance one, but this accident meant a great deal for the future of Texas, for Austin had become thoroughly discouraged and disheartened. On the return trip the elder Austin suffered such hardship, through being robbed and deserted by his companions, that his health was undermined, and he died in the following summer. Just before his death he received word that his application had been granted by the Spanish authorities, and he left an injunction with his son to carry out the project.

Stephen F. Austin, who deserves the title given him by Sam Houston of "Father of Texas," took up the work thus left incomplete by his father with tireless energy and unfaltering courage. He was now in his twenty-eighth year. At that time he was a circuit judge in the Territory of Arkansas. He was well fitted for this work of engineering a pioneer colony in a rough and unsettled country. He had lived in the midst of a wilderness surrounded by savage enemies, and it was amidst such scenes, where civilization was just beginning to diffuse its refinements, that his character was formed. In June, 1821, with two or three companions, he set out for New Orleans and found some Spanish commissioners waiting for his father at Natchitoches. Although his father had died ten days previous, neither he nor the commissioners were aware of this fact. A report reached him after he had started for Texas, but he continued his journey on to San Antonio. He informed Governor Martinez of the

[1] This German was the Baron de Bastrop, a native of Prussia and a soldier of fortune. He was then one of the alcaldes of San Antonio. It was he who sold, or ceded, to Aaron Burr four hundred thousand acres of land, lying on the Washita River, on which Burr expected to plant a colony as a nucleus for his expedition to the Southwest.

death of his father, and stated that he was ready to carry out the contract.

According to the concession of Austin, each head of a family was to have six hundred and forty acres for himself, in addition to three hundred and twenty for his wife, one hundred and sixty for each child, and eighty for each slave. This was a recognition of slavery as an institution. Single men of legal age were to have six hundred and forty acres each. The first party of settlers was conducted by Austin to the Lower Brazos in December, 1821. The new settlers had many sufferings and dangers to undergo during the first couple of years. A schooner, *The Lively,* had been loaded with supplies and agricultural implements at New Orleans, and sailed for the mouth of the Colorado. She was never heard from afterwards. The failure of supplies and game brought them to great extremity, and the colonists were too weak in numbers to protect themselves from the depredations of the Indians.

The Austin colonists were of a different stripe from the earlier American and Spanish immigrants. They may have been possessed with wild and adventurous spirits, but they were sturdy and honest. Likewise they were active, strong of limb, and inured to hardship from childhood. To them the free air of the prairie and the breath of the forest were like the salt sea breeze to the viking of old. It warmed their blood, but it stirred up real manliness. They were a hardy race, among whom hospitality and truth were almost universal. Many of these men had travelled from beyond the Mississippi in ox-teams, amid all the perils and hardships of the wilderness, and with scarcely a road or a trail to mark the way. The ready rifle supplied game for food and insured protection from savages. Every man knew that in his new home security of life must depend on a steady nerve and a sure aim with his rifle. Some were lost by the wayside, but the survivors were of the strongest and hardiest type of manhood. Some of them were uneasy when the smoke of a neighbour's chimney could be seen from their own cabin door.

Because of some difficulties that had arisen, owing to the change of government from Spain to the Republic, Austin went to the City of Mexico to have his grant confirmed. This entailed a journey of twelve hundred miles or more through a country very much disturbed and unsettled. Difficulties were encountered there because of the mutations of government which followed the independence of Mexico from Spain. A little later President Iturbide proclaimed himself emperor. By these various changes Austin was delayed there many months. The grant was finally re-affirmed, but changed to read that each colonist who engaged in agriculture should receive a "labour," about one hundred and seventy-seven acres, and each one who followed stock raising should be given a square league, or forty-four hundred and twenty-eight acres. Austin himself should be granted fifteen square leagues and two agricultural allotments for each two hundred families he should bring into Texas.

The revised grant was also changed to read that in Texas there should be "no sale or purchase of slaves, and that children of slaves born in the Empire were to be free at fourteen years of age." One important provision of the concession was that each colonist must be a Roman Catholic, or should agree to become such, and that all should be of steady habits and good character. The religious requirement was practically the only condition imposed upon settlers, except that certain improvements were to be made within two years under pain of

PRESIDENT TYLER

forfeiture. They were also obliged to take the oath of allegiance to Mexico. The authority granted to Austin was almost absolute. He was not only to govern the colony, and to administer justice, but was permitted to organize a body of militia, commanded by himself, to preserve good order and tranquillity. As a legislator he drew up an excellent code of laws, although no instructions were given him, and as a judge he administered these laws faithfully and impartially. Several were expelled from the colony under the severest threat of corporal punishment, if they returned, and in one instance he inflicted it. He was given the rank of Lieutenant Colonel. Thus he became commander, law-giver, judge —an unusual trust for one of alien birth.

When Austin returned to his colony in 1823, he found it almost disintegrated. Many of the original immigrants had returned to the States because of the hardships, and the new recruits had not arrived. He went at his work bravely, and conditions soon began to change. His zeal for his colonists knew no bounds. He founded the little town of San Felipe de Austin in the summer of that year, on the Little Brazos River. It was scarcely pretended that all the settlers were Roman Catholics, and the priests probably did not scrutinize their conduct very closely. The scarcity of priests made much trouble. As no marriage was legal unless performed by a priest, the system of provisional marriages by a bond entered into before a notary public was introduced. It was sometimes several years before the opportunity of a priestly sanction offered. Then they were joined in wedlock by the wholesale. But many not finding the marriage state to possess all the alluring charms which they had believed, burned up the bond and were as free as ever. They also paid little attention to the proviso concerning slaves.

Almost the entire work of organizing and directing this colony devolved upon Austin himself. For five years he sustained the burden, and many were the difficulties which he had to overcome. When he was relieved from the government of the colony of 1828, although still a young man, his health had begun to decline. It is quite likely that the tense strain of these years abbreviated his life, and brought about the early death which befell him.

San Felipe de Austin is almost unknown to-day, and yet it still is in existence with a small population. In this town, which in the days of Austin's colony was a mere collection of rude pioneer dwellings and business houses, was held the First Convention of Texas people in 1832, and likewise the Consultation of 1835. It was also the place where one of the first Texas newspapers, the *Telegraph and Texas Register,* was published. Four leagues of land were set aside originally for the town. Much of this land was sold a few years ago and invested, so that it enjoys the distinction of being the only municipality in Texas conducted without taxation. The revenue is more than sufficient to support the city government and the schools. The town is now known only as San Felipe, and the county is called Austin.

Mr. F. W. Johnson, who visited San Felipe de Austin in its early days, gives a good description of life on the frontier in those days: "San Felipe de Austin, though the principal town in the colony, was but a small place. However, it could boast a tavern, store and blacksmith shop and a few American and Mexican families. . . . We visited the store, owned and kept by Stephen Richardson and Thomas Davis, both good and true men. Their stock consisted of two or three barrels of whisky, some sugar, coffee, salt and a few remnants of dry goods, in value not exceeding five hundred dollars. Here we found a number of the *lords* of Texas. They seemed to be enjoying themselves; some were engaged at a game of 'old sledge' or seven-up at cards; others drinking whisky, eating *pelonce* (Mexican sugar), pecans; and all talking. We were kindly received, and soon felt ourselves at home. Here, in the course of conversation, we heard the words *caballada, corral, rieto, mustang,* etc., etc.—all of which were Greek to us, though we had heard the same words used time and again, but felt too diffident to ask their meaning."

Agriculture was conducted in a primitive way. The same writer gives the following account of the methods of the colonists: "We arrived at the busy season of preparing for and planting. Those of the settlers who had sufficient teams were breaking prairie, others were clearing what was called weed prairies, and bottom lands sparsely timbered, but with a thick growth of weeds. When the ground is cleared holes are made at proper distances with a stick, and a corn-seed put in the holes and covered. This done, it is left to grow and ripen and received no other work, except to knock down the weeds; the ground thus prepared and planted will yield twenty-five or thirty, sometimes forty, bushels per acre."

Even while Austin was in the City of Mexico, trying to secure a confirmation of his concession, a number of other persons were there seeking to promote similar enterprises. It was not until 1824, however, that a general law was passed under which such colonies could be formed. This law simply laid down certain provisions and left the actual granting of concessions to the states. It provided that no colonies should be located within ten leagues of the coast and twenty leagues of the boundary of a foreign country, without the consent of the general government, and that preference should be given to Mexican citizens.

In accordance with this law the State of Coahuila and Texas passed a colonization law March 24, 1825. This gave the opportunity of the *empresarios,* as the promoters were called, to enter this rich and new field. Each *empresario* was to receive five leagues and five "labours" for each hundred families introduced. Families engaged in farming at once received a labour of land. If they also engaged in raising cattle, this grant was enlarged to one league. Unmarried men received one-fourth this amount, but upon marriage were given the other three-fourths. If they espoused Mexican women, they received an extra premium of one-fourth more than the other settlers. A small payment in money was required. For ten years the settlements were to be free from all contributions to the state, except in case of an invasion by an enemy. When the towns were established it was provided that great care should be taken "to lay off the streets straight, giving them a direction from north to south, and from east to west, when the site will permit it."

In a short time the whole map of Texas was covered over with the claims of the *empresarios*. Austin himself obtained four additional concessions, permitting seventeen hundred families. In many cases the name *empresario* became almost synonymous with that of swindler. Everything connected with the settlement of the country seemed to be objects of barter and speculation. Hayden Edwards received concessions to settle eight hundred families. Benjamin R. Milam obtained authority to colonize two hundred families, David G. Burnett three hundred families, and Lorenzo de Zavala five hundred families, along with scores of others. Some of these grants

A SKYSCRAPER SPRINGS UP FROM THE PALMS
SAN ANTONIO

were annulled, and others were transferred. A number
of the contractors failed to introduce a single settler.

Immigrants did not come in so rapidly as might appear
from the number and magnitude of the grants. In 1827,
the population was estimated at only ten thousand, and,
in 1830, it had reached only twenty thousand. This, however, was an increase of probably five hundred per cent
in less than a decade. Most of the grants came to naught,
because of the failure of the promoters to fulfil the conditions. There were, however, a number of colonies actually established, but Austin's colony still remained the
predominant one, and, up to the time of the Revolution,
continued the most influential element among the Americans in Texas.

The tide of immigration continued to flow into Texas,
and some of the colonies became quite prosperous. The
Mexican authorities at length became affrighted at the increasing possibility of Anglo-American domination.
They perceived in it a menace to their own security.
Efforts on the part of the United States to purchase
either the whole or a part of Texas likewise excited apprehension in Mexico. In 1829, a decree was issued forbidding slavery within the Republic, and this was directed
toward Texas, which was the only Mexican state in which
actual slavery was practised. A law was passed forbidding further colonization in the border states of
Mexico by nations adjacent, or the importation of slaves,
and this enactment was also directed at the American
colonization of Texas.

An abortive revolution had its origin in Nacogdoches.
It amounted to little, but it was indicative of the general
unrest that was arising. It began at Nacogdoches, probably because that place was so remote from the Spanish
settlements, and was more overrun by intruders than

any of the other settlements. Its proximity to the Neutral Ground brought in many characters who were unwilling to submit to any laws or restraints limiting their absolute freedom of action. One, Hayden Edwards, had obtained a concession for colonizing an extensive territory here, although the authority granted to him was not so broad as that extended to Austin. Edwards undertook to assume powers not granted to him. This brought him in collision with the government of the State. It looked to him, also, as though the favours were all granted to Mexicans. Much confusion arose over titles that had been granted to settlers, who had fled several years ago, when Nacogdoches became depopulated at the approach of royalist troops. A hundred or more of these claimants of all ages, colours and nationalities had returned to the Edwards settlement. Old titles were manufactured by the authorities to order.

On December 16th, 1826, Benjamin W. Edwards, brother of Hayden Edwards, and during the absence of the latter, rode into Nacogdoches at the head of fifteen men and proclaimed an independent republic, which was named Fredonia. They took possession of the Old Stone Fort, and organized a so-called government. They made an offensive treaty against Mexico with the Cherokee Indians, who dwelt near there. Letters were written to many other leaders of colonies, urging them to unite in a common cause. Austin opposed this movement; he not only used his influence, but furnished some soldiers from his colony, for the Mexican government. The insurrection was not suppressed until there had been some actual fighting. Eleven white men and nine Indians opposed the forces sent to suppress them, and in the conflict that followed, one man of their party was wounded and one of the Mexican forces was killed. This was the

one battle of the Fredonian War. On the approach of
Mexican forces sent against them by the government at
San Antonio, the troops of Edwards disbanded and fled
to the United States. The Mexicans entered Nacogdoches in triumph, with the honours of a bloodless victory.

In the hope of giving the reader a more vivid idea of
the hardships endured by the early American settlers in
Texas than any general description can convey, I hereby
subjoin extracts from a letter written by a member of
Austin's Colony:

"COLORADO RIVER, COAHUILA AND TEXAS.

"December 1, 1823.

"Since I last wrote, our sufferings have been very
great for want of provisions. . . . There have been a
great many new settlers come on this fall, and those
who have not been accustomed to hunting in the woods
for support, are obliged to suffer. . . . Those of us who
have no families of our own reside with some of the
families of the settlement. We remain here, notwithstanding the scarcity of provisions, to assist in protecting the settlement. We are obliged to go out in the
morning, a party of us, to hunt food, leaving a part of
the men at home to guard the settlement from Indians,
who are very hostile to us. Indeed, we dare not go out
and hunt except in companies, as we are obliged to keep
on a lookout, lest the savages fall upon us; and one cannot hunt and watch too. Game is now so scarce that
we often hunt all day for a deer or a turkey, and return
at night empty handed. It would make your heart sick
to see the poor little half-naked children, who have nothing to eat during the day, watch for the return of the

hunters at night. . . . If the hunters return with a deer or turkey, the children are almost wild with delight, while on the other hand, they suddenly stop in their course, their countenances fall, the deep, bitter tears well up in their eyes and roll down their pale cheeks. 'Tis truly heart-rending to see us return home after a hard day's hunt without any game, knowing, as we do, that the women and children are entirely without food, and can have nothing until we find it in our hunt. No one can know our sufferings, or even imagine our feelings, unless they have been in similar situations. . . . It is surprising to see how bravely the delicate females bear up under their sufferings without a murmur or complaint. 'Tis only by their looks they show their feelings. When we seem the least discouraged, they cheer us with kind words, and looks, and strive to appear cheerful and happy. They do more when we are worried out with toil and fatigue—they take our guns in their hands and assist us in standing guard. . . . Were it not for the Tonkawa Indians, a small tribe who are friendly to us and supply us with dressed deerskins, we should be almost entirely destitute of clothing. . . . The common dress of men and children is made of buckskin, and even the women are often forced to wear the same.

"Your affectionate friend,

"W. B. Dewees."

CHAPTER III

THE STRUGGLE FOR INDEPENDENCE

THE revolution which had its centre at Nacogdoches, and in which the Fredonian Republic was proclaimed, proved abortive because the hour had not yet arrived. It required almost another decade before sentiment was crystallized to such an extent that a declaration of independence from Mexico was declared. In the meantime, under the liberal immigration policy of Mexico, Americans were thronging in by hundreds under the numerous promoters, or *empresarios,* of colonies. This accretion of the Anglo-Saxons must inevitably result in a separation from the Mexican states, for they would not submit to such an arbitrary government as Mexico possessed, especially when they greatly outnumbered the Spanish-speaking population.

The persistent efforts of the government at Washington to expand its territories toward the Rio Grande gradually aroused the suspicions of Mexico. In 1827, a million dollars was offered to extend its frontier to that boundary, but Mexico refused to consider any proffers. Another cause of suspicion was the comparative freedom of the colonies of Americans from attacks by the Indians, while these hostiles still continued their depredations against the Mexicans. This circumstance induced the authorities to believe that the colonists had some secret understanding with the red men. It was fallacious, but this suspicion was the genesis of a great deal of the trouble of the colonists. It induced repressive legislation against them. Had it not been that Mexico was in a perpetual state of revolution during these early years of her existence as a Republic, the colonists would either have been coerced or driven from the province before their strength was so great. Austin himself remained constant in his loyalty to the Mexican government, and endeavoured in every possible way to remain aloof from the party strife.

The decree abolishing slavery throughout Mexico was the first legislation that aroused general opposition among the Americans. There were probably not more than a thousand slaves in Texas at this time, but it was the principle involved. At the earnest representations of Austin, who feared that this interdiction would mean ruin for his colonies, Texas was exempted from the operation of this decree. Then followed a measure to establish Mexican colonists on the border, and also to prohibit the entry of foreigners from the northern borders without passports from Mexican agents. Convicts were also given the privilege of citizenship when their terms of punishment had expired, thus introducing a class of citizens who were utterly repugnant to the American colonists. The most irritating provisions, however, were those which stopped further colonizations, and that which forbade the introduction of more slaves into Texas. To enforce these laws considerable forces were despatched to Texas, and a number of military posts were established.

The principal port on the Gulf coast of Texas was Anahuac, at the mouth of Trinity River. An officer, an American by the name of Bradburn, was placed in charge of this port, and his methods of enforcing the laws aroused the general opposition of the colonists. He conducted himself with unwarranted license and brutality. The period of six years allowed for the free entry of supplies had expired, and it required a judicious policy to inaugurate the collection of duties. This was precisely the quality that this officer lacked. He became little more than a petty tyrant.

The colonists had consistently continued to evade the payment of duties in every way possible. In retaliation the commander at Anahuac placed under martial law a ten league strip of the coast, and declared Anahuac, a port so shallow that boats drawing more than six feet could not enter, the sole port of entry. In the execution of his duties, William B. Travis, afterwards of Alamo fame, and some other prominent men were arrested and imprisoned for alleged insubordination. Aroused by this act of violence, the colonists arose in force and marched on Anahuac. Bradburn promised to release the prisoners, but disregarded his word. Some desultory firing occurred, but there was no real battle. Bradburn was finally succeeded in command, and the Texans were delivered to their compatriots.

None realized better than the colonists that this violent act would mean serious trouble, if no plausible explanation could be offered. Santa Anna was then just scintillating upon the Mexican horizon as an opponent of the Bustamente government, so the men of the Anahuac expedition promulgated what are designated as the Turtle Bayou Resolutions. The resolutions elaborated upon the devotion of the colonists to the Constitution of 1824, and affirmed their unswerving support of the gallant chieftain, General Antonio Lopez de Santa Anna. It then set forth in detail the many alleged grievances of the Texans. It was indeed a politic move, and served these men, who otherwise would have been classed as revolutionists, an excellent purpose. The Turtle Bayou Resolutions so aroused the people that they decided to expel all the Mexican soldiers. Anahuac was captured after a spirited resistance. Velasco capitulated, and the Mexicans withdrew. The people of the municipality of Nacogdoches marched on their fortress and summoned the commander to declare for the Constitution of 1824, surrender, or fight. A fight followed in which the Texans were victorious. Thus all the Anglo-American settlements were delivered from the military, although there were still garrisons at the Mexican settlements of Goliad and San Antonio.

Santa Anna soon overthrew his opponents, and the Texans then became patriots and not revolutionists. When Santa Anna's commander and personal representative, Mejia, visited Texas, he was everywhere fêted by the Anglo-Americans and treated in every way as an honoured guest. For a brief period the name of Santa Anna was much extolled in Texas, and the colonists could not say enough in praise of his work and his character. But they had no conception of the man.

In August, 1832, a convention was called of the people of Texas. More than fifty delegates assembled at San Felipe, representing practically all the departments of the province with the exception of Bexar. In this convention it was particularly disclaimed that any effort was being made at separation from Mexico. A number of subjects were considered, and resolutions were adopted urging certain requests for the local government of the province. Among these was a demand that Texas be disunited from Coahuila. Reading between the lines, however, one can see that this convention was just as solicitous for any encroachment against its prerogatives, as it was to discharge its obligations to Mexico. Although

Austin was elected President, a third of the votes were cast for William H. Wharton, who was less conservative by far than his successful rival.

The Mexican authorities uniformly condemned this convention. "I deem it my duty," wrote Santa Anna himself, "to call special attention of the President to the condition of Texas. Satisfied I am that the foreigners who have introduced themselves in that province, have a strong tendency to declare themselves independent of the republic; and that all their remonstrances and complaints are but disguised to that end." The sagacious Mexican recognized the democratic tendencies of the settlers who came from the United States, and feared the result. In 1833 a second convention was convoked at San Felipe, and new delegates chosen. This time Wharton was elected chairman. The convention did little more than re-enact the resolutions and memorials of the preceding year. In the petition for separation, however, it went further. A constitution was drawn up, which was distinctly American. The preamble reads as follows: "We, the people of Texas, being capable of figuring as a state in the manner contemplated in the second article of the decree of the general congress of the nation, of the 7th of May, 1824, do ordain the following constitution; and do mutually agree with each other to form ourselves into a full and independent state of the Mexican Confederacy, by the name of the state of Texas."

There is no question that in the months following, the revolutionary impulse was gradually gaining strength. Austin proceeded to Mexico alone to urge the petition of the Texans for reforms of administration. He had a better knowledge of the Mexican government and also of the Spanish language than his compatriots, but he

undertook the mission with misgivings. In the statistics
which Austin carried with him he claimed the total population, including Indians, to be forty-six thousand and
five hundred. The organized municipalities were Bexar,
four thousand, Goliad, two thousand three hundred,
Gonzales, one thousand six hundred, Austin, twelve thousand six hundred, Liberty, four thousand five hundred,
Brazoria, four thousand eight hundred, and Nacogdoches,
sixteen thousand seven hundred. It must not be forgotten, as elsewhere suggested, that the Spanish municipality
covered a large territory, and included numerous small
towns and settlements. We would designate it as a
county. He reported that there were many cotton-gins,
and a number of saw-mills and grist-mills, some propelled
by water power and others by oxen or horses. "Fat
beeves," says he, "of from twenty to thirty *arrobas* (an
arroba is about twenty-five pounds), are worth from
eight to ten dollars. Fat hogs of from eight to twelve
arrobas are worth three and a half to five dollars each."

Austin laboured assiduously for half a year in an effort
to accomplish his mission, but he was compelled to depart with the matter still unsettled. The Mexicans
feared (and not without reason) American domination
if Texas was separated from Coahuila. After his departure from the City of Mexico, which was done openly,
the acting president decided to have Austin arrested, and
he was captured at Saltillo on his return journey and
conducted back to the Mexican capital. He was detained
there for a year and a half, several months of which was
in close confinement, or *incommunicado*. This means
that the prisoner is not allowed to communicate with
any one, not even an attorney. It is indeed a wonderful
system of jurisprudence.

"My room," wrote Austin in a letter to his brother,

"is about fifteen feet by thirteen—very high ceiling—
two doors, one flush with the outside surface of the wall,
the other near the inside surface and within the wall,
which is about three feet thick, of large hewn stone.
The latter door has an oblong hole large enough to admit
a plate, the other is solid. Both were always locked
and bolted until yesterday. No windows, a very small
skylight in the roof which barely afforded light to read
on very clear days, when the sun was high, say from ten
to three o'clock. Quite free from damp except such as
would naturally result from the want of free circula-
tion of air."

During this residence in Mexico, Austin accomplished
a part of his commission, but not the principal object.
Certain reforms in the administration of Texas were
granted, but it was not permitted a separate government.
Among the concessions was an act legalizing the use of
English in official documents, and a greater degree of
local self-government was granted for the Anglo-American portion of Texas. Four new municipalities were
created. Excitement and dissatisfaction in Texas continued to increase, however, and it was accelerated by
the long detention of Austin, the man who had been
most considerate toward the home government. Several
thousand Mexican troops were despatched to Texas, and
this augmented the inquietude. As a result the colonists
began to organize for self-defence, believing that a sanguinary struggle was before them.

When Austin reached Texas, in September, 1835, two
and a half years after his departure from Brazoria, the
leaders were all anxious to know his opinion. He expressed himself plainly in favour of the upholding of the
constitutional rights of Texas and in favour of a general
convention. His feeling toward Mexico had undergone

a radical transformation. Every one seemed to sense that war was imminent, and preparation went forward in many places with vigour. General Ugartechea had been ordered to Texas as the military commandant, and several thousand troops were under his command. The general impression among the colonists was that these troops, who were ostensibly sent to protect the settlements from Indians, were in reality intended to overawe and coerce the colonists. A proclamation disclaiming such a purpose did not alleviate the situation. Indignation meetings were held in nearly all the municipalities. Local committees of safety were organized, and volunteer companies for defence were banded together. As is usual among pioneers, every one possessed a weapon, and it was not difficult to gather equipment for soldiers. Even before members of the Consultation were elected, some blood had been spilled. In June, 1835, Travis, at the head of a small body of volunteers, had marched against and received the surrender of the garrison of Anahuac. But this victory was a bloodless one.

At Gonzales there was a small cannon, which had been furnished by the authorities of Bexar, and the Mexican commander demanded that the people give it up. The people claimed it as a gift and the demand was refused in a curt American way, which implied that if he desired the cannon he might come after it. As a result a cavalry troop of some hundred was sent to take it. The advance guard was captured by a ruse without a shot being fired. Large reinforcements arrived a few days later with positive orders to take the six-pounder. The answer of the Texans was "come and take it." The battle had scarcely begun before the Mexicans were in precipitate retreat. The cannon itself was a small affair, and had never been used by the settlers as they had no balls to fit it. Furthermore, they did not even understand how to shoot it if the occasion offered. They concluded to try it, however, before the Mexicans arrived. A gunsmith of the village hammered out a ball on his anvil to fit the cannon, and it was loaded at his shop. The gun was aimed at a small sycamore tree about three hundred yards distant. The tree was hit and considerably splintered. The gun was then loaded with slugs in anticipation of the approach of the enemy. During the skirmish it was discharged several times, as the gunsmith had provided an apronful of slugs for the purpose.

The engagement at Gonzales did much to consolidate the factions among the colonists. Resistance had become a reality—guns had been fired. W. H. Wharton issued a circular for all colonists to hasten to Gonzales "armed and equipped for war even to the knife." This circular was headed in the following striking way:

Freemen of Texas.
To arms! ! !   To arms! !
Now's the day, and Now's the hour!

A little army of Texans was organized to prosecute a campaign against Bexar. On the way they captured Goliad, where they obtained possession of considerable money and much needed arms and supplies. This little army, which had now increased to three hundred and fifty volunteers, with Stephen F. Austin himself as commander, proceeded against Bexar. The reduction of this town required a campaign of nearly two months. A detachment of forces under Colonel Bowie and Captain Fannin, who had been sent forward to select a position for the main army, defeated a force of Mexicans near Mission Concepcion. A short time afterwards occurred what is known as the Grass Fight. The horses of the

Mexicans were in need of fodder, so that a party of soldiers was sent out under cover of darkness to cut grass and bring it in. They succeeded in loading about fifty burros with the prairie grass, but they were discovered by the enemy. The Texans at once attacked and the Mexicans commenced a rapid retreat. The grass-laden burros kept the road, braying at every jump, and the Mexicans fired back as they ran. A rescuing party was also put to flight. It was a brilliant victory and aided in discouraging the besieged.

After several weeks the siege appeared to be useless. The Texans possessed three cannon but no suitable ammunition for them. About the only cannon balls they had were those fired by the Mexicans. "It was quite amusing," says a report, "to see two or three or half a dozen in chase of the balls, which, when recovered, were from time to time returned in compliment to the enemy." On the 3rd of December, a council of war was held, and it was resolved that the army should retire and go into winter quarters either at Goliad or Gonzales. But the army did not approve of this delay.

"Who will go into San Antonio with old Ben Milam?" shouted Benjamin R. Milam, in a moment of enthusiasm, as he made a ringing call for volunteers to follow him in an assault upon the city. Many shouted "I will," whereupon they were requested to fall into line. When finally assembled at dark for the storming, they numbered exactly three hundred and one. These were divided into two divisions. The attack began just before dawn; the Texans carried one barricade after another, dislodging the enemy in hand-to-hand fighting. At last General Cos hoisted the white flag, after the fourth day, and the garrison began negotiations for a surrender. The Mexicans were allowed to march out

and return beyond the Rio Grande.   Milam himself
was killed, but the Texan losses were small in comparison with those of the Mexicans.   This victory removed
all Mexican armed forces from Texas.

Milam was a native of Kentucky, and was at this
time about forty-five years of age.   He was six feet
high and a splendid specimen of manhood.   He had
distinguished himself in the War of 1812, and had
likewise fought in the Mexican struggles for •freedom
from Spain.   Because of opposition to Iturbide, however, he was thrown into prison at Monterey.   Escaping
‹from that prison, he came to Texas and enlisted with
the Texans.   His name is justly honoured by Texas and
the Texans.

It was during the siege of Bexar that the Consultation
gathered.   The term consultation was chosen, as the word
"convention" in the minds of some savoured too much
of revolution.   It was difficult to get a quorum together,
for so many of the members were taking part in the fighting at once place or another.   It was originally called for
October 16th, 1835, but because of lack of a quorum
was postponed until November 1st.   It was finally organized two days later.   Among the members of this
body were some of the ablest and best sons of Texas.
Like our forefathers, who composed the revolutionary
congresses, these men assembled and were animated by
the loftiest impulses.   Indignant at the misrule of Mexico, they were determined to establish a liberal government which they might leave as a proud heritage to
their children.   Although their election had been informal,
yet the stress of feeling was such that the best men were
undoubtedly sent.   It was not a struggle for place.

A committee of a dozen members, one from each
municipality, was appointed to draw up a Declaration

defining the attitude of the Texans. A minority, even at that time, favoured a Declaration of Independence for Texas. A majority of two-thirds, however, favoured pronouncing for the Constitution of 1824. Hence it was that this Consultation averred that the Texans had taken up arms "in defence of the republican institutions of the Federal Constitution of Mexico of 1824." The battle flags carried by the Texans in their engagements had printed on them in large figures "1824." A provisional government was provided for by this Consultation, establishing both a civil and a military administration. The powers were not very clearly defined, and a great deal of confusion soon resulted.

Henry Smith,[1] one of the extreme radicals, was elected governor by the Consultation, and Sam Houston, who begins to be very prominent, was made Major-General of the armies of Texas "to be raised." Stephen F. Austin, with two others, was made a commissioner to the United States. Governor Smith well stated the difficulties confronting Texas in his first message as follows: "You have to call system from chaos; to start the wheels of government, clogged and impeded as they are by conflicting interests, and by discordant materials. Without funds, without the munitions of war; with an

[1] Henry Smith was a native of Kentucky, and came to Texas in 1821 Owing to a serious misunderstanding with the Executive Council, an effort was made by the latter body to depose him as Governor. The controversy was still unsettled when the Provisional Government was displaced by the Government *ad interim*. He served as Secretary of the Treasury under Houston and filled the position with marked ability. A few years later he emigrated to California, where he died in 1853, at the very time he was making preparations to return to Texas. The origin of the Lone Star is traced to Governor Smith. It happened that the buttons on his coat had the impress of a five-pointed star. For want of a seal, one of the buttons was cut off and used. A little later the flag of the Lone Star was designed, although it passed through several evolutions before the final adoption of a flag by the Congress in 1839.

THE WATER TOWER, FORT SAM HOUSTON, SAN ANTONIO

army in the field contending against a powerful foe.
These are the auspices under which we are forced to
make a beginning."

Peace and harmony quickly vanished, for trouble
early arose between the Governor and the Council, which
was a sort of advisory body. The principal variance of
opinion was over the advisability of despatching an expedition against Matamoras, on the west side of the Rio
Grande. So many complications arose from this controversy between the two branches of the government
that the border defences were left unprovided for. At
no time prior to San Jacinto did the regular army exceed
one hundred, although Houston had made an impassioned
appeal for five hundred men. Finances were also troublesome. Some donations were received from the United
States, but the Texans themselves possessed little wealth
save in land. Austin offered his whole estate to be
mortgaged as the Consultation saw fit. Fannin tendered
thirty-six slaves, and numerous other patriotic proffers
of horses and land were made by the colonists. A loan
was finally floated in New Orleans and New York by
pledges of land.

Alarmed by rumours of a Mexican invasion to recover
Bexar, Lieutenant-Colonel Neill, who was in command
of the Alamo, sent an urgent request for re-inforcements.
General Houston despatched Colonel Bowie with a small
force to his aid. Instructions were given by Houston to
demolish the fortifications and carry off the artillery.
Governor Smith despatched Travis with the men in his
detachment. Soon afterwards Neill, because of ill
health, left for home, and Travis remained in charge
of the troops. This tragic event is treated quite fully
in another part of this work.

A body of troops numbering about four hundred, under

Colonel Fannin, marched to the old town of Goliad. It
had been ascertained that Mexican forces were invading
Texas in considerable numbers, and Fannin awaited
them at the fortress of Goliad. Houston sent orders to
Fannin to destroy the fortress and retreat to Victoria.
After a few days' delay, Fannin began his retrogression.
Before this time his forces had been weakened by small
detachments sent to Refugio and San Patricio in order
to rescue the citizens of those places. None of these
men returned. Most of them were captured and shot.
Several months later the bones of some of these unfortunates were discovered still tied to the trees where
they had been murdered. Word was received from
Colonel Travis of his desperate plight in the Alamo, and
Fannin first started for San Antonio. At a council of
officers, however, it was decided that it was impossible
to reach them in time for succour. The heaviest guns
were spiked, and only the small cannon taken along in
order to facilitate his movement. Five days' rations
and as much ammunition as he could carry were distributed to each man. But the impedimenta was all
drawn by oxen, and that rendered progress slow. The
entire force consisted of about three hundred, including
twenty-five mounted men. The troops were halted in
an open prairie to rest, and here it was that the Mexicans
overtook them.

"Here come the Mexicans!" was the cry that spread
over the camp. Fannin arranged his men in a hollow
square, with lines three deep in order to repel the cavalry
charge. The artillery were stationed at the four angles
of the square. The American cavalry made a recon-
naissance, but were cut off from the main body and compelled to flee. This was a serious loss. Charges from
three directions were simultaneously made by the Mexi-

cans, who numbered more than a thousand. The assault
was deadly, and bayonet met bayonet in some places,
but the Mexicans were finally compelled to retreat. The
fight then continued in a desultory way until sunset.
Anticipating a renewal of the conflict in the morning,
the Texans dug trenches and threw up earthen mounds
for protection. Fannin desired to retreat while this
might be done under cover of darkness, but the men expressed an unwillingness to leave their seventy wounded
comrades.

During the night three men deserted, but every other
man stuck to his post, determined upon victory or death.
Before the sun had fairly risen the Mexican forces were
astir and preparing for another attack. Large reinforcements had reached them during the night. Ammunition was now running short with the Texan forces.
The Mexican commander sent a flag of truce asking for
surrender "at discretion," in order to avoid the shedding
of more blood. Fannin refused this demand, stating
that he "would fight as long as there was a man left to
fire a gun before he would surrender on such terms."
Then General Urrea himself advanced and was met by
Colonel Fannin, and the terms of capitulation were
agreed upon. These were that the Texans should either
be held as prisoners of war or liberated on parole. These
terms were reduced to writing in both Spanish and English, and the English translation was read by Colonel
Fannin to his men, according to Mr. Duval in *Early
Times in Texas*. Santa Anna afterwards claimed that
the surrender was "at discretion."

The prisoners were conducted back to Goliad, and held
in close confinement for several days in the old mission
and the walls enclosing it. They were so crowded that
they could scarcely recline at night, and food was very

scanty. No intimation was given as to their final fate. "On the morning of the 27th of March," says J. C. Duval, one of the survivors, "a Mexican officer came to us and ordered us to get ready for a march. He told us we were to be liberated on 'parole,' and that arrangements had been made to send us to New Orleans on board of vessels then at Copano. This, you may be sure, was joyful news to us, and we lost no time in making preparations to leave our uncomfortable quarters. When all was ready we were formed into three divisions and marched out under a strong guard.

"One of our divisions was taken down the road leading to the lower ford of the river, one upon the road to San Patricio, and the division to which my company was attached along the road leading to San Antonio. A strong guard accompanied us, marching in double files on both sides of our column. When about half a mile above town, a halt was made and the guard on the side next the river filed around to the opposite side. Hardly had this manœuvre been executed, when I heard a heavy firing of musketry in the directions taken by the other two divisions. Some one near me exclaimed, 'Boys! they are going to shoot us!' and at the same instant I heard the clicking of musket locks all along the Mexican line. I turned to look, and, as I did so, the Mexicans fired upon us, killing probably one hundred out of the one hundred and fifty men in the division. We were in double file and I was in the rear rank. The man in front of me was shot dead, and in falling he knocked me down. I did not get up for a moment, and when I rose to my feet I found that the whole Mexican line had charged over me, and were in hot pursuit of those who had not been shot and who were fleeing towards the river about five hundred yards distant."

It would be hard to conceive of anything more brutal than this wholesale massacre of prisoners of war in this uncivilized way. The number of prisoners taken out to be shot like so many animals numbered three hundred and seventy-one. Twenty-seven were fortunate enough to escape in the confusion. The experiences of some of these men are almost past belief. Colonel Fannin, who was incapacitated by a wound, was not among the number. He was soon notified, however, to prepare for death. He was taken out to the square, seated on a bench with his eyes blindfolded, and shot to death. Thus died a brave son of old Georgia. The greater number of the men who were thus massacred were citizens of the United States, who had enlisted in the Texas army, and for that reason the Mexicans claimed, as a palliation for the deed, that they were filibusterers. This fact did not lessen the potency of the battle cry afterwards used: "Remember Goliad!" Together with "Remember the Alamo!" it served to thrill and stimulate the brave Texans at the Battle of San Jacinto.

In the city of Goliad, in Fannin Park, there stands a noble marble shaft. On the north side is engraved the battle cry of San Jacinto, "Remember the Alamo! Remember Goliad!"; on the west side, "Independence declared March 2, A. D. 1836, consummated April 21, A. D. 1836"; on the south, "Fannin; erected in memory of Fannin and his comrades," and on the east, "Massacred March 27, A. D. 1836." This forms at once an epitome of the history of the struggle for liberty in Texas.

In obedience to a resolution by the Council, new members of a Convention were elected by the various municipalities. They were to be "clothed with ample, unlimited, or plenary powers as to the form of government to be adopted: *provided,* that no constitution formed shall go into effect until the same be submitted to the people and confirmed by a majority thereof." This body convened on the first day of March, 1836, at the town of Washington, on the Brazos River. In a session of only seventeen days it accomplished work that has passed into history. It brought into existence the Republic of Texas. New men of the more radical type were in the ascendency in this body. Sam Houston was a delegate, but Austin was in the United States on business for the government.

It seemed to be a foregone conclusion that the independence of Texas would be promulgated. If there had been any uncertainty about it the news of the Alamo tragedy, which reached this body while in session, would have removed it. Everything now seemed to demand a formal declaration of independence. Public opinion had now been thoroughly aroused. The first work of the convention was to appoint a committee to draft a declaration of independence, which was reported on the following day. As finally approved, it set forth a number of causes of complaint which Texas had to make against Mexico. This instrument, which is now preserved in the State's archives, bears fifty-eight signatures. It includes nearly all of the greatest men of that day in Texas.

The next work of the convention was directed toward framing a Constitution. The Constitution of Texas was designed after the Constitution of the United States, only conforming to a single state instead of a federation of states. On the slavery question the Constitution provided that persons of colour, who had been slaves, should remain in bondage. Congress was forbidden to inhibit immigrants from bringing slaves with them, or to emancipate slaves within the Republic. No person was permitted to manumit his own slaves except by consent of Congress, unless he sent them out of the country. Free negroes were not allowed to dwell in Texas except by permission of Congress; but the African slave trade was forbidden, and negroes could only be introduced from the United States. This Constitution was subscribed by fifty members of the convention, three of whom were Mexicans.

The Constitution provided for a President, a Vice-President, an Attorney-General, and four secretaries, for the Departments of State, War, Navy and Treasury respectively. Because of the impossibility of holding elections, an ordinance provided that all the provisional officials were to be elected by the convention. There was also to be a Congress, consisting of two bodies. The President was to appoint, with the advice and consent of his Cabinet, all officers in public service. The government was authorized to borrow one million dollars upon the credit and faith of the Republic. David G. Burnet was chosen President, and Lorenzo de Zavala Vice-President of the government *ad interim*. The provisional capital was established at Harrisburg, on Buffalo Bayou. Sam Houston was appointed commander-in-chief of all the Texan troops, both regular and volunteers. He was to be subject to the general orders of the provisional government, until the election of a president in accordance with the constitution.

A few days after his appointment as commander-in-chief, General Houston started out at the head of his army to repel the Mexicans. Mrs. Dickinson, who had been in the Alamo, arrived with definite information concerning the fate of that fortress. A retreat was ordered. Houston withdrew from one place to another, leaving the settlements defenceless. The men under him were not

disciplined soldiers, but pioneers who were unused to
army life. They grew desperate and very disobedient.
Division, a general want of harmony, and lack of discipline, jealousy and insubordination were flagrant. There
was no regular term of enlistment, and no rigid rule of
discipline. The army had gathered under a sudden impulse, and every one came and went as he pleased. These
were common faults of an unorganized volunteer force.
Many of the companies were recruited from the United
States. Hence we find a battalion named "The New
Orleans Guard," and a company called "The Cincinnati."
There were "The Mustangs of Kentucky," the "Red
Rovers" of Alabama, and the Mobile "Greys."

During the revolutionary struggles of the "Lone Star
State," Texas was a powerful magnet toward which were
irresistibly attracted men of physical courage and restless appetite for adventure. These men, foregathered
from all parts of the country, had much in common, for,
by natural selection, they were all kindred spirits. What
to other men was tragedy was to these men commonplace.
War, adventure, scouting, Indian fighting were their
pleasures—a little diversion from the ordinary. Strange
and wild fellows many of these roving spirits were, often
of unusual stature, shaggy as lions and not less brave.
Such were the kind of men who, in the wars between
Texas and Mexico, and later, between the United States
and Mexico, formed the historic bands of scouts known
as the "Texas Rangers."

Houston's army continued to increase, even though
desertions were numerous. At one time as many as fifteen hundred men were enlisted under his standard. It
is not strange that the volunteers deserted in the manner
that they did. Although the men were eager to fight the
Mexicans, and could hardly be restrained, Houston con-

SAM HOUSTON

tinued his retreat without explaining his plans to any one. It was not until they had reached the far bank of the Trinity River that Houston turned to face the Mexicans under Santa Anna. With this victory of San Jacinto the forces of the Mexicans were annihilated, and it was several years before any further struggles followed between the Texans and the Mexicans.[1] The Republic of Texas was now an accomplished fact, for actual independence had been achieved.

[1] For an account of this battle see Chapter VIII, "Houston and San Jacinto."

CHAPTER IV

THE LONE STAR REPUBLIC

As a result of the Revolution, which culminated at San Jacinto, a new Republic was projected into the family of nations, seeking recognition as an independent country. It is not strange that the great powers of the world did not tumble over themselves in their efforts to recognize the Republic of Texas. It was inevitable that such action would affect the relations of the country with Mexico herself. The United States was the first to grant recognition, in March, 1837. France followed a couple of years later. Holland and Belgium entered into treaty relations in 1840, but Great Britain did not do this until 1842, through a series of treaties which began two years earlier. England was consistently favourable from the very beginning, however, for she desired a market for her merchandise "without having to climb over the United States tariff," as one of her ministers expressed it.

It was many years before friendly relations were restored between the Mexicans and the Texans. The Texans could not efface from memory Goliad and the Alamo, and the Mexicans demanded revenge for the loss of so great a territory. Mexico undoubtedly dreamed of reconquering Texas. The borders between the two had never been defined. There was a great strip of neutral ground between the two republics over which neither exercised absolute jurisdiction. The Congress of Texas defined the boundary of the Republic to extend from the mouth of the Rio Grande to its source, and this included all of the neutral ground, but she never exercised authority over it.

Texas possessed a navy, which made itself felt on the Gulf of Mexico. The *Invincible* and the *Brutus* would scarcely be a desirable target for a submarine to-day, but they boldly cruised around the blue waters of the Gulf and wreaked considerable havoc. The *Independence* was finally added to the galaxy. The *Independence* was captured by the Mexican navy after a spirited fight in which the Texans behaved most gallantly. The *Invincible* was unable to enter the harbour of Galveston when pursued by the enemy. She struck on the breakers and soon went to pieces. The *Brutus* was foundered in an equinoctial gale. Thus ended the old navy of the republic. The *Zavalla* with eight guns, the *Austin* with twenty guns, the *San Jacinto* with five guns, and some other small vessels were afterwards added to the navy. At one time several of them were loaned to the revolutionary government of Yucatan, that government agreeing to defray all expenses and render other compensation as well, so long as it operated against a common enemy.

When Houston was inducted into office the second time, such was the situation of the navy. He recalled the vessels, and they proceeded to New Orleans for repairs. Months passed, and the ships were still at anchor either there or at Mobile. The Secretary of War ordered them back to Texas, but the commander refused to obey. He claimed that he had invested largely of his personal means in refitting the vessels, since the government had failed to send remittances. A commissioner was sent by President Houston. The commander evidently convinced him of the justice of his cause, for he and the commissioner sailed off on an expedition to Yucatan.

This enraged Houston, and the commander was relieved by a proclamation which declared any future acts piratical. This pronouncement brought the ships back to Galveston, but the sympathies of the people were with Commander Maher. Four of these boats were still in commission at the time of annexation, and were by the treaty to be added to the navy of the United States. It is said, however, that they never did reach that destination.

Spurred on by the renewed rumours of annexation, both in the United States and Texas, Mexico began to despatch small military parties into the country, evidently with the hope of maintaining her shadowy claim. Unheralded and unexpected, General Vasquez, at the head of a force of five hundred men, marched against San Antonio in March, 1842, and captured the city, which he held for as much as two days. He then retreated to the west side of the Rio Grande. Another body of Mexicans took possession of Refugio and Goliad for a day or two.

To say that these expeditions aroused great excitement in Texas is superfluous. The tension was intense; hundreds of volunteers were soon enrolled and ready to attack the enemy. But the Mexicans escaped across the Rio Grande. Santa Anna boldly proclaimed that Mexico would not cease her hostility until she had planted her eagle standard on the banks of the Sabine. A few months later another attack of Mexicans, under General Woll, was made just as unexpectedly, and San Antonio was once more in the Mexican toils. The District Court was in session, and the presiding judge was captured. On this occasion the occupation continued for more than a week. The whole of Texas was immediately aflame with anger, and the demon of war was once more aroused.

A call was issued by President Houston for volunteers

to gather at San Antonio for the purpose of making an invasion of Mexico. The two raids had enkindled anew the martial spirit in Texas. Moreover, a number of Texans were held as prisoners in the southern republic, including the members of the Santa Fe Expedition. Hence it was not difficult to secure volunteers. General Somerville was placed in command against the wishes of the troops. The men expected to cross the Rio Grande at Laredo, but Somerville remained on the Texas side. They finally crossed, but only a couple of days later re-crossed the river. Then an order disbanding the army fell upon the soldiers like a thunderbolt.

These men of the outraged Republic, who had enlisted to avenge both personal and national insults, were astounded. About three hundred refused to disband and crossed the Rio Grande into Mexico once more. A commander of their own choice was elected. The town of Mier was made the first objective point. The skirmishing began in the town. The Mexicans were soon retreating and firing from housetops as they retired. During a temporary lull the Mexican commander, who had received reinforcements, sent a flag of truce asking for surrender. Up to that time the Texans appeared to be in the lead. Colonel Fisher had been wounded, however, and, fearing defeat, surrendered with more than two hundred men. While being conducted south toward the Mexican capital most of them tried to escape, but they were recaptured. The men were then compelled to draw a bean from a box in which every tenth bean was black—and this meant death. They requested to be shot from the front, and even this poor boon was denied them. They were blindfolded, secured, and made to sit down with their backs toward their executioners. Slightly more than one hundred finally reached home a year and a half after their capture. In its experiences as a Republic, Texas cannot be said to have covered itself with glory. It was practically bankrupt the greater part of the time, and was constantly in trouble with its creditors because of the depreciation of the script currency that was issued. It was not, in fact, until the closing years of the Republic, that the financial condition experienced any relief. Texas did produce some splendid types of manhood. The emergency of a new nation developed men of the type needed, just as it did in the Thirteen Colonies. There were legislators, judges, generals, and cabinet members who deserve high places on the roll of fame of these United States. A number of them did fill high places in the State and nation after annexation.

In one of his messages to Congress (1841), Houston says: "There is not a dollar in the treasury. The nation is involved from ten to fifteen millions; we are not only without money, but without credit, and for want of punctuality, without character. Patriotism, industry and enterprise are now our only resources—apart from our public domain, and the precarious revenue of the country."

The administration of Provisional President Burnet [1] was inaugurated in the gloomiest period of the war. The Alamo had fallen, and Santa Anna's main division was advancing toward the very heart of the republic. The seat of government was moved here and there as exi-

---

[1] Burnet was born in New Jersey, but had lived in Ohio, and was a lawyer. Like Houston, he had dwelt among the Indians (Comanches) for several years. He became a citizen of Texas in 1826. He served as Vice-president under Lamar, and was really acting president for several months during the latter's absence on account of illness. He was Secretary of State under the first governor after admission as a State. In 1866 he was elected to the United States Senate, but was not permitted to take his seat. He died at Galveston in 1879 at the age of eighty-three years.

gencies arose. Considering Washington on the Brazos too exposed, President Burnet had established himself at Harrisburg. The approach of Santa Anna drove him to Galveston Island. After the Battle of San Jacinto, and because there were no accommodations on the island, a change was made to Velasco. A few weeks later found the government at Columbia. The army was troublesome and insubordinate. It refused to acknowledge the man sent to command, while Houston was at New Orleans receiving treatment for his wound.

In the midst of such confusion definite policies were not to be expected. The President simply faced problems as they arose, and dealt with them as he could. Prior to the Battle of San Jacinto, such time as the wanderings of the Government permitted was employed in efforts to pacify the fugitives, strengthen the army, and obtain supplies. These efforts were not conspicuously successful. The message of President Burnet to the first Congress speaks of these things in the following words:

"Sometimes, when Texas was a moving mass of fugitives, they have been without 'a local habitation' and scattered to the cardinal points; again they have been on Galveston Island, without a shelter, and almost without subsistence, and never have they been in circumstances of comfort and convenience suitable to the orderly conducting of the grave and momentous business committed to their charge. That errors should have been committed under such circumstances will not surprise those who have an honest consciousness of their own fallibilities. But that those extraordinary powers have not been perverted to any sinister purpose, to the damage of the country, to personal aggrandizement, or to the creation or advancement of a party, or to the success of a speculation, I assert with a modest but firm and assured confidence."

The first regular election was held in September, 1836, at which Stephen F. Austin, Henry Smith and Sam Houston were candidates for the presidency. The natural habit of worshipping the successful warrior carried the hero of San Jacinto into office with a tremendous wave of enthusiasm. He received four times as many votes as his two opponents. The Constitution was also ratified. Houston immediately appointed Austin Secretary of State and Smith Secretary of the Treasury, in an effort to harmonize all factions. His term of office did not begin until December, but President Burnet resigned in October and Houston was immediately inaugurated.

A national seal and standard for the Republic were adopted December 10th. The former consisted of a single star with the letters "Republic of Texas" circular on the seal, which was also circular. The national flag was to have an azure ground, with a large golden star central, and to be denominated the national standard of Texas. With regard to the territorial extent of the infant Republic, Congress was not backward in defining the boundaries. By an act of December 19th it was declared that the civil and political jurisdiction of Texas extended from the mouth of the Sabine to the mouth of the Rio Grande, thence up the principal stream of the latter river to its source. The initial session of the first regularly elected Congress was guided by a spirit of patriotism and singleness of purpose worthy of emulation.

During this brief term of President Houston, the debt of the new Republic was augmented to two million dollars. A loan of five million dollars had been authorized

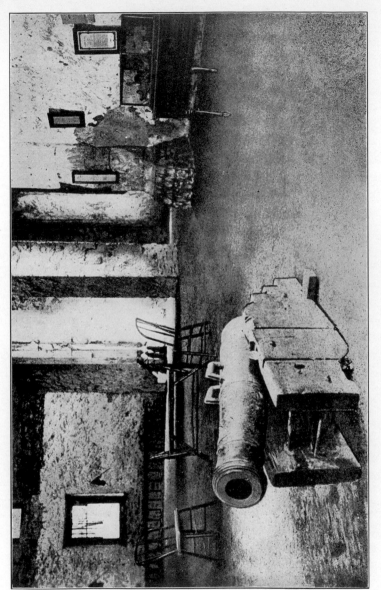

INTERIOR OF THE ALAMO

by Congress, but it was impossible to float it. The Government was accordingly compelled to institute the issue of paper money. For a time the army was reduced to a destitute condition for the want of food and clothing. The salaries of officials went unpaid. The Constitution provided that the first president should serve only two years, and should be ineligible for election to succeed himself, but the succeeding presidential terms were extended to three years.

At the election in 1838, Mirabeau B. Lamar was almost unanimously elected. Houston and his friends were strenuously opposed to Lamar, believing him to be visionary rather than practical, and imbued with extravagant ideas for the conducting of governmental affairs. They were unable, however, to pick a strong man as his opponent. After this the whole country became divided into the "Houston Party" and the "Anti-Houston Party," and all the elections hinged on the policies advocated by Houston or those opposed to him. Lamar was opposed to the annexation of Texas to the United States, and his inaugural address pictured eloquently and at length the advantages of independence. He could not "regard the annexation of Texas to the American union in any other light than as the grave of all her hopes of happiness and greatness." His administration is most celebrated for its vigorous advocacy of public education. During his term a modest provision was made for the endowment of schools and colleges. Three leagues of land in each county were set aside for the establishment of primary schools or academies. Fifty leagues of land were to be surveyed and devoted to the establishment or endowment of two colleges or universities thereafter to be created.

The financial problem continued to grow more and more serious. As the paper issues increased, deprecia-

tion followed apace. At the close of Lamar's term the
debt exceeded seven million dollars, and the value of
the government script had depreciated to about fifteen
cents on the dollar. These treasury notes were generally called "red-backs" from the colour of the paper
upon which they were printed. The finances and credit
of the republic had utterly collapsed. His administration
has generally been condemned for its extravagance and
lack of judgment. Distinguished though Lamar was as
a patriot of unquestioned integrity and exalted courage,
as an administrator he was an utter failure.

The Indians were very troublesome, and provocation
was not wanting. Incoming settlers did not hesitate to
push out in the Indian country and occupy the rich lands
of the aborigines. Surveyors and speculators penetrated
into districts which hitherto had been generally recognized as their hunting grounds. As a result, there were
isolated tragedies without number, and several organized
revolts of the savages. Many of the chiefs were likewise
incited to revolt by Mexican emissaries. An abortive
scheme to organize the Republic of the Rio Grande was
entered into by some adventurers consisting of both Texans and Mexicans. This new republic was to include
Southern Texas, which was practically a neutral ground.
An army advanced into Mexico as far as Saltillo, but
Texas absolutely ignored the movement.

The most notorious instance of lack of judgment was
the Santa Fé Expedition, which ended in disaster. It
was undertaken without the sanction of Congress and
against its protest. The expedition numbered about
three hundred men. Its object was to extend the actual
jurisdiction of Texas over that portion of the republic
now included within New Mexico, but which was still
administered by Mexico. If the inhabitants were will-

ing, the authority and protection of Texas was to be offered. Should the people there be found hostile, the expedition was to return after disposing of the merchandise carried along for trade.

It must be remembered that Texas had always claimed the Rio Grande as its boundaries, and Santa Fé is situated a number of miles on the eastern, or Texas, side of that stream. It is true that Texas had never been able to establish her jurisdiction over that remote section, because of its isolation, but that was probably no reason why she should not at some time attempt such exercise, unless prudence and good judgment warned against it. The guides did not understand the route well, and the party became bewildered and finally lost. Provisions gave out, water was very scarce, the Indians troublesome, horses were stolen, and occasionally men, who straggled off from the main body, were killed. The survivors reached the vicinity of Santa Fé in a starving condition. Here they were betrayed into a shameful surrender, and all were sent as prisoners to Mexico.[1]

"But what, the reader will ask," says Mr. Kendall, a member of the party, in his *Santa Fé Expedition*, "induced so large a body of young men to start upon an expedition of this kind? What objects could they have in view? The answer is easy enough. They were actuated by that love of adventure, which is inherent in thousands of our race; they were anxious to participate in the excitements ever incidental to a prairie tour. . . . We were to pass over a portion of country entirely unknown to the white man, and might reasonably expect to meet

[1] After annexation Lamar served as Division Inspector under General Henderson during the Mexican War. At the taking of Monterey he displayed conspicuous gallantry. On his return to Texas he was elected to the Legislature. For a short time he was United States Minister to Argentina. He died at his home in Texas, December 19th, 1859.

with a larger share of adventure than usually falls to the
lot of the Western travellers."

In 1841 David G. Burnet and Sam Houston were the
only candidates for the presidency, and Houston was
again elected. The financial situation was all but desperate, and Congress was in the mood for economy.
Necessity also demanded such a move, for the limit of
credit had been reached. Houston had evidently profited
by his previous experience; a number of offices were
abolished, while the salaries of others were appreciably
reduced. By this means the expenditures of the Government were reduced until they were actually less than
the receipts. The problem, nevertheless, continued a troublesome one throughout the life of the Republic and,
at the close of 1845, the public debt was estimated at
nearly twelve million dollars. Houston's second administration was a stormy one. The financial difficulties,
the Mexican raids, the seat of government controversy,
and other incidents all contributed to its tempestuous
character. The official intercourse between the executive
and legislative departments was not always characterized
by the spirit of urbanity.

The Indian policy of President Houston caused a great
deal of discussion, as there were radical differences of
opinion. He advocated treaties with the red men rather
than continuous efforts to exterminate them. In pur-
suance of this policy, a number of treaties were actually
entered into with them. The names of the Indian chiefs,
whose signatures appear on these treaties, as revealed in
the *Secret Journals* of the Senate, are rather amusing.
Among these are Colonel Bowl, Big Mush, Corn Tassel,
The Egg, Roasting Ear, Red Bear, Chicken Trotter.
Some of the chiefs and tribes lived up to their obligations,
but many of them repudiated their solemn word. Un-

doubtedly they had much provocation from unscrupulous settlers and traders.

In spite of all the political turmoil, and the discord between the executive and legislative branches of the Government, upon his retirement in 1844, both houses joined in a resolution commending Houston for his patriotic statesmanship. He was succeeded by Anson Jones, who had been serving as Secretary of State. Jones was the choice of the Houstonites. The Republic was in the most favourable position that it had ever been. The finances were excellent, while the assurances of peace and tranquillity were becoming stronger each day. The Indians were remarkably tranquil, and there was less disturbance upon the frontier during this administration than at almost any period in her history. Even with Mexico the prospects for peace and the recognition of independence were flattering. President Jones had been an ardent patriot, and had occupied numerous official positions with unusual ability. By this time annexation was the all-absorbing issue, and the domestic affairs of the Republic were of relatively small importance to the public at large.

The people of Texas were beginning to be fairly prosperous, but the country was unwittingly a shuttlecock of stronger powers. Immigration had been rapid since the Battle of San Jacinto, and by 1845 there were probably a hundred thousand white inhabitants, most of whom had emigrated from the United States. Next in number were the German immigrants, with here and there an occasional Englishman or Frenchman. A renaissance of the *empresario* system had been instrumental in hastening the development of the unsettled portions of the State on the western and northwestern frontier. Crops were excellent, commerce was increasing, and indications were evident that the hardest days of the Republic were over.

The Republic of Texas occupied a comparatively large place in the diplomacy of three of the principal powers of the world—the United States, England and France, without a mention of Mexico. This was due in general to the refusal of Mexico to recognize the independence of Texas. The fact that such a small number of Anglo-Americans were able to achieve independence, and then to maintain it for about ten years, in spite of a powerful enemy on the border and in the face of tremendous financial difficulties, is one of the marvels of the century. There were indeed brave men and true in Texas. In the words of Henry van Dyke:

> "O question not, but honour every name,
> Travis and Crockett, Bowie, Bonham, Ward,
> Fannin and King, all who drew the sword
> And dared to die for Texan liberty!
> Yea, write them all upon the roll of fame,
> But no less love and equal honour give
> To those who paid the longer sacrifice—
> Austin and Houston, Burnet, Rusk, Lamar
> And all the stalwart men who dared to live
> Long years of service to the lonely star."

CHAPTER V

THE LONE STAR STATE

"THE Lone Star of Texas, which ten years ago arose amid clouds over fields of carnage, obscurely seen for awhile, has culminated and, following an inscrutable destiny, has passed on and become fixed forever in that glorious constellation which all freemen and lovers of freedom in the world must reverence and adore—the American Union. Blending its rays with its sister States, long may it continue to shine, and may generous Heaven smile upon the consummation of the wishes of the two Republics now joined in one. May the union be perpetual, and may it be the means of conferring benefits and blessings upon the people of all the States, is my ardent prayer. The final act in the great drama is now performed. The Republic of Texas is no more!"

These were the concluding words of the valedictory of President Anson Jones when he turned the Government over to General J. Pinckney Henderson, the governor-elect.[1] During this address, which was delivered in front of the old capitol in Austin, intense emotion thrilled every bosom while tears trickled from the eyes

[1] This first Governor of Texas was a native of North Carolina. He came to the Republic in 1836 at the head of a company of volunteers. At the inauguration of Houston as President he became Attorney General and afterward served as Secretary of State. He was Minister to both England and France, and a Special Minister to the United States. In 1857 he was elected to the United States Senate, but died before taking his seat.

of many weather-beaten Texans. They felt that Texas was being stricken from the galaxy of nations.

As the retiring executive uttered the words, "The Republic of Texas is no more," he lowered the lone star emblem of that passing State, and hoisted the starred and striped banner of the greater Republic of which Texas became a member. Thus was consummated one of the most remarkable events in the civil history of the world, in which a nation voluntarily surrendered its sovereignty. The hillside was covered with people, and many a strong man wept to see the lone star come down. They had sustained that flag for almost ten years on many a battlefield, and they dreaded a future conflict over African slavery in the United States, for the war clouds were even then gathering.

In a vote taken by the Texans the same year in which independence was declared, the Texans had expressed themselves almost unanimously in favour of annexation with the United States. The political situation in that Republic was such, however, that the proposal did not meet with favour. In the first place this proposition was promulgated at a time when the contest between the slave States and the free States was ebullient. The imminent possibility of extending slave territory to such an extent as the admission of Texas would mean did not receive favourable consideration in the North. Another impediment was the probability that the admission of Texas at that time presaged a war with Mexico, which was not at all desired. The best that could be considered was the recognition of the new Republic.

It was not until 1843, in the reign of President Tyler, that fresh overtures from the Texans were received with encouraging favour. But England was not indifferent. She exerted every controlling influence that she could interpose to prevent its accomplishment. The Mexican Government announced that it would consider annexation as in fact a declaration of war. Deterred by neither of these threatening complications, a treaty was actually presented to the Senate in April, 1844. President Tyler, the "president without a party," had been so unfortunate in his political affiliations, however, that he had alienated the support of the Whigs, and, with only a partial support from the Democrats, the treaty was defeated by more than two to one. In the election which followed shortly afterwards, the Democratic party declared for annexation in its platform, and its candidate, James K. Polk, was elected. Thus it was that the annexation of Texas became a question only of time and method. Tyler succeeded in robbing his successor of a little of the glory by forcing a resolution providing for annexation through the combined houses of Congress a few days before his office terminated. This method was declared to be unconstitutional, but such an announcement had no effect upon the action of the legislative body.

The attitude of Texas herself threatened to become a stumbling-block at this time. Many of the public men were opposed to annexation, desiring to link their names with the rise and destiny of an independent nation. For a while it appeared as though annexation had been too long delayed by the United States. President Anson Jones himself was considered by many as an opponent of annexation. In his inaugural address he studiously avoided all reference to this subject, which everybody was thinking about, while the ninth and last Congress of the Republic in its regular session, which ended February 3rd, 1845, omitted to take any action on the matter. Jones was probably misjudged. And yet so intense did public feeling become on this question, that there was actually talk of deposing him and introducing a government *ad interim*.[1] As soon as the joint resolution was passed by the United States Congress, President Jones summoned a special session of the Texas Congress, and also called a State convention to pass upon the subject of annexation. At this time a treaty of peace between Texas and Mexico was presented by the latter country, providing that the independence of Texas would be officially recognized, in the event that Republic would pledge itself against annexation. The Congress, which met on June 16th, did not hesitate long, for on the fifth day it unanimously rejected the treaty with Mexico, and on the seventh day unanimously declared itself in favour of annexation. In October the State constitution, which had been prepared, was submitted to the vote of the people, as well as the question of annexation. Thus the uncertainty was relieved, and the preliminaries necessary to the union were arranged as speedily as it was possible so to do.

It required great care to prepare these preliminaries for statehood while the country was still a republic. In

[1] Anson Jones was a Massachusetts man and had come to Texas to practice medicine. He soon afterwards deserted medicine and entered the field of active politics. He was one of the earliest advocates of Texas independence. He had participated in the Battle of San Jacinto. President Jones never recovered from the unpopularity aroused by the feeling that he opposed annexation. After annexation he retired to his place in Washington County, and for eleven years remained in private life. Others were honoured with high positions and he felt that he had been slighted. At last his name was brought out as a candidate for the United States Senate, but he was defeated. On the 7th of January, 1858, he was at the old Capitol Hotel in Houston. He then seemed in low spirits, and in a sad tone remarked to a friend: "Here, in this house, twenty years ago, I commenced my political career in Texas, as a member of the Senate, and here I would like to close it." Not long afterward, a pistol shot was heard in his room, and Dr. Jones was found in a dying condition. The country was shocked at this sad occurrence.

December an election for State officials was held, and by proclamation the Legislature was convened for February 16th, 1846. It was on this date that the transfer of authority took place. The Constitution drawn up was worthy of a great State. It is short, and exhibits many successful attempts at self-restraint.

War between the United States and Mexico closely followed annexation. The question as to whether the United States was right or wrong in its actions, which provoked the conflict with our neighbouring Republic, has been adjudged with varying opinions by historians and students of international affairs. It is undoubtedly true that the attitude of President Polk was more unyielding than a powerful nation should have conducted itself toward one relatively so weak. Mexico had uttered threats, but every one knew, and none better than Washington, that Mexico was too weak to follow up her defiance.

The one question that was of great importance to Texas, and, therefore, to the United States after annexation, was the establishment of a definite boundary between it and Mexico. It is generally conceded that Texas, while a Spanish province, and subsequently a political division of the Republic of Mexico, did not touch the Rio Grande River at any point. In Southern Texas, on the Gulf, the dividing line was the Nueces River, which empties into the Gulf of Mexico near Corpus Christi. At another point the dividing line was the Medina River, flowing a few miles southeast of San Antonio. Farther west its boundaries were still more remote from the Rio Grande.

According to a treaty entered into with Santa Anna, the Mexican president, when a prisoner, and therefore under a sort of duress, it was provided that Texas ob-

ligated herself not to lay claim to anything west of the
Rio Grande River, but this entire treaty was afterward
repudiated by the Mexican Government. In 1836 the
Congress of Texas had passed a resolution declaring
the boundaries of that Republic on the south and west
to be the Rio Grande. From a legal standpoint this signified nothing more than if that legislative body had
asseverated that the Pacific Ocean should be their frontier. At no period in her history did Texas succeed
in establishing her jurisdiction as far as the Rio Grande.
The Santa Fé Expedition was the only attempt made to
push the frontier westward, and that was a fiasco.

The conflict between Mexico and the United States
could have only one result, but, as this subject is not
especially pertinent to a study of Texas, it will not be
considered any more extensively. Suffice it to say that in
the Treaty of Guadalupe Hidalgo, in 1848, the international boundaries were finally adjudicated, and the Rio
Grande was established as the Texas frontier. There
is no doubt that the war was really welcomed by the
Texans, as it provided the opportunity for her adventurous sons to make the execrated Mexicans feel the
blighting effects of a sanguinary struggle carried to
their altars and firesides. It was a costly experience for
Mexico, and the nominal sum paid by the United States
for the lost territory did not moderate the bitterness of
the compulsion.

The limits of Texas were not yet finally determined.
On two occasions, since the admission of Texas as a
State, have the boundary lines of that expansive commonwealth been changed. The first of these developed a
controversy that aroused a bellicose attitude on the part
of Texas which threatened serious trouble. As Texas
was admitted it extended as far north as latitude forty-

two, and followed the Rio Grande River in its course through New Mexico. Appended to the final treaty with Mexico was a map on which the western frontier of Texas was outlined as claimed by that State. A number of questions at once arose. During the war with Mexico Federal troops had taken possession of Santa Fé. Almost immediately after peace was declared the people of New Mexico in a convention adopted an anti-slavery petition to Congress, in which protest was made against the claims of Texas. Thus the question of the limits of that State became inseparably bound up with the struggle over the expansion of slavery.

Texas organized the County of Santa Fé, but the officer appointed to assume charge was opposed by the United States officials, who claimed exclusive authority. The contest assumed the proportions of a national problem. Texas had been admitted as a slave State, and its boundaries reached far above the line established by the Missouri Compromise. Although there was a clause stating that that portion above thirty-six degrees thirty minutes should become free when erected into a separate State, there appeared little likelihood that such action would be taken. This placed the anti-slavery forces against Texas. Newspapers of Texas published inflammatory editorials, and the governor besought of the Legislature authority to enlist several thousand rangers.

When Fillmore succeeded to the office of chief executive, upon the death of General Taylor, a spirit of concession developed and the Compromise of 1850 was enacted. Texas needed money to pay off the obligations left over from the Republic. In consideration of ten million dollars delivered to the State in United States bonds, bearing five per cent interest and due in fourteen years, Texas relinquished all of her assertions to territory beyond the present outlines. This excised territory comprised parts of Oklahoma, Kansas, Colorado, Wyoming, and New Mexico. The exact boundaries were not surveyed until half a century subsequently, but no serious complications resulted. As a further consideration for the money paid, Texas ceded to the United States her forts, her navy, and her customs-houses with the revenue therefrom. After the many old obligations of the Republic of Texas had been satisfied, this still left a sufficient sum to rehabilitate the finances of the new State into a healthy condition. Texas had also been prudent enough to retain possession of all of her public lands. This placed the commonwealth in possession of immense resources, which have aided very materially in the development of that State.

By a decision of the United States Supreme Court as recently as 1896, Texas lost what was known as Greer County, which was added to Oklahoma. This was the adjudication of an antiquated claim dating back to 1819, in the treaty between the United States and Spain. By this treaty the boundary line of the two countries was to extend from the "Gulph of Mexico" up the Sabine River to the thirty-second degree of latitude, then north to the Rio Roxo, or Red River, and then to follow the Red River westward. The Red River has two branches, however, and the question in dispute hinged upon whether the demarcation was the north fork or the south fork. Texas naturally interpreted it to be the north fork, which gave her the greater territory, and actually exercised jurisdiction over that disputed territory, but the highest tribunal of the United States decided in favour of the south fork. She thus lost a territory greater than our two smallest States.

Statehood for Texas was very fortunate. She sacrificed a certain degree of independence, but she was released from a tremendous financial burden owing to the necessity of a diplomatic and military establishment. The population of the Republic of Texas was so meagre, and the territory so large, that the strain would have become infinitely greater as the years passed. The war with Mexico recorded the beginning of a period of rapid growth in the population and wealth of the State, which was arrested only by the paralyzing effects of the internecine struggle between the States. The disposal of New Mexico unburdened the State from its staggering debts, and placed a good working balance in the treasury. Thus Texas could offer not only low taxes, a protected homestead, fertile lands, and a genial climate, but an opportunity for adventure.

Immediately after annexation immigration began to pour into the new State in increasing numbers. In the decade preceding the Civil War, Texas was exceeded in growth by only four States. Whereas at the time of the Declaration of Independence the white population did not exceed thirty thousand, a year or two after annexation it had been augmented to more than a hundred thousand. In 1860 there were almost half a million Texans, and the value of property had increased in even a greater proportion. The rapid growth in population signified the occupation of large areas of the former wild lands. The rapidity with which the frontier receded is strikingly indicated by the lists of new counties created and organized during those years. In 1856 sixteen counties were established, and the highest mark was reached in 1858, when thirty-five new counties were presented to the commonwealth.

The growth and expansion in population was outstripped by the accretion in wealth. The taxable values in 1860 were eight hundred per cent greater than those at the initiation of statehood. With this development came a demand for improved transportation facilities. Work was begun on a number of projects for the improvement of bays and rivers. As it was possible for the waterways to serve only a small portion of the country, the construction of railways was advocated and encouraged. Then followed the era of railroad construction.

The first railroad in Texas was the "Buffalo Bayou, Brazos and Colorado Railroad," which was started west from the town of Harrisburg in 1852. Twenty miles were completed by August 1st, 1853. This was the beginning of the Sunset System of railroads. The name afterwards became the "Galveston, Harrisburg and San Antonio," which name still remains for a portion of the system. The next iron road was the Galveston and Red River, begun at Houston in the following year, and designed to traverse the State to the north. The name was afterwards changed to the "Houston and Texas Central," which it still bears. This company operated its first locomotive on the road in 1856, at which time it had completed two miles of track out of Houston. The Washington County Railroad had reached from Hempstead to Brenhan, a distance of twenty-one miles, by 1860. The Galveston, Houston and Henderson in 1859 constructed a bridge across the bay and reached Galveston, providing that island its first connection with the mainland. It is needless to enumerate all the early railroads, but this brief description will give a little idea of the beginning of railroad construction.

The greatest problem that confronted Texas during these years was that of the Indians, whose tepees were within her boundaries. Some of these tribes were friendly, but the Comanches who roamed the western

LIVE OAK TREE IN ONE OF HOUSTON'S NEW PARKS

prairies were exceedingly troublesome. Their special enemies had been Mexicans during the Republic, but if the brown Mexican enemies were scarce they were satisfied with whites. Furthermore, there were many hostile raids of the red men from the Indian Territory over into Northern Texas. A report submitted to the Legislature in 1850 outlined a list of one hundred and seventy-one persons killed, seven wounded, and twenty-five carried into captivity during the preceding year.

The reason for this unusual casualty list was that the Federal troops had been withdrawn almost entirely. Several companies of volunteers were called into service by the State, and they did effective work. But there was a vast expanse of territory to be protected, much of it being trackless and almost waterless areas over which the foot of white men had seldom if ever trod. There were fastnesses and places of retreat known only to the savage. The State constabulary, known as the Texas Rangers, performed effective service, but they could not be everywhere along the border. The Indians were finally colonized on lands appropriated by the State, but even this did not entirely solve the problem. Stray bands would occasionally break away and plunder horses and other valuables from the settlers, sometimes even killing those who resisted. Such disturbances as these, however, were not peculiar to Texas, for border troubles occurred from our northern border to our southern border in the onward march of civilization toward the West. At a later date, with the exception of a few in Polk County, and near El Paso, all the aborigines were removed beyond the borders of the State.

The feeling between the Mexicans and the Texans was not always of the best. The Mexicans were accused of stealing horses and stimulating opposition of the slaves

to their masters. An escaped slave was never restored
to its owner by Mexico. In this way a racial opposition
was engendered which caused a number of unfortunate
occurrences between Mexicans and Texans. In some
counties resolutions were adopted in mass conventions
which forever forbade any Mexican from coming within
the limits of the county, and those living there were
expelled. At Brownsville a Mexican band, under the
leadership of a daring border chieftain, took possession
of that city and killed several Americans who had in-
curred the leader's hostility. He was defeated and driven
back into Mexico with considerable losses on both sides.

The so-called "Cart War" also caused considerable
disquietude. Mexican cartmen had been engaged for
many years in hauling goods between San Antonio and
the Gulf. On several occasions they were attacked by
lawless bands of persons who fired on them. At Goliad
a meeting was called, which declared that "the presence of
the greasers or peon Mexicans as citizens among us is
an intolerable nuisance and a grievance which calls loudly
for redress." One of the chief causes for the bitterness
of feeling was the fact that the Mexicans carried goods
cheaper than their American competitors. The militia
were called out, and the "war" collapsed.

No State in the Union has made more history than
Texas. The Texans have contributed their full share of
thrilling experiences. By the year 1860 there were one
hundred thousand and more negro slaves owned within
the borders of Texas. The greater percentage of immigrants had migrated from States where slavery was a
recognized institution. Texas had likewise dropped into
the Democratic column. No more than natural was it,
therefore, that Texas should withdraw from the Union
along with the other Southern States in the concerted

movement which followed the defection of South Carolina. The judgment, passions, and prejudices of an overwhelming majority of the people of Texas favoured secession. It must not be forgotten that a considerable portion of her population had lived there when Texas was a nation. The question of slavery in Texas, they considered, had been settled when Texas entered the Union as a slave State only fifteen years before. Had that privilege been denied, Texas never would have considered annexation. The so-called "higher law" of the "Black Republicans" could not be considered.

Alone, and almost unsupported, there was one public man who stood like a stone wall against secession. This man was the hero of San Jacinto, who was then governor. In his inaugural address, Houston had said: "Texas will maintain the Constitution and stand by the Union. It is all that can save us as a nation. Destroy it and anarchy awaits us." He had been elected as an independent over the regular Democratic candidate. He was still a man of powerful influence on the platform, and, as ever, was aggressive in everything which he undertook. Heedless of a tremendous clamour, Houston refused to summon the Legislature in session. The people had recourse to an extraordinary action. A convention was called by some unauthorized State officials, to which twice as many delegates were to be elected as there were members of the Legislature. This was ordered to meet on January 28th. Houston then yielded and convened the Legislature one week earlier. Five States had already seceded when the Legislature assembled.

When the South Carolina Resolutions were transmitted to the Legislature, Governor Houston recommended "the adoption of resolutions dissenting from the assertion of the abstract right of secession." The temper of the as-

sembly is shown a few days later by the adoption of
an ordinance of secession by a vote of one hundred and
sixty-seven to seven. The convention, which had been
called, met, and before the vote of the people had been
taken, elected delegates to the Congress of the Southern
States already called, and appointed a Committee of Public Safety. This Committee immediately inaugurated
steps to secure the arms and military property of the
United States in Texas. This was very large, because
the uncertain condition along the border had made necessary a number of army posts in which were an abundance of military stores. This was all surrendered by
General David E. Twiggs, the commander of this department. When Twiggs, who was himself a Southerner,
demurred a little, probably for propriety's sake, a display
of force was made by a volunteer body, and Twiggs then
wrote out an order for the surrender of all government
military property in Texas to the Texans.

It is worthy of note that the early military move-
ments in Texas preceding and following secession were
conducted under the Lone Star Flag. Whenever the
Stars and Stripes were lowered, this banner was hoisted
in their place. The employment of this former emblem
was evidence of quite a general desire to resume State
sovereignty, and simply work in harmony with the newly-
formed confederacy. The members of this party, however, were greatly out-numbered as events developed.

That Houston at one time considered open resistance
to the secessionists appears quite evident, but he evidently abandoned the idea and calmly submitted to the
trend of affairs. Perhaps it was because of his age and
infirmity. In some sections the union party was powerful, and a resourceful leader like Houston could have
involved the State in a sanguinary civil war of its own.

BOOT CANYON, CEDARS OF LEBANON, CHISOS MTS.

On February 23rd, the ordinance of secession was balloted upon by the electorate, and was carried by a vote of almost three to one. Texas delegates joined with those of the other recalcitrant States in establishing a provisional government of the Confederate States, at Montgomery, Alabama. It was not long until the internecine war was fully under way.

Fortunate indeed was it for Texas that she was located so far from the scene of active military operations. She lay entirely outside the path of the terrible storm that devastated her sister States. Proximity to Mexico provided a comparatively safe outlet for cotton and inlet for supplies of various kinds. Almost ninety thousand Texans affiliated with the Confederate Armies during the war. Hood's Texas Brigade and the Terry Rangers achieved for themselves laurels on many a bloody battlefield. Her officers won high places. Few conflicts, and those of a minor nature, occurred on Texas soil. For a while Galveston was in possession of Union troops, and there were some other isolated skirmishes at various places. The recapture of Galveston and the defence of Sabine Pass are the most brilliant fights. These struggles, however, were unimportant when compared with the bloody fights that took place in the Eastern States of the Confederacy.

There was absolutely no fighting in the interior of Texas during the entire Civil War, and all the skirmishes happened somewhere on the border. The cultivation of the soil continued very much as it did preceding the war, with the exception that the ranch owners and farmers were handicapped by the paucity of men to perform the work. These men had taken their places on the fighting line at other points. But the financial burden of Texas was unusually onerous, for she was

compelled to protect her own borders from Indian depredations as well as satisfy the almost unprecedented
demands of the Confederacy.

It was indeed a scene of great disorder and confusion
that Texas presented at the close of the war. Soldiers,
who had proved their bravery on the battlefield, and
who had endured frightful hardships without complaint,
now became lawless brigands. Finding their cause lost,
and having received no pay for months, they demanded
a division of all Confederate property. It was seized
and taken possession of wherever found. The utmost
confusion reigned. The country swarmed with men out
of funds and devoid of employment. The civil authorities confessed themselves impotent to deal with the situation. Guerillas and highwaymen almost openly plied
their vocations everywhere. An abortive attempt was
made to rob the penitentiary at Huntsville. The State
treasury was actually looted, but there was little of value
in it. The war had exhausted all the available resources.
An interregnum of several weeks intervened between the
departure of the principal State and Confederate officers
and the arrival of Federal officers, and this afforded the
opportunity.

From June 8th to October 13th, 1865, there are only
blank pages in the fiscal ledger, "mute evidences of the
end of a disastrous struggle, and of the temporary dis-
solution of state government." A. J. Hamilton, a Texas
Union man, was appointed provisional governor. Reconstruction presented many problems in Texas, as it did
in the other Southern States. Union men who had been
driven out of the State by secession were inclined to be
unyielding and uncompromising when the tide of events
placed things in their control.

"Rid of the incubus of slavery," says Mr. Garrison in

his *Texas, a Contest of Civilizations* (1903), "and
with her government again in the hands of her people,
Texas received a new progressive impetus that has
seemed to grow and strengthen with each succeeding
year. It would appear as if the industrial and moral en-
ergies of the State were emancipated along with the
slaves, and the record of its development during the
last quarter of a century has been really wonderful. In
population, in wealth, in education, and in general culture, the increase has been equally striking. The grain
of Anglo-American mustard seed planted in the far
Southwest has grown to a stately tree, in which many
of the best ideas and impulses of the whole outer world
have come to nest."

CHAPTER VI

CHARMING AND HISTORIC SAN ANTONIO

SAN AN-TON-I-O and Al-a-mo—there is something pleasing and euphonious about these very names. The one is reminiscent of the Dons and monks of Spain who once dwelt here; the other is a memory of unexcelled bravery and stoicism. But each would lose half its charm if translated into the prosaic English of Saint Anthony and Cottonwood. I have visited San Antonio several times, and each time I have been charmed the more. There is something restful and quieting about the city that one does not find in our large Eastern cities. The strenuous activity of those congested centres is absent, and life moves along in a far easier way. People have time to pause for a moment on their way to business and exchange confidences with their neighbours. There is just the least bit of that *mañana* spirit of old Mexico distinguishable. In short, it is a city that is different, with an atmosphere and a charm peculiarly its own. The sun does not always shine, as some San Antonians would have you believe, but when it does shine there is a blueness of the sky and a balminess of the air which is so seductive that you are likely to forget you had any intention of journeying farther.

San Antonio is a sort of meeting-place between the East and the West, the North and the South, the old and the new. It is a gateway to the West, where changes begin to evolve that are peculiarly Western. It is on

90

the main highway to Old Mexico, the land of burros and *sombreros*. It is also the juxtaposition of the Latin and the Anglo-Saxon civilization, for you can find here the old Spanish *patios* in the interior of the houses. You will also discover numerous plazas scattered over the city, just one block in extent, which are riotous with bloom and reminiscent of the plazas to be found in Spanish towns. Your ears will be assailed on all sides by the soft and lisping accents of the Castilian tongue. Built upon the foundations of an eighteenth century town, and still retaining many of the features of the earlier order, San Antonio is one of the most distinctive of American cities. It will always be regarded by loyal Texans as the shrine of early Texas history, while the old missions and other remains of the Spanish era are quaint and picturesque landmarks which attract visitors from every State and every country.

San Antonio is an old city, as Texas cities go. The cowled and frocked Franciscan monks tramped three hundred leagues across the deserts of Northern Mexico in their numerous journeys which led them to this site. Many fell by the wayside in this fearful enterprise. It was the report of the discovery of the Gulf of Mexico by La Salle, the famous French explorer, that prompted Spain to make conquests in this territory. With the priests went soldiers clad in helmet and mail, who sought gold and adventure. The sword and the cross marched hand in hand, as is usual with the Spaniards, and in this way the site of San Antonio was first visited by white men.

A number of springs bubble up here out of the earth and form a beautiful little stream of wonderfully clear water; and it is to this fact that San Antonio owes its location. These streams, which furnish an abundant sup-

ply of water, and the verdant vegetation caused by a
constant supply of moisture, attracted the attention of
these Franciscan monks, so that they decided to erect a
mission here for the Indians who were numerous in this
neighbourhood. The first mission was established at the
head springs of the San Pedro by Don Martin de Alar-
con, in 1718. He called it the Mission de San Antonio
de Valero. The mission was not a new one, but was removed from its former location on the Rio Grande. At
the same time he created the presidio of San Antonio de
Bexar, or fort of San Antonio, declaring it to be his monarch's capital in this country. This was probably located
near an Indian village known to be there. The domin-
ion he named the Province of Bexar (pronounced bear).

An old Spanish chronicle reads as follows: "In this
province (Bexar) are some beautiful springs. So great
is their volume that they send out within a short distance a considerable river which they form. This stream
is called San Antonio. Across the river on its eastern
bank and about two gunshots is the Mission of San Antonio de Valero (now the Alamo). This mission was
founded on the First of May, 1718, by order of the most
excellent Marquis de Valero. It was the first college of
the Holy Cross that in its zeal for the salvation of the
natives was planted in the province of Texas. The records show that since its formation and up to this date
(1762) seventeen hundred and ninety-two persons
have been baptized here. At present there are seventy-
six families here, which, counting widows, orphans, and
other children, comprise two hundred and seventy-five
persons."

The natives did not welcome the intrusion of a paler
race, and hostilities arose almost immediately. They
had hitherto enjoyed undisputed possession of the spark-

ling springs, and they cared not to share their boon with any other people. A couple of years later reinforcements, both clerical and military, arrived, and a new and stronger presidio arose on the site of the present Military Plaza, or Plaza de Armas. The river ran through one side of it which guaranteed an inexhaustible supply of pure water. One-storied buildings were erected on the four sides of the parallelogram, and this was surrounded by a stout stockade composed of a wooden wall. Piercing this at intervals were loopholes for fire-arms.

Of the three permanent Spanish settlements in the early days of Texas, that of San Antonio was by far the most important. It was the western outpost of Spanish authority in Texas, as was Nacogdoches, the easternmost outpost. It was the capital of the province during practically the whole of the Spanish and the Mexican occupation. It became the scene of the most desperate fighting in the struggle for freedom from the Mexican yoke. A number of legends date its settlement back to the last decade of the seventeenth century, but this claim is not supported by trustworthy evidence.

From its founding almost, San Antonio was a combination, or aggregation, of mission, presidio (fortress) and villa (village). The three did not always dwell in peace and harmony, as the early records disclose many controversies. As the lawmakers and judges were so distant, the colonists were compelled to settle their petty quarrels among themselves. As a result, the minutes of the local assemblies are a record of petitions and trivial discussions. They are of no interest to-day other than the light they throw on the public questions of that day.

A constant call went out for settlers after the establishment of the eastern missions. This call was finally answered by the establishment, in 1731, of a villa, or civil

settlement, designated as San Fernando, in honour of
the Spanish king.   The colonists were secured in the
Canary Islands.   A royal decree provided that four hundred families should be transferred to Texas, but only a
small proportion of this number came.   These colonists
were landed at Vera Cruz, and were compelled to make
the long and wearisome march overland.   The government paid all expenses of the settlers, and the most elaborate plan was formulated for their well-being.   The de-
crees of the viceroy provided for their welfare as a father
would look after his children.   It was even decreed that
they become *hidalgos,* that is, gentlemen of the realm.
But they seem to have made little of this honour.   The
settlement was to become a *ciudad,* or city.   These colonists became the "Canary Island" settlers, whose members and descendants have occupied quite a prominent
place in the history of San Antonio.

Although the missions were convenient to the settlement of San Fernando, the settlers demanded a parish
church of their own.   In response to these demands the
corner stone of San Fernando was laid in 1744.   This
church was used as the central place of worship in San
Antonio for a century and a quarter.   The present cathedral was then built around and over the old church.
All that now remains of this historic structure is the curious polygonal portion with its Moorish dome at the western end.   In the early days there was a constant triangular quarrel between the three discordant elements mentioned above.   Some of it was of the most trifling nature,
and the conduct was childish.   In 1793 the mission known
as the Alamo was abandoned, and one of the discordant
elements disappeared.   The real name of the settlement
was long in doubt.   San Fernando was applied only to
the civil settlement.   As the presidio and villa gradually

TYPICAL VIEW ON A TEXAS RANCH

united and merged into one community, there was a constant struggle between Bexar and San Antonio, but the latter gradually supplanted all other designations.

All the writers of the early days tell of the obsequiousness of the Spaniards in Bexar towards the Indians, and the contempt with which the Indians treated the whites. Here is what one historian says of this period:

"Encouraged by the passive submission of the Mexicans of mixed blood, they (the Indians) carried their insolence so far as to ride into Bexar, and alight in the public square, leaving their horses to be caught and pastured by the obsequious soldiers of the garrison, on pain of chastisement. To raise a contribution, they would enter the town with a drove of Mexican horses, stolen by themselves, and under pretence of having rescued the caballado from hostile Indians, would exact a reward for their honesty! They openly carried off herds of cattle and horses from the settlements east of the Rio Grande, sparing the lives of the herdsmen, not from motives of humanity, but because they deemed it impolitic to kill those who were so useful in raising horses and mules for the benefit of the Comanches."

San Antonio did not grow very fast. When Zeb Pike passed through here in the early part of the last century, he writes of it as a city of "perhaps two thousand souls, most of whom reside in miserable mud wall houses, covered with thatched grass roofs. The town is laid out on a very grand plan."

In 1834, a colonist who visited San Antonio gives us the following description of the city:

"Bexar is one of the poorest, most miserable places in this country. The Indians steal all their horses, rob their rancheros, and, nearly every week, murder some one or two of the inhabitants. From want of union and energy, they tamely submit to this outrage, which all admit is inflicted by a few Tahuacanas."

Even at a much later period San Antonio was quite crude, for F. L. Olmstead, writing in 1856, says: "The street life of San Antonio is more varied than might be supposed. Hardly a day passes without some noise. If there be no personal affairs to arouse talk, there is some government train to be seen, with its hundreds of mules on its way from the coast to a fort above, or a Mexican ox-train from the coast. A government express clatters off, or news arrives from some exposed outpost, or from New Mexico. An Indian in his finery appears on a shaggy horse, in search of blankets, powder and ball. . . . The street affrays are numerous and characteristic. . . . More often than otherwise, the parties meet upon the plaza by chance, and each, on catching sight of his enemy, draws a revolver, and fires away. As the actors are under more or less excitement, their aim is not apt to be of the most careful and sure, and consequently it is, not seldom, the passers-by who suffer. . . . If neither is seriously injured they are brought to drink together on the following day, and the town waits for the next excitement."

With the advent of Texas sovereignty, obsequiousness toward the Indian ceased. He was taught that the white man was lord of the place. The most sanguinary event that transpired with the red men in San Antonio was the famous Council House Fight in 1840. The Comanches had expressed a desire for a conference concerning ransom for captives. The commanding officer had told them that they could come if they brought all their white captives, but not to come otherwise. On March 19th a party of sixty-five Comanches, including a dozen chiefs, arrived at San Antonio. They brought with them only one prisoner, Matilda Mary Lockhart, who, together with her sister, had been carried into captivity a couple of years before. The chiefs were conducted to the Court House, which stood at the northeast corner of Market Street and the Main Plaza. At that time, however, Market Street was called Calle de Calabosa, because the jail fronted on it just across an alley from the Court House. In this palace of justice the chiefs took seats on the platform together with the officers. Soldiers were stationed both within and without the building.

" 'Where are the prisoners you promised to bring in to this talk?' was asked.

"Muke-war-rah, the chief who held the last talk with us, and made the promise, replied: 'We have brought in the only one we had; the others are with other tribes.'

"A pause ensued because, as this answer was a palpable lie, and a direct violation of their pledges, solemnly given scarcely a month since, we had the only alternative left us. He observed this pause, and asked quickly, 'How do you like the answer?' "

The above is from the official report of the officer in charge to President Lamar. During the whole of the proceedings the chiefs kept a keen and scrutinous watch upon every movement of the whites.

The girl was questioned, and said that she had seen several other prisoners only a few days previous, and that the Indians had determined to bring them in one at a time to extort large ransoms. She also told of the brutal treatment she had received. The chiefs listened in haughty and defiant silence. The soldiers were then stationed at the doors. Colonel Fisher then reproached the Indians for their perfidy. They were reminded of the terms of the conference. He said: "You have come against our orders. Your women and children may depart in peace, and your braves may go and tell your people to send in the prisoners. When these prisoners are returned, you and the other chiefs here present may likewise go free. Until then we hold you as hostages."

The interpreter at first refused to translate this, saying that a conflict would undoubtedly follow. As soon as he uttered the words, he left the room. True to his prediction, the chiefs strung their bows, and drew their knives. A rush was made for the door. The order was given, "Fire, if they do not desist." The Indians fought desperately, and a general order to fire was given. In a short time every one of the chiefs lay dead upon the floor. The Indians in the plaza outside took up the fight and contended like wild beasts. The Indian boys, who had been shooting at marks, killed some of the whites, and even the squaws fought like fiends. Only one warrior, a renegade Mexican, escaped. Thirty-five Indians were killed. The women and children were detained as prisoners. A number of Texans, seven in all, were slain. One squaw was released, mounted on a good horse, and sent back to her people with the message that the prisoners would be released when the white prisoners were brought in. A short time afterwards a party of Comanches, displaying a white flag, appeared on a hill a short distance from San Antonio. The band brought in several white children. Their own people were released and the Indians hurried away.

The modern city of San Antonio now houses more than two hundred thousand people, and is the third city in Texas. At the time of the massacre it was a typical Mexican town of about seven thousand. The city was then on the opposite side of the river from the Alamo. It has now grown up to and around that old structure.

ALFALFA FARM, NEAR EL PASO

San Antonio has zealously preserved her sacred shrines as the expanding city has enveloped them. Here in the very heart of the city, in the shadow of towering sky-scrapers, is a two-century-old cathedral in daily use and the old Governor's Palace, recently restored to its original state, where the grandees of Spain held sway for almost a hundred years. Much of the material was imported from Hispania.

San Antoino is truly a charming city, with a riotous panorama of flowers, shrubbery and semi-tropical plants on every side. There are many little parks, or plazas, comprising a single block, after the Spanish fashion. On Milam Square is a monument marking the grave of that hero. At Travis Park rises an imposing memorial to the "Lost Cause" and bearing the significant inscription "Lest we Forget." San Pedro Park was a gift of the King of Spain in 1720. The San Antonio River meanders around lazily for many miles, and in the down-town district breaks the monotony of business structures. There are many unexpected glimpses of its palm-dotted banks, graceful bends and many bridges, all of which are extremely pleasing. The waters are clear and sparkling.

Outstanding among the attractions of San Antonio is Brackenridge Park, a fascinating bit of woodland, where every effort has been made to preserve the natural beauty of the site. It adjoins the springs which form the source of the San Antonio River, which winds through it between vine-laden trees. Live oaks, festooned with Spanish moss, form shaded driveways. Feathered songsters fill the air with their entrancing melodies. Seldom have I seen and heard so many birds as in this park so close to nature, and Texas boasts more species than any other state in the union. In the park is located one of the finest zoos in the country, where more than sixteen hundred specimens are kept in captivity.   Monkey island, the barless bear terraces, and the hippopotamus pool, where these animals are kept amidst natural surroundings, as well as many rarer animals and wild waterfowl will interest one.

One of San Antonio's slogans is "the city where sunshine spends the winter."   Of course this claim will be disputed by many other places, but this historic old city is treated exceedingly well by old Sol.   It has also the advantage of an elevation of seven hundred feet, which tempers the summer heat.   Blue ridges form the horizon. Some thirty miles distant is Medina Lake, one of the largest private irrigation projects in our land.   Surrounded by a circle of low mountains it presents a picture of remarkable beauty and, being stocked with game fish, it is a favorite resort for anglers.   There are splendid roads, and San Antonio is now the leading gateway to Old Mexico by way of Laredo and Nuevo Laredo.

If Davy Crockett or James Bowie were to revisit San Antonio, they would have great difficulty in recognizing the modern city.   It has not changed so much as to be unrecognizable, for the old has not been destroyed.   It is the growth, the tall buildings, the paved streets, the brilliant lighting that would confuse.   There is still an old Mexican quarter that is very much Mexican.   There are still many of the one-storied, flat-roofed adobe buildings with water spouts jutting out over the street.   Frequently the walls rise a couple of feet above the roof, thus forming a ready-made breastwork for the street fighting so common in some Spanish-American countries.   Señoras and señoritas go about clad in the black shawl so much worn south of the Rio Grande.   In the Mexican quarter vendors of *dulces* (candies), pottery, baskets, trinkets and Mexican foods display their wares in sidewalk bazaars. Drawnwork, which represents so much labour, can be purchased cheap. At night Haymarket Plaza, which is by day a fruit and vegetable market, becomes the center of outdoor life. Young and old, gay caballeros as well as demure señoritas, join their voices in song to the plaintive airs of the homeland romantically played upon stringed instruments.

San Antonians pride themselves upon their history and do everything possible to preserve the traditions of the past. Hence many of the new buildings, both public and private, have retained in a greater or lesser degree the Spanish type of architecture. Arcades and permanent awnings covering the sidewalks are an evidence of a sunny climate. Some of the streets have been widened, but others are as narrow as when the booted and spurred Spaniards trod them.

From Government Hill, the most prominent elevation in the city, Fort Sam Houston, claimed to be the largest military establishment in the United States, looks down upon San Antonio. From four to five thousand enlisted men and several hundred officers are usually stationed here, so that the sound of the bugle and the sight of uniforms are very familiar to San Antonians. This has been true ever since the Mexican War when troops were concentrated here. Before that it was a Spanish and Mexican military headquarters. The only interval was during the war between the states when federal troops were removed elsewhere. Fort Sam Houston now occupies five square miles adjoining the city limits. Seventeen miles distant is Randolph Field, where millions have been spent to create an ideal military aviation center. Several hundred aeroplanes can take off within a few minutes. Most of our great military leaders have seen service at Fort Sam Houston, among them Grant, Lee, Hood and Sheridan. Remember also that San Antonio was the rendezvous of the famous regiment of "Rough Riders" raised for service in the Spanish-American War.

The day of the picturesque frontier forts has almost passed. Many of them have been abandoned, and those where the soldiers are still quartered have been rebuilt and modernized. The names of many of the old forts still appear in the nomenclature of towns, such as Fort Smith, Fort Worth, Fort Scott, and others, but their military character has disappeared. Civilization and development have made the patrolling of the plains less necessary, and new barracks have been erected at central points, such as those at Fort Houston, to harbour the troops that the Government considers it necessary to maintain. The different regiments are shifted from one barrack to another, a change usually being made every few months.

The magnificent buildings which constitute Fort Sam Houston are situated on a hill which looks down upon the Alamo, and across the prairie to the other old Spanish missions. Few people visit San Antonio without a trip to Fort Sam Houston, for the buildings themselves are attractive, and the view which it affords of the surrounding country well repays the little exertion required. The red and brown sandstone of which the buildings are constructed gives a beautiful tint to everything. The Water Tower is a most artistic erection, every line of its exterior being a line of beauty, and the outlook from the balcony near the top is superb.

The life of the soldier is not all play. From the first notes of the morning bugle call until the last strain of Retreat is sounded, the hours are filled with drills, gymnastics, sham battles, target practice and other occupations. At sunrise the soldiers' day begins. As the light breaks across the rolling prairie on the eastern horizon, the roar of the morning gun disturbs the silence of the city. Then follows the lively music of the Reveille, to which the soldiers have set the following words:

> "I can't git 'em up, I can't git 'em up,
> I can't git 'em up in the morning,
> I can't git 'em up to-day."

Then the sleepy soldiers have to turn in for the morning march and answer to roll call. Three times each day comes the mess call with its rather hum-drum music. To this the soldiers have also set their own words. The day is otherwise filled with the sick-call, guard-mounting, inspection, review, etc., everything being announced by the trumpets. As sunset illumines the western sky the band plays the *Star Spangled Banner*, and the flag is slowly lowered from the flagstaff. The darkness deepens, the reds, pinks and purples become fainter, and soon Fort Sam Houston is outlined in dark shadows against the evening sky. Uncle Sam has endeavoured to look after his soldiers well. Fine grounds for football, baseball, and other games are provided for the leisure hours of the soldiers, and they are encouraged to engage in them; reading courses and a well-stocked library are maintained, as well as concerts for officers and men. The mess department is in charge of competent help, and the Government aims to provide the best of food, even if the variety is not as great as a Broadway hotel.

As Texas has far more history than many of our American States, so San Antonio has been the centre of all its history. San Antonio was the scene of minor engagements between the French and Spanish, and also between the Texas-Mexicans and the Spaniards in the revolutionary struggles which resulted in the independence of Mexico. Several years after independence it was twice occupied by Mexican troops, but only for a little while each time. The capture of the city so aroused the surrounding country that in a very short time hundreds of gallant Texans were on their way to free San Antonio from the invaders, and the city was evacuated. The city was the point of rendezvous for a number of expeditions fitted out for the invasion of Mexican territory.

The old Veramendi Palace, so noted in San Antonio history, has disappeared. It was a typical one-storied Mexican building with plastered front, but it should have been preserved. The rulers of the Province of Bexar long dwelt within its walls. James Bowie won his bride, the daughter of Governor Veramendi, there. For permitting his daughter to wed a Texas patriot, the Governor and his family were later exiled by Santa Anna. It was in this building also where General Twiggs surrendered to the Confederate commissioners all supplies and authority under his control. The heavy double doors were scarred and battered by shot and shell, and it was almost at its portal that Ben Milam received his death wound in the very hour of victory. To-day every evidence of the existence of the building has been effaced, but the doors with their bullet scars are still preserved in the city.

Of all the battles and struggles for supremacy that have occurred in Texas, one may truthfully say that the siege of the Alamo fills the largest place in history. It is the most superlatively dramatic episode in the history of the United States. The fall of the Alamo, and massacre of its garrison, caused a profound sensation throughout the entire United States, as well as Texas. It is a part of American history, and it is the kind of history that has been soul thrilling from the very beginning of time. The heroism of the defenders has been ranked with that shown at Thermopylæ and at the charge of Balaklava. It is not remarkable for the numbers engaged on the Alamo side, for they numbered less than two hundred, but it is notable because of the courage and patriotism of the defenders who fought until the very last man had fallen. Greater bravery or grander heroism could no man show. As has been said: "Thermopylæ had its messenger of defeat, but the Alamo had none." Among these was Davy Crockett, who is still an undimmed hero among boys. But the patriot Travis, the commander; James Bowie, the designer of the bowie knife; Lieutenant Dickinson, and a hundred and more obscure heroes were equally brave, and yet they have not a monument erected to their individual memory.

The old mission of the Alamo, which was probably the chapel of the original mission, stands at one side of the Alamo Plaza in San Antonio and faces the west. It is not imposing in appearance, as one might be led to believe, for the walls are not high. In size it is about seventy-five feet long by sixty-two feet wide. Originally designed as a place of worship, it was secularized in 1793 and used as a citadel of defence against the incursions of the Indians. At that time there were only a few score Indians attached to the mission. The baptismal records reveal the surprising number of one hundred distinct tribes represented in the various services during the religious career of this mission. With walls four and a half feet thick and twenty-two feet high, it was well adapted for defence against the light arms of that day. The walls are severely plain, with the exception of the ornate carvings on the arched doorways and side pillars.

The Alamo has recently been restored more nearly to its original condition at the time of this famous struggle. At one side of the mission was an enclosure, surrounded by a high wall, in which were some buildings that had been the living quarters of those connected with the monastery.

The old document, quoted above, also says of the Alamo: "It contains a convent, or monastery, fifty yards square with arcades above and below. In the monastery are the living-rooms of the religious, the porter's lodge, the dining-room, kitchen and office. The mission has a well-built stone chapel eleven yards long. Among its ornaments is a stone cross two yards high and capped with silver. In the cross are hidden the reliquaries, four in number, and each containing its own relic. The altar is adorned with carved and painted images.

"There are seven rows of houses for dwellings for the Indians. These are made of stone and supplied with doors and windows. They are furnished with high beds, chests, metates, pots, flat earthen pans, kettles, cauldrons and boilers. With their arched porticoes, the houses form a beautiful plaza through which runs a canal skirted with willows and by fruit trees and used by the Indians. To insure a supply of water in case of blockade by an enemy, a curbed well has been made. For the defence of the settlement the plaza is surrounded by a wall. Over, the gate is a large tower within whose embrasure are three cannons, some firearms, and other appropriate supplies for warfare."

This was probably the condition of the Alamo at the time of the tragedy. That part of it outside of the mission is just as sacred as the chapel itself, for here it was that the greater part of the struggle took place, and the final act only was enacted within the mission walls. The walled enclosure around the convent, which adjoined the church on the north, now appears in its original condition, but the buildings have not been restored. The larger area, however, which was in front of the church, and on the west side of the convent enclosure, has entirely disappeared. A part of it is included in the Plaza. This area was about one hundred and fifty-four yards long and fifty-four yards wide, and enclosed by walls nine to twelve feet high and nearly three feet thick. Into this area several doors opened from the convent enclosure, and their locations can be seen in the restored wall. The area of all the enclosures probably amounted to two or three acres. The church itself was used as the powder magazine.

After the conflict the Alamo was roofless, and remained so for many years. At the close of the Mexican War, the United States leased the entire group from the Catholic Church. It was occupied as a quartermaster's and commissary depot up to the beginning of the Civil War, after a complete restoration of the buildings. It was then surrendered to the Confederacy. After the collapse of the Confederacy, the buildings were again used by the United States until 1876, when the quartermaster's depot was removed to Fort Sam Houston on Government Hill. The chapel was purchased by the State some time ago, but it was only recently that the convent portion was added through an enabling act of the Legislature. A syndicate was endeavouring to secure it as a site for a hotel.

"Save the Alamo" was the appeal sent broadcast over the State by the "Daughters of the Republic of Texas." When the voluntary contributions were insufficient, the State stepped in. But there has been much discord. One faction wanted to tear down all but the church. The other desired to restore the monastery. My sympathies are strongly with the latter faction. The entire fortress should be restored as nearly as possible to its original appearance.

As has been mentioned elsewhere in this work, the Texan soldiers were mostly volunteers. They were pioneers in a new land, accustomed to take the initiative, and consequently very independent in their actions. On January 17th, 1836, Houston wrote to Governor Smith: "Col. Bowie will leave here in a few hours for Bexar, with a detachment of from 20 to 50 men. . . . I have ordered the fortifications in the town of Bexar to be demolished and, if you should think fit, I will remove all the cannon and other munitions of war to Gonzales and Copano, blow up the Alamo and abandon the place, as it will be impossible to keep up the station with volunteers." [1]

Colonel Bowie reached San Antonio as quickly as possible, for, on February 2nd, he wrote to Governor Smith as follows: "Relief at the post in men, money and provisions is of vital importance. The salvation of Texas depends on keeping Bexar out of the hands of the enemy. . . . Col. Neill and myself have come to the same conclusion, that we will rather die in these ditches than give it up to the enemy. These citizens deserve our patriotism, and the public safety demands our lives rather than evacuate this post to the enemy. Again we call aloud for relief. . . . Our force is very small. The returns this day show only 120 men and officers. . . . I have information just now from a friend that the force at Presidio is 2,000 complete."

Colonel Travis was not then at San Antonio. On Jan-

[1] This correspondence is from *A History of Texas and Texans*, by Johnson and Barker, published in 1914.

uary 28th he wrote to Governor Smith from Burnham's on the Colorado: "In obedience to my orders I have done everything in my power to get ready to march to the relief of Bexar, but owing to the difficulty of getting horses and provisions, and owing to desertions, etc., I shall march to-day with only about thirty men, all regulars, except four. I shall however go on and do my duty if I am sacrificed, unless I receive new orders to countermarch. . . . You have no idea of the exhausted state of the country—Volunteers can no longer be had or relied upon—A speedy organization, classification and draft of the Militia is all that can save us now. . . . The patriotism of a few has done much; but that is becoming worn down—I have strained every nerve—I have used my personal credit and have neither slept day nor night since I rec'd orders to march—and with all this exertion I have hardly been able to get horses and equipments for the few men I have."

On February 12th, Travis again wrote, this time from Bexar: "Santa Anna . . . has issued his proclamation denouncing vengeance against the people of Texas, and threatens to exterminate every white man within its limits. This, being the frontier post, will be the first attacked. We are illy prepared for their reception, as we have not more than 150 men here and they in a very disorganized state. . . . For God's sake and for the sake of our country, send us reinforcements. I hope you will send to this post at least two companies of regular troops. . . . Yet, should we receive no reinforcements, I am determined to fight to the last, and should Bexar fall, your friend will be buried beneath its ruins."

The most famous of all the messages of Travis, and which has been called the most heroic document in American history, is the following, which is here given in full:

"COMMANDANCY OF THE ALAMO, BEXAR,

"Feby. 24th, 1836.

"To the People of Texas and All Americans in the World:

"FELLOW CITIZENS AND COMPATRIOTS: I am besieged by a thousand or more of the Mexicans under Santa Anna. I have sustained a continued Bombardment and cannonade for 24 hours and have not lost a man. The enemy has demanded a surrender at discretion, otherwise, the garrison are to be put to the sword, if the fort is taken. I have answered the demand with a cannon shot, and our flag still waves proudly from the walls. *I shall never surrender or retreat.* Then, I call on you in the name of liberty, of patriotism, and everything dear to the American character, to come to our aid with all dispatch. The enemy is receiving reinforcements daily, and will no doubt increase to three or four thousand in four or five days. If this call is neglected, I am determined to sustain myself as long as possible and die like a soldier who never forgets what is due to his own honour and that of his country. VICTORY OR DEATH.

"WILLIAM BARRETT TRAVIS,

"Lt. Col. comdt.

"P. S. The Lord is on our side. When the enemy appeared in sight we had not three bushels of corn. We have since found in deserted houses 80 to 90 bushels and got into the walls 20 or 30 head of Beeves.

"TRAVIS."

In response to a note received by him, Andrew Ponton and thirty-two men marched from Gonzales and passed through the enemy's lines on the night of March 1st. Governor Smith published an appeal in the form of a handbill, and sent it broadcast. On March 3rd Travis got through a final message, which gave an account of the siege up to that date. "A blood red banner," says this letter, "waves from the church of Bexar, and in the camp above us, in token that the war is one of vengeance against rebels. . . . Their threats have had no influence upon me or my men, but to make all fight with desperation, and that high-souled courage which characterizes the patriot, who is willing to die in defence of his country's liberty and his own honour." He ends it with these words: "God and Texas—Victory or Death." I quote thus freely from these various messages to elucidate clearly the fact that the actions of these brave men were deliberate. Many men can be brave when suddenly confronted by an emergency, but it requires the very highest degree of courage and patriotism to do as these men did and deliberately face annihilation.

"All who wish to leave stand in their places. Every man who will die with me, come across the line! Who will be first?" These words, so we are told, were spoken by Colonel Travis.[1] As he spoke the words, he drew a

[1] Colonel Travis was a native of North Carolina, only twenty-eight years of age, and a lawyer by profession. In appearance, he was six feet in height, erect and manly in carriage, with blue eyes, reddish hair and a round face. Davy Crockett came from Tennessee. He had spent his life in the forests, and was known all over the frontier as a mighty hunter. He had served in a State legislature and also two terms in the United States Congress. Defeated in his ambition for a third term, Crockett came to Texas to try and renew his fortunes. He had arrived only about three weeks before the beginning of the siege of the Alamo. He dressed in buckskins, wore a coonskin cap, and always carried his favorite long rifle named "Betsy."

line on the ground with his sword. Every man leaped over the line but two, so we are told. One of these was James Bowie, a famous frontiersman, and he was so ill that he could not get up from his cot. "Boys, move my cot over the line," he said. Bowie was a Georgian, who is best known as the inventor of the knife that bears his name. He was about six feet tall, with fair complexion, and had a fierce look. But he was not quarrelsome. "He had a wonderful art of winning people to him, and was extremely prodigal of his money," we are told. One man, and one only, refused to cross the line, and he attempted to escape. But he was never heard of afterwards.

A band of Mexicans, under Santa Anna, numbering about five thousand, besieged the fortress on the outside. The demand for surrender on February 23rd was answered by Colonel Travis with a cannon shot. The flag of the Constitution of 1824 was nailed to the staff so that it could not be lowered. Day after day shells came hurtling over the walls from dawn until dark, and from dark to dawn. On March 1st, thirty-two soldiers from Gonzales arrived and entered the fort. The last courier was sent out on March 3rd. By that time ammunition was running low, and the Texans seldom fired. It was not until ammunition failed that the assailants made any headway against the brave defenders. Santa Anna called a council of his officers and an assault was decided upon. There were to be four columns of attack. At four o'clock on the morning of the 6th, a Sunday, the bugle sounded, and the whole line advanced to the attack. The Texans were ready and met them with a shower of grape and rifle balls. Twice the assailants reeled, but each time they rallied. The third time an entrance was secured into the enclosed yard. One of their guns was captured and immediately turned upon the defenders. But the enfeebled garrison could not hold out against such overwhelming numbers. The church was the last place entered by the foe, and the few who had taken refuge there were soon despatched. A couple of women, two children, and two slaves alone remained.

The spirit that animated the Alamo has always filled Texas. "Remember the Alamo!" is a cry that has never failed of enthusiastic response. At the time it aroused a sensation throughout the United States. All the details have never been learned, for the simple reason that not a single combatant of the last struggle survived to tell the tale, and the official reports of the enemy are not reliable.

Don Francisco Ruiz, the Alcalde of San Antonio, wrote an account, from which the following extracts are made:

"On the 6th of March (1836) at 3 a. m., General Santa Anna at the head of 4,000 men advanced against the Alamo. The infantry, artillery and cavalry had formed about 1,000 varas from the walls of the same fortress. The Mexican army charged and were twice repulsed by the deadly fire of Travis's artillery, which resembled a constant thunder. At the third charge the Toluca battalion commenced to scale the walls and suffered severely. Out of 830 men only 130 were left alive.

"On the north battery of the fortress convent, lay the lifeless body of Col. Travis on the gun carriage, shot only through the forehead. Towards the west, and in a small fort opposite the city, we found the body of Col. Crockett. Col. Bowie was found dead in his bed in one of the rooms on the south side. Santa Anna, after all the Mexican bodies had been taken out, ordered wood to be brought to burn the bodies of the Texans. He sent a company of dragoons with me to bring wood and dry branches from the neighbouring forests. About three o'clock in the afternoon of March 6, we laid the wood and dry branches upon which a pile of dead bodies were placed, more wood was piled on them and another pile of bodies was brought and in this manner they were all arranged in layers. Kindling wood was distributed throughout the pile and about 5 o'clock in the evening it was lighted.

"The gallantry of the few Texans who defended the Alamo was really wondered at by the Mexican army. Even the generals were astonished at their vigorous resistance and how dearly victory was bought. . . . The men (Texans) burnt were one hundred and eighty-two. I was an eye-witness, for as Alcalde of San Antonio, I was, with some of the neighbours, collecting the dead bodies and placing them on the funeral pyre."

Requiescat in pace, heroes of the Alamo!

A FLOWING ARTESIAN WELL

CHAPTER VII

THE old missions erected by religious orders in some parts of our Southwest were the forerunners of the civilization that was to follow. To fully appreciate their significance one must allow his imagination to run back a century or two, and try to picture to oneself conditions as they then existed. The adventurers who first visited this part of the New World had two objects in view. The first was to add to the new dominions of their sovereigns; the second to extend the Christian religion. The establishment of missions accomplished both these purposes. It gave possession of the country, and at the same time provided for the conversion of the aborigines.

The missions of Texas are probably not so well known as the similar institutions of California. They are, nevertheless, almost speaking monuments of the early history of the marvellous State of Texas, just as are those in California of the early history of that great State. At that time the wide-stretching plains of Texas were dotted with the wigwams of the wandering Indian tribes. Unlike the peaceful Pueblo Indians of New Mexico, who were easily Christianized and who made little trouble for the early missionaries, the Indians of Texas belonged to those nomadic and savage tribes which have never yet been Christianized. The most troublesome were the Comanches and Apaches. The missionaries who went among them did so in great personal danger. Hence

115

it is that we find the missions which are grouped around
San Antonio built close together for the purpose of defence and mutual aid in times of trouble, while those
of California are separated by a day's journey.

Together with the military posts, or presidios, which
were established with them, the missions formed an outpost of Spanish power and aided in extending the domain of the Golden Lions of Castile into new lands. The
presidio, or fort, was the instrument of military occupation. It was used when defence or the protection of arms
was necessary. There was generally at least one for
each exposed group of missions, and it was so located
as to be most effective as a protection for all. If there
was no presidio, a little guard of soldiers was generally
stationed at the mission itself. The soldiers assigned for
such duty, however, were generally of such a low type
that the padres frequently preferred to be without them.
Their outrages not only interfered with the work, but
frequently aroused the Indians to retaliatory acts which
endangered the safety of all.

And yet, even if the soldiers had not contributed much
to neutralize the efforts of the missionaries, the difficulties
of the work would have been almost insurmountable.
The method of confining the roving Indians, who were
accustomed to a free and nomadic life, in pueblos in a
condition closely approaching to slavery, and forcing
them to perform a daily round of labour, as well as to
attend a continuous programme of formal services, did
not instil much love either for Christ or the Spaniards.
They remained while gifts were abundant, but when these
failed they disappeared.

"In 1691," says an old writer, "the province of Asais,
or Texas, as it was called by the Spaniards, was settled
by some emigrants, and visited by fourteen Spanish

monks, who were anxious to devote themselves to the conversion of the Indians, and a garrison and a mission were at that time established." The location of this establishment cannot now be positively identified. One of the earliest known missions was that of Adaes, not far from Natchitoches. The fort here was intended as an outpost against the French, but the mission was designed for the conversion of the Indians in that neighbourhood. Our knowledge of the history of these grand old missions is extremely meagre. The locations of the earliest ones can now hardly be identified. The Indians were so troublesome that frequent removals took place. Nearly all of them were founded by the monks of the Order of Saint Francis, who came up from Querétero and Zacatecas in Mexico. The task was hard.

"It was necessary," said one of the padres who laboured in Texas, "first to transform these Indians into men, and afterwards to labour to make them Christians." How vastly different were the conditions here than among the Aztec population across the Rio Grande. That non-resisting race at least passively received the new religion. The Christianization, at any rate the baptizing, of the millions of that race is a record such as the world had never before witnessed. A single priest baptized in one day, according to his own report, five thousand natives, and he did not desist until he was so exhausted that he could not lift his hands. Another priest wrote that "an ordinary day's work is from ten to twenty thousand souls." In the course of a few years baptism had been administered to millions. These new converts, of course, were very immature Christians. They might be able to make the sign of the cross, and still be ignorant of what that symbol meant to humanity. But the important fact is that these priests, who had laboured

among a pliant and receptive people, were here thrown
out into the wilderness among a race of real savages who
had never developed a civilization of their own.

Not only were converts difficult to secure in Texas, but
it was necessary to be constantly on the alert to prevent
attack from marauding bodies of these savages. Even
then they were not immune from disaster. In 1757 there
was founded on the San Saba River, in what is now
Menard County, the mission of San Saba, by a company
of fathers from Santa Fé. For a time everything went
well, and the Apaches maintained friendly relations with
the ecclesiastics, although they refused to form a pueblo
around it. At first the Apaches made various excuses,
but finally frankly said that they preferred a wandering
life. But the Apaches were at war with the Comanches,
and the latter came one day and fell upon the defenceless
missionaries during the absence of the soldiers from the
presidio, a league and a half away. Not a priest or a
domestic escaped the fury of the red men. This terrible
fate of San Saba resulted in a recommendation that the
idea of dealing with the Apaches by missions be abandoned. At any rate it had been an absolute failure from
the time of its inception.

One of the early missions established in Texas was
that known as San Francisco de los Tejas, which was
founded by the padres soon after the destruction of Fort
Saint Louis. The exact location of this mission is unknown, but it was somewhere between the Trinity and
Neches rivers, and forty or fifty miles southwest of
Nacogdoches. As the Indians refused to live in com-
munities, and the soldiers became troublesome, its abandonment was ordered by the viceroy. In 1693 the padres
buried whatever property they could not carry with them.
In 1716 the mission was revived, and a few years later

THE PECOS RIVER

was transferred to the bank of the San Antonio River. As the buildings of the original mission were of timber, all landmarks have disappeared. This was true of a number of the earlier missions established in Eastern Texas, which were the earliest ones, for the lack of suitable stone caused the use of the more perishable materials. For this reason the old mission at Nacogdoches has disappeared. In the West, stone was plentiful and wood scarce, so that the buildings erected there were massive and enduring. To this fact is due the preservation of those splendid monuments of the Mission Period that are found in the neighbourhood of San Antonio.

It was in the year 1689 that the first representative of Spain arrived at the location where San Antonio is now located. The Indians who then lived there greeted the arrival of Don Alonzo de Leon and his followers with the cry of "Tejas! Tejas!" The natural attractions of this location, and the abundance of the pure water, moved Don Alonzo to believe that here was a site where a settlement should be established, and where a mission should be built to convert the savages living in the vicinity. This was the beginning of the string of missions for the worship of the Almighty and the spread of the Gospel in Texas. It was during the years from 1690 to 1719 that the most of the missions of Texas were built and made a part of the established church. The Alamo is the most noted of these missions around San Antonio, and its grey time-stained walls stand in the centre of the city. Its history has been written in the blood of the bravest of the brave. It was first used as a place of worship, but later principally served as a citadel of defence against the incursions of the Indians. It is probably due to this secular use that the name Alamo supplanted its earlier name of the religious fathers. Its history has been treated of elsewhere.

The Mission Concepcion, or Nuestra Senora de la Purisima Concepcion de Acuna, which is situated only two miles from San Antonio, is generally known as the First Mission. After that of the Alamo, it is the most celebrated of any of these establishments in Texas from an historical standpoint, for it was one of the favoured spots of the Texas patriots. It has been the scene of a number of gatherings participated in by many of the heroes whose names are now venerated by the people of Texas. It was also the site of one of the thrilling and bloody contests between the Mexicans and Texas during the momentous times when the people of that territory were striving to overthrow the yoke of Mexico.

On the 27th of October, 1835, General Austin sent a party of ninety men, under James Bowie and James W. Fannin, on a reconnoitring expedition to select a good location for his army near San Antonio. They encamped that night at a horseshoe bend in the San Antonio River, near the Mission Concepcion. It was a strategic position, for the river and a skirt of timber protected the rear, and there was a depression in the front which constituted a sort of natural fortification. The Mexicans discovered the camp and attempted to surround it during the night. The creak of an artillery wheel aroused Colonel Bowie, so that when the Mexicans advanced the little force was prepared to receive them. The Mexicans fired in reckless volleys, while the Texans made every bullet count. They succeeded in firing their little four-pound cannon five times, but without effect. The rifles of the Texans picked off the gunners. Three times the Mexicans sounded the charge, but all in vain. The Texans hurled them back and remained masters of the field. Although the Mexican forces numbered fully four hundred, they were compelled to flee. Their casualties were greater than the entire force of Texans, while the latter had one man killed and none wounded. Knowing that defeat meant death, and that surrender could not even be thought of, these Texans had fought with the same bravery as was afterwards shown at the Alamo.

The Mission Concepcion was established in 1716, and rebuilt on its present site in 1731. It is modelled after the Moorish style, which was then a favourite model with Spanish builders. As early as 1762 a writer dwells with great pride on this mission. He speaks of the beautiful architecture of the building, the finely sculptured images of stone, the mural decorations, the abundance of ornaments and the rich vestments of the priests. It has a square front with dome-covered belfries on either side. The front door is surmounted by a curious triangle, and in the centre of the arch is a coat of arms. The walls are covered with cement, ornamented with geometric designs, and the floor is covered with a native tiling. There is a curious stone altar, and services are occasionally held here, but vandalism and time, the two great destroyers, are rapidly making a ruin of this splendid old structure.

A few miles farther out from Mission Concepcion lies the Mission San José de Aguayo, being named in honour of the patron saint, Saint Joseph, and a former governor of Texas. It is doubtless the most imposing and beautiful of the several sacred edifices known as missions in and about San Antonio. Although the dome and portions of the arched roof have fallen in, San José still bears witness to the wonderful manner in which the Spaniards and the priests carried the art of the Old World into the wilderness of the New. The remarkable carvings which ornament the stone facings of the doorways, and the great oak and cedar doors themselves, would reflect credit upon the religious establishments of Spain herself. A celebrated artist was sent out from Spain, who spent years in carving the statues and other ornamental work of this mission.

The Mission San José was founded in 1720, and the construction was finished in the following eight years. It also stands on the right bank of the San Antonio River, and is located only four miles from the city of the same name. Like the other missions, the walls are several feet thick, and the doors are made of heavy oaken planking of massive construction. The mission is to-day wholly in ruins, and the ruins are the most extensive of any of the missions. Vandal hands have defaced some of the statues. One may still see the spiral stairway to the belfry, and the antique cedar ladder which leads to the belfry and was used by the monks when they wished to ring the bells for mass. This is one of the striking reminders of the early days. After the secularization of the missions, this mission was discontinued and the land distributed to the Indians. When this mission was visited by Lieutenant Pike in 1807, there were left hardly enough Indians to perform the household duties. Standing in solitary grandeur upon a beautiful plateau, it is annually visited by thousands who can but admire this monument of the zeal and enterprise of the Franciscan fathers of the last century.

The Mission San Juan de Caprisana is located at a distance of two miles from that of San José, or almost six miles from San Antonio, and also on the bank of the San Antonio River. This mission was completed about 1716, but for some reason must have been soon abandoned by the friars and permitted to lapse into decay. It seems never to have been prosperous. The proba-

bilities are that it was too remote from the settlements
and the military force within the city of San Antonio,
so that the monks and others living there were in too much
danger from the savage Indians. Very little but ruins
are left of this Mission San Juan, but the imposing bell
tower and some of the moss-grown walls remain
to impress the visitor with the grandeur that once existed here two centuries ago, when the cowled monks
and the booted and helmeted cavaliers of Spain trod
this wilderness, and laboured to erect a bulwark of state
and church. It was a war of conquest, in which greed
and religion were very closely allied.

San Francisco de la Espada (sword) is another of
the group of missions around San Antonio. The name
signifies that those who founded this establishment belonged to the church militant, and as such were obliged
to wield the literal as well as the spiritual sword. Time
has not dealt gently with this sacred edifice. It was
early abandoned and then rebuilt, but it was again relinquished soon afterwards. For many years the handi-
work of the early architect and builders has been disintegrating. The queer old sword-shaped tower still rears
itself skyward, and portions of the walls have resisted
Time, the destroyer. It is to be hoped that the further
encroachments of destructive influences will be arrested
or counteracted, so that these ruins will not fall into
absolute and irremediable decay.

From the very beginning of the Mission Period, there
were those who distrusted this method of colonization.
It was not long until the objections were loudly outspoken. In 1727, an official who made a tour of inspection reported all of them in bad condition. As a
result of his recommendation some of them were abandoned when official protection and support were with-

drawn. Each official visit resulted in another report adverse to the friars. One of the effective arguments against them was the great cost and the meagre results. The settlers were decreasing in numbers rather than increasing. It was urged that the money spent in maintaining these establishments could be more profitably employed in paying the actual expenses of the colonists for a number of years. But the padres were not disheartened by the official attitude, and we cannot but admire their courage and persistence. After the destruction of San Saba, the missionary activity rapidly subsided. The padres themselves could not make a good showing for their work, and could only indulge in hopes for the future. It was in 1794 that the order came for the secularization of the missions, and the support from the royal treasury was withdrawn. The process began at once, but it was not completed for a number of years afterwards. In 1812 a few Indians still dwelt around the missions, but they were finally dispersed by the Spanish government.

Let us look for a moment at the life that was lived at these establishments. The Indians attached to the missions were reduced almost to the condition of menials. The attitude of the Spaniards toward them is well expressed by the term used to describe them. This was *Indios reducidos,* or "reduced Indians," to distinguish them from the *Indios bravos.* By the Spanish law they could be detained in the pueblos by force, and, if they ran away, could be brought back forcibly. In 1762, there were probably twenty-five hundred Indians connected with the San Antonio missions. Twenty years later there were not more than five hundred. The following description of the village connected with the Mission Concepcion, near San Antonio, is most interesting and enlightening

as to the common life at the missions; it is translated
from a report of the missionaries in 1762:

"The pueblo is composed of two rows of stone houses
and huts in which the Indians live, which are furnished
with boilers, flat earthen pans, pots, and other domestic
utensils, the pueblo being also surrounded by a wall for
its protection and defence. It has its inclosed fields, the
necessary supplies of water, a flowing irrigation ditch
with its stone dam, and a ranch with its dwellings for
the families who look after its two hundred mares, one
hundred and ten horses, six hundred and ten head of
cattle, and twenty-two hundred head of goats and sheep.

"Every day all the Indians recite in concert the text
of the Christian doctrine according to the catechism of
Ripalda, in the morning before work and in the evening
after it. Three or four times a week the ministers in-
struct their Indians, with reference to the same text of
the catechism, in the mysteries of our holy faith, and the
obligations of Christians, with similes and arguments
adapted to their inexpressible rusticity. . . . All those
who are of sufficient age confess and receive the sacra-
ment, according to their respective ability to understand,
during Lent and on any festivals when they wish. . . .
The missionaries have paid special attention to the tem-
poral assistance of the Indians, both because this is their
personal business, and because it is one of the most important means of subsistence for those who live at the
missions, and for the attraction of those who inhabit the
woods, who observe and consider the advantages the
others enjoy.

"The corn crop is consumed by giving the Indians what
they need for all purposes; and they are also furnished
beans, pumpkins, watermelons, melons, pepper, salt, and
sugar, which is made from cane that they take care to

plant at each mission annually, because this is the best
thing to regale the Indians and the most pleasing to their
appetite. . . . The horses are used in looking after the
cattle, gathering the flocks, and in other services of the
missions to which they belong; most of them being lost
or stolen, either by enemies or by the Indians of the missions themselves when they escape. The Indians are
assisted, when they are sick, with medicines which this
country furnishes, and some which are brought in for
the purpose. They are visited by the fathers and by other
persons who have been charged with the care of them;
and in serious cases they are fed from the kitchen of the
fathers, and in all they are relieved from work.

"The labour of the Indians is to plant the fields, look
after the cattle, to water the crops, to clear away weeds,
and to gather their grain, to erect their dwellings, and
other buildings of the missions to which the community
attends; but with such slowness and carelessness that it is
always necessary for some Spaniard to be directing them,
and four of them are not sufficient for what could be done
by one. They work, with a lack of energy corresponding
to their inborn laziness, some at weaving and in the
forges, and others as carpenters and bricklayers, in which
trades instruction has been furnished them by the missionaries with no small endeavour for their comfort.
They have been provided also with the proper tools for
all these occupations. The employment of the women
and children is to spin with *malacates,* and to comb cotton. All this labour constitutes no impediment to their
spiritual welfare or the help due their families, but is
very moderate and comfortable to their want of culture,
little talent, and great sloth."

THE RIO GRANDE

CHAPTER VIII

HOUSTON AND SAN JACINTO

"Site of capital of the Republic of Texas, 1837-38, '39 and '42. Commemorating days when after her glorious struggle Texas stood an independent nation."

This inscription on a tablet placed at the entrance to the leading hotel in Houston discloses the pretension that this city has to eminence. It must not be forgotten that Texas for almost ten years was a full-fledged Republic with a complete government. She maintained diplomatic representatives in the courts of a number of European countries and at Washington. In the capitol at Austin are preserved a number of original treaties negotiated between that Republic and these governments. They are all inscribed in longhand, and a heavy seal, weighing several pounds, is attached to them.

The city of Houston came into existence in August, 1836. It was in the same year that the Texas Congress, which was then a sort of perambulating body, having shifted from place to place according to the exigencies of the occasion, decided to establish the capital at the newly-founded settlement until 1840. After Texas had achieved her independence, the possession of the seat of government was a prize eagerly contended for by nearly all the actual and prospective municipalities, within the limits of actual occupation. Individuals and companies which were prospecting town sites extended proffers for the capital, because of the prestige this would bestow.

127

Texas commerce had been only slightly developed, and it was obvious that the capital city, owing to its political importance, would have superior advantages over its rivals.

The city was located on Buffalo Bayou, and was appropriately named after General Sam Houston, who had just been elected President. The Allens, who were promoting the town, had agreed to erect the capitol at their own expense. These men had purchased more than two square miles of land for about what one foot front would now bring in the heart of the city. Circulars were issued with drawings representing a large city, showing churches, court house, market-house and other improvements, at a time when the site was nothing more than a camp. The first sale of town lots was held January 19, 1837, and many were attracted to it as the first permanent capital. Among these were many men around whom history has since thrown its aureola. The Allens fulfilled their contract and erected a frame building for the government offices, which was afterwards converted into a hotel upon the removal of the seat of government.

Texas was by this time attracting the attention of the whole world. The heroism of those who had fallen at the Alamo, the brutal massacre at Goliad, and the accomplishments of the Texans in the other skirmishes, which had culminated in the remarkable victory of San Jacinto, with resulting freedom from the yoke of Mexico, suggested to the world the marvellous deeds of heroes of the past. The naturalist Audubon came here on a search for new varieties of birds in 1837. He writes of Houston in his diary, as follows:

"We landed at Houston, the capital of Texas, drenched to the skin, and were kindly received on board the steamer *Yellow Stone*, Captain West, who gave us his stateroom to change our clothes, and furnished us refreshments and dinner. The Buffalo Bayou had risen about six feet, and the neighbouring prairies were partly covered with water: there was a wild and desolate look cast on the surrounding scenery. We had already passed two little girls encamped on the bank of the bayou under the cover of a few clap-boards, cooking a scanty meal; shanties, cargoes of hogsheads, barrels, etc., were spread about the landing; and Indians drunk and hallooing were stumbling about in the mud in every direction. These poor beings had come here to enter into a treaty proposed by the whites; many of them were young and well looking, and with far less decorations than I have seen before on such occasions. The chief of the tribe is an old and corpulent man.

"We walked toward the President's house, accompanied by the Secretary of the Navy, and as soon as we rose above the bank we saw before us a level of far-extending prairie, destitute of timber and rather poor soil. Houses, half finished, and most of them without roofs, tents, and a liberty pole, with the capitol, were all exhibited to our view at once. We approached the President's mansion, however, wading in water above our ankles. This abode of President Houston is a small log house, consisting of two rooms and a passage through, after the Southern fashion. The moment we stepped over the threshold, on the right hand of the passage, we found ourselves ushered into what in other countries would be called the ante-chamber; the ground floor, however, was muddy and filthy, a large fire was burning, and a small table, covered with paper and writing materials, was in the centre; camp beds, trunks, and different materials were strewed around the room. We were at once presented to several members of the Cabinet, some of whom bore the stamp of men of intellectual ability, simple, though bold, in their general appearance.

"We first caught sight of President Houston as he walked from one of the grog-shops, where he had been to stop the sale of ardent spirits. We reached his abode before him, but he soon came, and we were presented to his Excellency. He was dressed in a fancy velvet coat and trousers trimmed with broad gold lace, and around his neck was tied a cravat somewhat in the style of '76. He received us kindly, was desirous of retaining us for a while, and offered us every facility in his power. He at once removed us from the ante-room to his private chamber, which, by the way, was not much cleaner than the former. We were severally introduced by him to the different members of his Cabinet and Staff, and at once asked to drink grog with him, which we did, wishing success to the new Republic. Our talk was short, but the impression which was made on our mind at the time by himself, his officers, and the place of his abode can never be forgotten."

The initial capitol of the Government here in Houston was a small log house which has disappeared, but the residence of the President, now nothing more than a small unpretentious clapboard house with only two rooms, still survives the changes of time, in a dilapidated condition. Garbed in a scarlet waistcoat, and boots with red tops and finished at the heels with silver spurs, Houston certainly made an impressive picture for the head of a Republic in the wilderness. When the first diplomatic agent from England arrived in Houston, and found the President of the Republic to which he was accredited living in such unpretentious quarters, he was indeed astonished, and doubtless much disappointed.

Houston at that time, although the capital of an inde-

HOME OF A MEXICAN FAMILY IN THE JUNGLE

pendent republic, was unworthy the name of a town, for nothing more than tents and temporary shanties of clapboards and pine poles were scattered along the banks of the bayou. Even the substantial log cabins, which were so commonly built by the pioneers, were rare. The howling of the wolves and wildcats, so we are informed by those who dwelt there at that time, was common, and the settler usually kept his shotgun convenient to use if occasion arose.

In the first issue of the *Telegraph,* the first newspaper established in the city, a racy account of the editor's experiences is given. He says: "Fortunately, we have succeeded in renting a shanty, which, although like the capitol in this place, is

> "Without a roof and without a floor,
> Without window and without a door.

"N. B.: Our troubles have not yet ended. The shanty is falling about our ears, two massive beams have dropped down upon the stands, made a disgusting *pi,* and have driven the workmen to seek safety outside. The devil alone looks smiling at the mischief."

Gradually the wolves, the wildcats, and the Indians disappeared, however, and a new order arose in Houston. The houses increased in number and waxed larger, streets of generous width were laid out; flower gardens began to bloom, and shade trees were planted. The old-fashioned, white-topped wagons, with their many yokes of oxen, were a distinguishing feature of Houston. In the early days these wagons were the sole means of communication with the rest of the State and with the adjoining States, for it was many years before the last spike of the first railroad was driven. The teamsters were men of great fortitude, for they were forced to brave not only storm and exposure but also the menace of lurking savages on their long journeys across country.

Sam Houston and Stephen Austin, the two most noted men in the early history of Texas, were bitter rivals. Their political ideas and ideals rarely harmonized. Their methods of accomplishing their ends were certainly different. Each had a following of devoted partisans. Although milder in his manner, Austin was also inclined to be unyielding and not very compromising. Houston was domineering in his manner and could not brook opposition. He was naturally very anxious that the city bearing his name should remain the permanent capital; but the friends of Austin, after his death, were equally determined to have the permanent capital named in his honour. The crude buildings, the unhealthfulness of the location and the muddy streets were all urged as reasons for the removal of the seat of government. Their efforts were so successful that about the middle of September, 1838, the official archives were loaded on wagons and hauled to Austin, President Lamar and his cabinet following soon afterwards on horseback.

Houston is the real wonder city of Texas. Its growth has been phenomenal. In 1915 it was the third city in the state, with a population considerably less than one hundred thousand. To-day it has passed the three hundred thousand mark, and among southern cities is the largest city between Los Angeles and New Orleans. It is a city that pleases the eye, for the streets have generous width and the new additions made necessary by the city's growth have been designed with a regard for the artistic, which is not always true in growing municipalities. The mild climate is an advantage in the work of beautification. They are able to develop shrubbery and ornamental plants

much more quickly than in the north, for the winters are
short and mild and vegetation will grow practically every
month in the year.   Ornamental palms thrive, and the
live oaks are particularly beautified by clinging Spanish
moss, which adds an indefinable charm.

Houstonians boast that they brought the ocean to their
doors, which is a true statement of fact.   The early
rivalry of Houston was with Galveston.   Before the advent of railroads the only outlet was by water, and that
meant rendering tribute to the island city.   Although the
produce could be floated on tugs down the sluggish Buffalo Bayou for shipment from Galveston, Houston was
still at a tremendous disadvantage in cost of importa-
tions.   Her enterprising business men succeeded in attracting several iron highways to the city, which partially
removed the handicap and made it a distributing centre
for quite a large area, but it was still commercially dependent upon Galveston in a large measure.

The Houstonians began to look upon the shallow Buffalo Bayou with longing eyes.   Could it be deepened and
widened into a real ship canal?   Government engineers
were called to make a survey and submitted a favourable
report.   Congress made liberal appropriations to which
large sums were added by both city and county.   The
result is that a ship canal with a uniform depth of thirty
feet and with a width of one hundred and fifty feet at
the bottom now unites Houston with the Gulf fifty miles
away.   This will, it is claimed, accommodate any vessel
now sailing the Gulf of Mexico.   This canal is twice as
long as the one connecting Manchester, England, with the
sea, which made that inland city a rival of Liverpool.   It
is longer than the Panama Canal, but did not present the
engineering problems of that international waterway that
severed North and South America.   The total cost ex-

ceeded twenty-five million dollars, and it was money well spent.   Furthermore, it is all a municipal enterprise.

The magical growth of Houston dates from the completion of the canal, which made it an inland port.   Each year the number of vessels sailing up its quiet waters has increased and each year the annual tonnage has run into larger figures.   It has undoubtedly detracted considerably from Galveston's prestige and commerce.   It is now the greatest cotton port in the United States, so it is claimed, and enough of this snowy material passes out to sea to clothe a large part of the world's humans.   It is also sixth in order in the value of its total foreign commerce.   This is a remarkable achievement in the short space of about a score of years.   It speaks well for the energy and enterprise of the Houstonians.

The business section of Houston is attractive, partly because most of it is new.   There are many "cloud scratchers," as the Germans call our tall buildings, so that the city has an impressive sky line.   A great many factories have located there, but next to shipping, both by rail and water, distribution is of greatest importance.   A very large area draws its supplies from the hundreds of wholesale houses.   There are splendid churches, excellent educational institutions, fine hospitals, and spacious parks. One of the features of the city is the magnificent municipal auditorium.   It was this feature, together with the hotel facilities and liberality of the citizens, that drew the Democratic National Convention to Houston in 1928.

William Marsh Rice, whose murder by his valet a number of years ago was one of the sensations of the time, gave to Houston the Rice Institute, which will ever prove a rich memorial to the memory of this philanthropic millionaire, who met such a tragic end.   The original endowment of nine millions has increased to fourteen mil-

lions, making it one of the opulent educational institutions
of the country, few of which have started out under such
favourable auspices. Hence it never has been compelled
to pass through a period of adversity such as so many
institutions have faced and still face. It is a university
of liberal and technical training in which the scientific side
is given the greatest stress. Men and women are admitted on an equal footing, for it was the founder's desire
that they should have this opportunity for advanced training at a minimum cost. The endowment is in the hands
of a self-perpetuatory board of seven members. A site
of three hundred acres was selected in the southern part
of the city, which now presents the appearance of a semi-
tropical park. Ten buildings have already been erected,
and the plans call for thirty buildings. The standard is
high, and it has already developed into one of the outstanding scientific institutions of the country, and the
Southwest in particular. Opportunity is written all over
the Southwest, and the Rice Institute means much to the
future development.

Under the Spanish rule the entire country was included
in the municipality of Harrisburg. When the Republic
was established, it was enacted into a county and the name
changed to Harris, in honour of a prominent early settler.
Under President Burnet the little hamlet became the temporary capital until the day before the arrival of Santa
Anna. The twenty stores, houses and shops were all
burned by that villainous general. But the settlers returned, and it arose from the ashes. The superior enterprise of the Houstonians, however, secured the first
railroads so that the little town of Harrisburg is now an
unimportant suburb of its larger neighbour.

Just twenty-two miles from Houston, and easily reached
by an excellent motor highway, lies one of the most

historic spots in the State of Texas. It is the battlefield
of San Jacinto, and is on the bank of the ship channel
leading to the Gulf. The site has now been developed
into a beautiful park and playground, which is visited
by thousands of people every year. One of the splendid
shell roads for which this county is noted leads out to
the park, which affords a delightful drive by automobile.
Monuments and markers indicate the position of the
troops of both contending parties in this decisive engagement. Most Americans are but slightly acquainted with
the history of the heroic struggle of Texas for liberty
from the oppression of Mexico. The Battle of San Jacinto occurred after the slaughter at the Alamo, and the
equally brutal butchery at Goliad. It made possible the
Republic of Texas.

General Houston, in charge of the Texas forces, had
retreated before the onward march of Santa Anna, who
was bent on annihilating the Texans. He at first fell
back to the Colorado, and then decided to retreat to the
Brazos River. The wildest confusion seized the whole
of this country. The forces of the Mexican general were
flushed with victory, and they destroyed everything in
their pathway as they charged across the country. Up
to that time the Mexican leader had never suffered defeat.
The engagement would doubtless have occurred a few
days earlier, had not Santa Anna learned that Harrisburg was undefended. Abandoning his original plan,
he hastened to this town, hoping to capture the President
and other officials. Arriving there too late, he was informed that the Government had departed for Galveston
Island that very morning.

On the night of April 19th, 1836, the Texans had
bivouacked in the timber less than a mile from the Mexicans, whose bugles they could plainly hear. They had

crossed over Buffalo Bayou, a narrow but deep stream, which was then running bank full. The grove was of heavy live oak, hung with weeping Spanish moss and free from underbrush. To the left was the San Jacinto River, and at their back was the bayou. In front extended an open prairie for a couple of miles, which was bounded on one side by a marsh. In all there were about seven hundred and eighty-three men under General Houston. On the following day the first collision took place between the opposing forces. When Santa Anna learned that the Texans were near at hand, he is said to have become very much excited. In the afternoon of that day some of Houston's pickets were discovered, and a little skirmishing followed. But nothing decisive occurred on this day. Santa Anna established a new camp, and erected hastily constructed breastworks.

The morning of the 21st rose bright and cloudless. The Texans impatiently awaited the order for battle. They could see reinforcements advancing to the Mexican lines. At a council of war, called about midday, it was decided to postpone the engagement until the following morning. But this decision was sullenly received by the impatient troops, and the question was then submitted directly to them. The decision was in favour of immediate attack. It was not until half-past three that Houston gave orders for the troops to be formed in line of battle. The only music which the Texan army had was a solitary drum and fife. They struck up the air, *Will You Come to the Bower?* Two brass, six-pounder cannon, which had been sent from Cincinnati, and named "The Twin Sisters," were advantageously placed. Houston placed himself in the centre of his forces. Thus it was that the Texans advanced toward the improvised breastworks of Santa Anna. Deaf Smith had been com-

missioned by Houston to destroy Vince's bridge, so
as to cut off one source of the enemy's retreat, and also
to hinder the approach of any additional reinforcements.[1]

It must be remembered that here was the merchant,
who had but recently stepped from behind the counter.
He stood side by side with the farmer, who had hastily
abandoned his plough in the field, and the doctor, who had
probably brought his drugs and pills with him. All
these men were handling a long rifle, with shotpouch and
powderhorn over the shoulder, instead of the more
familiar implements of their trade. When Houston endeavoured to effect a little better discipline into his ranks,
those volunteers did not take kindly to restraint. They
had but little respect for the enemy's fighting ability, and
chafed at every delay of the commander. The cowards
and scalawags had long since deserted this body of
determined men. All were there in the presence of a
well-disciplined army, with but one object in view—
freedom from Mexican tyranny.

"Remember the Alamo!" and "Remember Goliad!"
were the battle cries. The Mexicans outnumbered the
Texans at least two to one. But Santa Anna had given
up all idea of an attack that day, and was enjoying a
siesta in his tent. Many of the other officers were dozing.
When the Texan army was seen approaching in battle
array, there was the greatest alarm and confusion. Santa
Anna ran out of his tent and ordered his men to lie
down. The "Twin Sisters" spoke sharply and often.

---

[1] Deaf Smith is one of the unique characters of Texas. "This singular
individual," said the *Houston Telegraph*, "was one whose name bears with
it more of respect than sounding titles. Major, Colonel, General, sink into
insignificance before the simple name of Deaf Smith. That name is identified with the battlefields of Texas. His eulogy is inseparably interwoven
with the most thrilling annals of our country." He survived San Jacinto
only a little more than a year.

The Mexicans had barely time to seize their muskets and give a scattering volley before the charging line was over the barricade. The Texans clubbed their rifles and drew their bowie knives. They captured the Mexican cannon, and turned them into the ranks of the Mexicans themselves. The fight lasted but eighteen minutes, when the Mexicans fled, having been completely routed.

The losses among the Mexicans exceeded six hundred in number, and those who surrendered almost equalled in number the entire forces of the victors. Many fled into the morass and became bogged in the quagmire, where they were despatched by the infuriated Texans. Some fled over the prairie, but they were pursued by fleeter steps than their own. A few escaped by swimming across Buffalo Bayou. Some would throw up their arms and cry: "Me no Alamo!" Many arms and much camp equipage, together with a small sum of cash, fell into the hands of the Texans as booty. The soldiers voted two thousand dollars for the national navy, and distributed the rest among themselves. They received about seven dollars and fifty cents each, which was all the compensation paid them for the entire campaign. The losses of Houston's army were almost infinitesimal. Two were killed and twenty-three wounded.

On the day after the battle a scouting party observed a man crouching in the tall grass and covering his head with a blanket. His horse had mired, and he had continued his flight on foot. He was clad in the soiled suit of an ordinary Mexican soldier, consisting of linen trousers, a blue cotton jacket, a cap, and red worsted slippers. Covering his head was a dilapidated straw hat, but it was observed that his shirt was of the finest linen, and in it were gold buttons. Upon being questioned, the captive finally admitted that he was Santa Anna, and re-

quested to be taken to the residence of General Houston.
The latter was then reclining on a pallet under a large
tree, little more distinguished in appearance than his captive, while a surgeon was dressing a wound in his leg.
His horse had been killed beneath him, and he himself
had been shot through the ankle.

As soon as the news spread that the famous and infa-
mous Mexican commander was a prisoner, curiosity drew
a large crowd whose only object was to catch a glimpse
of him. Santa Anna himself was very much disturbed
for fear that the spirit of revenge would animate these
men, whose hearts were still bleeding over his misdeeds.

"I am General Antonio Lopez de Santa Anna, President of the Mexican Republic, and I claim to be a prisoner
of war, at your disposal. . . . That man may consider
himself born to no common destiny who has conquered
the Napoleon of the West. It now remains for him to be
generous to the vanquished."

"You should have remembered that at the Alamo,"
rejoined Houston. Santa Anna then endeavoured to
excuse himself for that action.

General Houston, instead of wreaking retribution upon
the head of the Mexican chief, who was also president
of the Mexicans, sent him to honourable captivity. An
armistice was arranged, according to which the Mexican
troops were to withdraw beyond the Rio Grande. By a
secret treaty Santa Anna was to be released on his solemn
promise to use his influence to secure a recognition of
Texan independence. Because of the indignant protests
of the enraged army, however, this was abandoned by the
Government, and he remained a prisoner for several
months. At last he was released and sent to Washington.
It has long been a question whether Houston acted wisely
in being so magnanimous, for Santa Anna caused a great

deal of trouble for his own country as well as ours during the remaining years of his life.

To those who believe in retribution even in this life, I would give a picture of this man by Rev. William Butler, who visited Santa Anna about a year before his death on the 20th of June, 1876:

"Santa Anna was living in an obscure street, neglected and forgotten by all parties. On entering the apartment we found the old man sitting on a sofa, behind which hung a picture of his wife, 'her serene highness, Dolores Tosta de Santa Anna,' arrayed as a vice-queen. The magnificence of the painting contrasted sadly with the poverty-stricken aspect of the room and furniture. To him, however, this could make but little difference, as we soon saw that he was totally blind as well as feeble and broken in spirit, with a tendency to mental weakness." He was buried in the cemetery at Guadalupe, just outside the Mexican capital, without honours or recognition by the Government, and his remains still rest there. As I gazed upon his tomb, I could not help thinking of the horrible events in the history of Texas with which his name is associated.

CHAPTER IX

FOLLOWING THE SETTING SUN

"IF I owned hell and Texas, I would rent Texas and live in the other place." This is a statement attributed to that picturesque old warrior, Phil Sheridan. His acquaintance with Texas was while a lieutenant on duty on the frontier of that frontier State prior to the Civil War. Taking this statement, put in such an epigrammatic way, as their clue, many correspondents and newsmongers have coloured their pictures of Texas in harmony with it. That State has likewise been depicted as the abiding place of the most diabolical villains that the fertile brain of the most extravagant writer of fiction has been able to conceive. But there is a closed season for "bad men" in Texas now, and that "off" season extends from January 1st to December 31st of each year. If the county officials become a little remiss in their duties, the Texas Rangers may be trusted to put on the finishing touches. Not only is gun-carrying tabooed, but you cannot even play an innocent little game of "seven-up" on a train in Texas.

"Dry, did you say? Well, it is somewhat anhydrous in big sections of the map. Texas, let me inform you, is one of the driest States in the Union. In the six hundred miles from San Antonio to El Paso there is scarcely a 'wet spot.' You can travel for two hundred miles without discovering a single oasis for irrigating a parched throat. You might think that the counties in this arid

142

belt would welcome every sort of moisture, even of the distilled or fermented kind. But they do not." These words were written before national prohibition went into effect. Nearly every one of the extreme western counties, which were supposed to be the wildest and woolliest sections of Texas, had gone dry under local option. They remained the strongholds of prohibition afterwards. It was in the eastern counties, those lying nearest to the "effete" and cultured East, where the opposition was strongest. In the west the thirsty inhabitants lined up at the long counters in the drug stores and washed down the dust with soft drinks, a habit which is still much in evidence today, although there are some wet spots now appearing.

The cowboy saves his money now after pay day, so I was told, for he can no longer ride pellmell into a nearby town and carouse as he did in the days of old. "We are not sorry that the cowboys with their guns and unquenchable thirst are gone," said a rancher, "for in their place we have a finer lot, who will do more and stand more than the old ones. They're an odd lot of ducks, but we couldn't do without them."

In going west from San Antonio the traveller gradually approaches the most arid section of Texas until in the northern part of Hudspeth and Culberson counties it is a close approach to a desert. On one occasion I motored ninety miles without passing a filling station or a place where one might fill up the radiator. There was not the slightest sign of human habitation.

Ranching overshadows every other industry. Instead of a solid velvety green the coarse grass usually grows in clumps, but it is extremely nourishing and palatable and stock eagerly eat it. Even a severe forest does not kill it or render it distasteful to animals, and it is owing to

this fact that cattlemen have succeeded so well throughout all this territory.

"A farm of one section is small here," said a Texan to
me. "Ten to fifty sections are far more common."

The mesquite which, near San Antonio, is large and
thick, gradually becomes dwarfed and thinner. This mesquite is said to be one of the finest of hardwoods, and is
used in a great many ways. The small size and twisted
contour of the trunk, however, bars it from many uses
to which it would be well adapted. Mixed with other
thorny shrubs as an undergrowth, all together called
chaparral, it frequently forms over acres together an
almost impenetrable mass when there has been no effort
at clearing. The prickly pear is quite thickly scattered
over the ground in many places, and one will find many
other plants which grow only where rain is infrequent.

It is not long after San Antonio has faded from view
until the Sunset Route reaches the lands occupied by
the old Castro Colony, which is mentioned elsewhere.
D'Hanis was likewise a settlement of Alsatian colonists.
Uvalde and Del Rio (meaning "by the river") are fairly
good sized county towns, which are passed on the journey
toward the disappearing sun. Uvalde County for a long
time occupied a prominent position on the southwestern
frontier. It was infested with Indians, and they, together with American and Mexican outlaws, made it an
insecure dwelling place until the construction of the
railroad introduced settled conditions.

The Canyon de Uvalde was a favourite resort for the
savages, since it provided them with shelter and a natural
defence. Just a few miles south of the city of Uvalde was
located Fort Inge, which was an important military post
in the middle of the last century. The mail routes to
the more distant west and to Mexico here intersected, and

the pony express riders were a common sight in Uvalde.
It was under the protection of this fort that the first settlers located in this neighbourhood in 1851. The city is
now a flourishing municipality, and is a commercial centre for the great stock country all about. More honey
is said to be shipped from here than any other city in
the United States, for the bees make a most excellent
honey from the flowers of the range.

Many were the forts scattered over this western country at one time or another. One of these interesting advance outposts of the Anglo-American occupation to
follow was that known as Camp Verde, which may still
be found as the name of a small place in Kerr County,
a little north of Uvalde. This old and historic frontier
post was established in 1855, and it is a reminder of one
of the strangest innovations ever attempted by our Government. Forty camels were imported from the Orient,
together with a dozen Armenian drivers and their families. A sketch had been made of a caravansary in Asia
Minor, and this camp was reproduced at Camp Verde
in every minute particular. It was constructed in a
rectangular shape, except the north wall which made an
angle, the distance from each corner of this angle being
exactly one hundred and fifty feet. This wall was sixteen
feet high and made of concrete and timber, the latter
having been transported all the way from Florida.

The idea of employing camels on the Texas frontier
was an idea which had its inception with Jefferson Davis.
He believed that camels could cross the desert country
with more ease and quicker than horses. Because they
could go longer without water, their employment would
greatly facilitate the carrying of despatches and following of the Indians, so he represented. This might have
proved true, if the western country had consisted of

desert sand. Camp Verde, however, was situated in a mountainous and rocky country, over which the camel with his soft and spongy feet could make but little progress. The tough little Spanish pony could outdistance him. The camels, being a failure so far as following Indians was concerned, were sold in 1868. The forty had increased at that time until the original number was more than doubled. A few of the camels escaped to the *Llano Estacado,* and it is said that their descendants are still occasionally seen in that section of Texas and New Mexico. Many stories are told of the frights experienced by the Indians and white men when these strange apparitions came unexpectedly upon them.

Del Rio is rather an attractive place, only a couple of miles from the Mexican border. An abundant supply of excellent water is provided by a number of large flowing springs. The largest spring is about fifty feet across, and an almost incredible amount of water issues from it. It was the neighbourhood of such an unfailing supply of pure water that determined the first settlements here. These settlements gradually grew into the present city. At the present time Mexicans seem to predominate among the population. Away from the valleys here in the great Valverde County, the general surface is rough and broken, but in the valleys there is considerable land that will lend itself to irrigation. Development by irrigation on a considerable scale has been initiated with water from the Rio Grande, and it promises considerable success here as at other places along that international waterway.

Have you, gentle reader, been harbouring the belief that the whole of Texas was either level or rolling prairie? Then let me proceed to dispel this phantasy. Proceeding westward in obedience to the command given

SAW MILL, EAST TEXAS

young men some time ago, we find that there is a gradual rise in the level of the land. The traveler soon learns that far from being all prairie, there are mountain peaks in Texas which overtop anything east of the Mississippi. Some of the scenery is exceedingly beautiful, for these Texas mountains have a charm all their own. While the Rockies have an awfulness that oftentimes repels the timid onlooker, these uptilted lands attract and charm. The motorist who follows the main highway, which closely parallels the railway, will get many a thrill as he winds around the peaks and across the valleys. At Paisano the divide is crossed at an altitude of a mile or more. There are many peaks in sight ranging from five to eight thousand feet above sea level, with broad valleys between them. These lofty mountains outlined against the distant horizon look wonderfully impressive in the translucent atmosphere.

The traveler who loves to get away from the beaten path will enjoy a motor trip through this enchanted region. The counties are princely in dimensions. Brewster County is larger than Connecticut, but there is only about one inhabitant to each square mile, of whom half are Mexicans. The adjoining county of Presidio, only slightly smaller, claims twice as many people, but even then there is no need to tramp on each other's toes. Outside of some irrigation along the rivers not much land is under cultivation, for the rainfall is insufficient. Out of two and a half million acres in one of these divisions, only a few thousand are classed as "improved lands." But if the human population is slight, these regions are not uninhabited, for tens of thousands of cattle, sheep and goats are pastured on the ranches and thrive exceedingly well. Alpine is the chief city and it is a delightful place to linger, if the traveller is not urged on by the mania of haste.

Brewster County contains some of the loftiest mountains to be found in Texas. There is another Grand Canyon here that has walls which in places rise perpendicularly almost two thousand feet. In these mountains and canyons and valleys considerable mineral wealth has been discovered. One of the largest quicksilver mines in the United States is in operation here, besides those which produce many other minerals, such as lead, iron, copper, and silver. Because of a lack of transportation, however, and an inadequate water supply, the great mineral wealth has not yet been fully developed. It certainly required indomitable pluck and unconquerable energy to push the Southern Pacific railroad out across the vast and—the then—almost unknown plains and mountains of Texas. It began with the old Galveston, Harrisburg and San Antonio Railroad. Mile by mile, almost foot by foot, struggling against difficulties seemingly insuperable, this railroad was pushed forward from Houston until it reached .San Antonio, where its engineers were greeted with ovations by the delighted inhabitants. Thence it crept westward into the sunset. But another railroad was also headed eastward, which likewise aimed to cross the expansive leagues of Texas. The outcome was a compromise, and the two roads became the Southern Pacific, by which the East and the West were again united.

The nearer we approach the western boundary of Texas the more noticeable become the signs of aridity. A wit made the remark that it was so poor here a crow "would have to tote his rations over it." Another wag averred that it would take the moisture from a couple of acres to rust a nail. In places it might hustle an active goat to get a good day's feed from an acre. The sagebrush and the graceful Spanish bayonet are practically the only signs

of vegetable life at times.   It is a country of barbs and
spines and bayoneted shrubs, which tear and fret the
hands of any who come in collision with them.   The
sun also sheds a glare, which accounts for the wide hats
and the gathered wrinkles nesting at the corner of men's
eyes, because they have been squinting at it for years.
Nevertheless, the hundreds of windmills at work demon-
strate the fact that water is present not far from the surface.   In some of the towns a windmill will be found in
almost every yard.   As El Paso is approached the landscape becomes a dreary waste, until a dozen miles away
irrigation begins.   The fertility of the soil is indicated
by the eagerness with which it responds to the application
of water.

"No se Ingles" (I do not understand English), is a
common expression heard throughout this section of
Texas.   It may come from some one who looks as white
as you or I.   He is a Mexican, but has none of the Indian
blood in him.   Isolated thatched houses are encountered
which might come from interior Mexico.   The women
may be seen rolling and patting *tortillas* on the *metate,*
just as they do in their native home.   Strings of chili and
garlic ornament the outside of the doorway.   The don-
keys, the pigs, and the chickens have the entrée to the best
the house affords.   An equal number of lean and hungry
dogs infest the doorway.

Many reach El Paso via the Old Texas and Pacific
from Dallas or Fort Worth.   Not far distant from the
latter city on the southwestern journey is the dividing
line between the black waxy belt and West Texas.   Diversified farming is still followed for some distance, until
at length the rainfall diminishes to such an extent that
either dry farming methods or irrigation are necessary.
Indian depredations were common here until long after

reconstruction and quiet started after the War of 1860.

Most transcontinental motorists, who choose the southern route to-day, follow the Bankhead Highway, which closely parallels the Texas and Pacific from Fort Worth to El Paso, across Texas. For about one hundred and fifty miles it is as fascinating a road as one would wish to find. It ascends, descends and winds about constantly. The slopes of the hills are covered with scrub timber, largely oak, and mesquite grows on the more level land. In the spring hundreds of acres, in patches as large as an acre, will be covered with the beautiful Texas bluebonnet, which has been adopted as the state flower. It seems to prefer a thin gravelly soil to the richest of black loam.

Most of the towns are new and show it in their appearance. The few settlers who were there prior to annexation were a sort of advance guard against the forces of barbarism. The real development began with the completion of the railroad. The vanishing bison were succeeded by the hardy longhorns and the old-time stockmen who were, for a time, the lords supreme. But to-day, with much land under cultivation, there are probably more and better cattle than in the palmiest days of the old ranchers.

The motorist can journey across Texas without sacrificing any of the luxuries to which he has been accustomed. The tired traveller can rest his weary body each night on a comfortable bed, and dine on satisfying foods. A modern town will be found every fifteen to thirty miles, and a regular mania for building hotels swept across Texas during the boom years. The traveller to-day reaps the benefit. The discovery of oil may be credited with much of this transformation, for many little municipalities owe not only their prosperity but their very existence to this fluid mineral. Few of the oil pools lie directly on

SPINDLE TOP, BEAUMONT

the highway or railroad, but towns sprang up here because of the transportation facilities afforded by both.

There are many little cities between Fort Worth and El Paso, but a description of all would be tedious reading. Mineral Wells is different, for its growth and prosperity has been due largely to the healing waters yielded by scores of wells and now distributed over the entire country. The visitors who flock there support many hotels and boarding houses. Abilene is the largest of these municipalities. It is a lively little city and increased from ten to twenty-six thousand in the decade between 1920 to 1930, largely owing to oil discoveries in adjoining counties. Sweetwater has developed into a railroad centre of considerable importance. From it the steel rails radiate to all points of the compass. And yet a county government was not organized here until about half a century ago.

About seventy miles south of Sweetwater is San Angelo, the chief city of an agricultural empire as large as Ohio. Like the Panhandle this section began an era of rapid development about fifteen or twenty years ago. Small farmers flocked there because the spring-fed streams provided water for stock and irrigation as well. The rainfall is about twenty-two inches. San Angelo has grown rapidly until it is a city of twenty-five thousand and has become a great wool and mohair centre. In the score of counties contributing to San Angelo two million angora goats and six million sheep graze. This agile can-eater, a native of Asia Minor, is celebrated for its beautiful silky hair, which attains a length of about eight inches, and is used principally to manufacture mohair. More mohair is produced here than in all the rest of the United States put together. One animal will yield a little over four pounds, which is considerably less than the wool from a sheep, but the value is normally much greater.

West of Sweetwater the rainfall gradually decreases and the change in vegetation reveals the aridity. But many places have an abundant supply of underground water and windmills dot the landscape. Big Springs was so named because of the large flowing springs located near the little city. The early settlers and stockmen found the gushing waters as refreshing as did the Indians and buffalo. In some places the population is sparse, even to-day, only three or four to the square mile. In Winkler County up to the discovery of oil a decade ago, there were not over five hundred people. To-day the population exceeds six thousand.

A mile east of the thriving little city of Pecos the highway crosses the Pecos River, one of the most important rivers in Texas. Rising in the Sangre de Christo (Blood of Christ) Mountains of New Mexico, it flows six hundreds miles through these two states to its mouth, bringing fertility to thousands of acres of thirsty soil through a number of irrigation projects. For several decades the Pecos was considered the dividing line between organized and unorganized society. "Law West of the Pecos" meant just such primitive regulations as any community might adopt for self-protection. There were no elective or appointed officials. Each big rancher maintained order on his own range, and some of them were as unscrupulous as the cattle rustlers themselves. Many of the cowboys were little better than desperados. It was necessary to be a good shot and quick on the draw, if one had any regard for his own safety. Scenting an opportunity Roy Bean, a dispenser of liquor at Langtry, on the high bank of the Rio Grande, added the title of "Justice of the Peace" to his other accomplishments and proceeded to dispense "Law West of the Pecos" to whoever sought his aid. Although absolutely without legal authority "Judge" Bean held court, pronounced sentences, performed marriages and even granted divorces. Many and weird are the strange tales told of his ideas of justice, but his decisions were usually accepted by the litigants. He sometimes held court with a whisky bottle in one hand and a revolver in the other, and there were frequent adjournments to the bar for stimulating refreshments.

Soon after leaving Pecos[1] the Bankhead Highway begins to skirt around the group of mountains, which may collectively be called the Davis Mountains, although they bear a number of designations. The views at times are marvellously beautiful, with detached peaks arising two or three thousand feet above the general level of the plateau. But a more interesting route, although somewhat longer and more mountainous, is to historic old Fort Davis in the heart of the mountains and county seat of Jeff Davis County, by the way of Balmorhea, and again joins the main highway at Van Horn. It is a region of rugged mountains covered with the eternal green of junipers, cedars, piñins and tall pines against a background of azure skies. It is a place to linger; to bask in the beauties of nature and breathe the stimulating ozone. It is the best hunting territory in Texas, where the bear black-tailed deer, wolf and mountain lion will be found as well as the smaller game, both four-footed and feathered. Fort Davis, now abandoned and in ruins, has a history running back to 1854, when Jefferson Davis, then Sec-

[1]Note: For anyone desiring to visit the famous Carlsbad Caverns, Pecos is a good starting point. They lie in the Guadalupe Mountains, seventy-five miles north and just across the New Mexico line, and over a fairly good highway. The visit to these remarkable caverns, one of nature's greatest wonders, will more than repay the extra day required. A direct road will take the motorist to El Paso.

retary of War, ordered its establishment. It served as
a protection against the bloodthirsty Apaches and Comanches for a good many years.

On the way to El Paso low ranges of mountains are
crossed, but there is little development until the land becomes more level so that irrigation is possible from the
Rio Grande. A dozen miles from El Paso is one of the
oldest settlements in Texas. This village began as a
refuge for a band of Tigua Indians, who had been driven
from a pueblo of the same name not very far from Albu-
querque, New Mexico, by an anti-Christian uprising.
These friendly and christianized Indians were colonized
here in 1682 by the Spanish governor.

Although two and a half centuries old, Ysleta has had
little part in the development of Texas. Until quite recently it was almost a pure Indian town. The intention
of the priests was to found a mission like those in California, but in this they were not very successful. Mexicans now dwell all about the few Indians who still linger
within the shadows of the old church, which is well preserved. The outside walls have been replastered, but the
black-robed priests still conduct their ceremonies before
the same altar where the Spanish padres intoned their
prayers in the long ago. The hand-beaten bells of bronze
ring out joyously as they did in the seventeenth century
when "The Priest was Lord of the Land," summoning
the faithful to worship. Ysleta is one of only three or
four places where any Indians still remain in the great
state of Texas, once the home of tens of thousands of the
most savage of the red men.

The western gateway to Texas, and the only large city
in that section of the State, is El Paso, which nestles at
the foot of Mt. Franklin and close up to the New Mexico border. It is a great relief to land in this modern

city, with every convenience for comfort and pleasure, after a long journey across the arid plateaus in midsummer. There is a reason for El Paso, which means The Pass. The banks of the Rio Grande are here low and easily approachable. This is the lowest pass across the continental divide between the Arctic Sea and the Isthmus of Tehuantepec. Several of the oldest trails established by the white men passed through here, just as does one of the leading transcontinental highways to-day. Coronado crossed the river at this point on his famous expedition to the Santa Fé country in 1540. In 1598 Juan de Oñate with more than one hundred colonists and several thousand cattle followed this route on his way to the upper Rio Grande region. He took possession of the country in the name of the King of Spain, calling it Nuevo (New) Méjico.

The plateau immediately surrounding El Paso is the nearest approach to a genuine desert that one will find in Texas. But this fact, combined with an elevation of three-fourths of a mile, makes what her citizens proudly term "the most delightful all-the-year-round climate in the world." The altitude tempers the heat, which otherwise might render the summer temperature uncomfortable. The most disagreeable feature is the sandstorms, which sometimes sweep down over the city. It is the largest city between San Antonio and Los Angeles, a distance of fifteen hundred miles. To the north there is no large city nearer than Denver. It is one of the main gateways to Mexico. Due to these advantages El Paso has developed into a great natural concentration and distributing point and a very important railroad centre.

Even though the surrounding plateau has the appearance of desert, the soil is very rich and only needs moisture to bring out the dormant fertility. The average precipitation is less than ten inches, which comes principally in summer rains. For many years there has been much irrigation both up and down the Rio Grande with water drawn directly from the river. Here will be found pear and plum orchards on a large scale. With the completion of the Elephant Butte Dam, one hundred and ten miles north of El Paso, the waters of the Rio Grande are now impounded in a reservoir forty miles long with an average width of one and one-half miles. The depth, in places at least, is almost two hundred feet. This tremendous volume of water is expected to be sufficient to tide over three or four dry years. Since its completion in 1915 the irrigated area has been greatly expanded, for the water is brought thirty-five miles within the Texas border. These fields of cultivated land contrast vividly in their varied grass with the gray alluvial hills and dull rocky slopes, imparting an indescribable charm to the landscape. About two hundred thousand acres are now irrigated. Under an agreement with Mexico it is necessary to deliver sixty thousand "acre feet" to the republic each year in return for its consent to the project.

The contrast in civilization and races is readily seen on crossing the international bridge to Ciudad Juarez. This city was originally called El Paso del Norte, but the name was changed in honour of Mexico's most famous president. The Mexican city had a much better start than its American rival, for there was no settlement of any size on the north bank until it came under American sovereignty, and Juarez then boasted thirteen thousand inhabitants—a large population for that period. It was an outpost of Spanish and then Mexican power and civilization.

The Juarez of to-day, with a population of forty thousand, bears little resemblance to El Paso with its towering skyscrapers, imposing business block and beautiful homes. Here adobe buildings predominate, and most of the streets are not presentable. It is true that its progress has been greatly hampered by the recurring revolutionary disturbances, during which it has changed hands many times. The most conspicuous buildings are the railroad station and the Plaza de Toros (bull-ring). The most flourishing enterprises are the race track and gambling of every sort. It is not much to our credit that the promoters and managers of the races, bull-fights and gambling, and especially the least creditable ones, are generally our fellow countrymen. But such is the fact. One will find the same conditions all along the border, at Tia Juana, Agua Caliente, Mexicala, Nogales in Sonora, Naco, Agua Prieta, Nuevo Laredo and Matamoras. Men who have been driven out of the United States by enforcement of the laws against vice drift across the border in order to continue the fleecing of their countrymen.

The tourist will enjoy a visit to the old church of Nuestra Señora de Guadalupe. Tradition claims its founding as far back as 1549. The bells were brought overland from Vera Cruz, one thousand miles away. To-day the rude walls are covered with rather crude pictures of the saints, while the ceiling beams are composed of rudely carved logs that were brought from distant mountains. The worshippers, mostly peons, come and go as they have for many generations, kneeling and crouching upon the floor in the dim light and before the chancel altars with their many burning tapers.[1]

El Paso did not grow rapidly for a good many years and had the reputation of being a tough place. Border outlaws from both sides of the river visited it and they

[1]Anyone interested in our neighbouring republic will find *Mexico and Her People of To-day* by the same author and published by L. C. Page and Co., Boston, an informing book.

came around with deadly guns. Many were the casualties. Every kind of vice flourished. Describing El Paso of 1885, a well-known writer said: "The town—whose inhabitants will doubtless be mortally offended because I did not call it a city—is about half a mile across, and situated in the centre of a verdureless, mud-coloured plain, with a semicircle of gravelly hills on one side and the Rio Grande on the other. Its buildings are mainly new, as houses of wood and brick are fast replacing the old adobe hovels." Since then the city has been transformed in more ways than one. The open gambling houses were cleaned out years ago. Many deplored this, for they said these institutions were a necessary evil, but the better citizens said "No." Business began to forge ahead at once, and the character of the inhabitants likewise improved.

The most influential and wealthiest man on this side of the river during the Mexican rule was Juan Marie Ponce de Leon, whose ranch house stood in the very heart of the modern city, where palatial hotels, busy retail stores and lofty office buildings now rise. He held a monopoly of public transportation with his wagon trains. He fought with his country during the Mexican War, but the United States troops took possession of the country very soon after peace was declared. A large military post, called Fort Bliss, was established, which has ever since been maintained. The present fort occupies an elevation overlooking the city and is the largest cavalry post maintained by Uncle Sam. During the war between the states El Paso was alternately occupied by Confederate and Federal troops. After that it was little more than an isolated border town until the railroad connected it with the outside world in 1881.

El Paso is now stretching out toward Fort Bliss and

SHIP CANAL, PORT ARTHUR

up the slopes of the overhanging mountain, whose up-turned strata show that there has been a tremendous upheaval of nature at some time in the past. It is a city of substantial homes. The bungalow type of dwelling is most popular among the cheaper homes. The streets are generally wide, thus giving abundant opportunity for a park between sidewalk and curb. The homes are beauti-fied by a profusion of flowers, vines, shrubs and trees. Water is plentiful even if rainfall is scant, and an ampli-tude of sunshine is nature's choicest gift to El Pasoans, for it brings thousands of health seekers from afar. The city is now the home of more than one hundred thousand people, the fifth city in the State.

El Paso has experienced much excitement since the Diaz Revolution in 1910, and the nearness of Fort Bliss was a source of satisfaction to El Pasoans on many occa-sions. For months at a time several thousand extra troops were stationed here to guard against threatened raids, so that the khaki was a familiar sight on the streets. Thousands of Mexican refugees came across to the American side, the well-to-do to preserve both lives and property, and the poor peons to avoid conscription in the armies. Fortunately, these conditions have improved and travel between the two countries is increasing rapidly.

CHAPTER X

THE GULF COAST

THOSE were indeed stirring times when the early explorers on this continent were treading the pathless wilderness and sailing over uncharted waters. It required no lurid melodrama to provide any needed thrills, for the dangers of the way and the treachery of the red men supplied an abundance of excitement. One of the most fascinating incidents in connection with the Gulf Coast of Texas is that involving its discovery by the Chevalier de La Salle. This intrepid explorer found his way down the Mississippi and into the great inland sea known as the Gulf of Mexico. One by one the Great Lakes had been discovered. Joliet and Marquette reached the Mississippi, and followed that stream as far as the Arkansas in 1673. But apprehension caused them to return. In 1681, La Salle, with a body of fifty followers, started on the same journey and sailed the Mississippi to its mouth in the following year. Unaware that the Spaniards had already been there, he named the country Louisiana in honour of his king, and claimed the territory for France.

"Henceforth," proclaimed La Salle, "my God and my king are supreme, forever, over the innumerable souls and immeasurable lands of this great Continent." Shortly afterward he returned to France to report his discoveries. Louis XIV was at this time at the very zenith of his glory. The prospect of a new empire appealed to his vanity, as well as to his judgment. La Salle was no doubt fully as enthusiastic as the project warranted in his interviews with the monarch. At any rate, when La Salle retraced his steps for the New World, in 1684, he was accompanied by four ships, with a captain of the royal navy in command of one.

La Salle intended to establish a military post at the mouth of the Great River, in order to protect the French settlements to be established farther up. His good fortune had ended, however, as succeeding events proved. One ship was captured by buccaneers in the West Indies. But the severest trial of all was that he missed his destination, and finally succeeded, in February, 1685, in effecting a landing at Matagorda Bay, on the coast of Texas, hundreds of miles southwest of the river sought. La Salle firmly believed this bay to be one of the mouths of the Mississippi, and so established a temporary camp on the shore. In entering the bay another vessel was wrecked, and shortly after landing the naval officer sailed for France with a third, because he could not work in harmony with his rather irritable chief. Thus only one rather small vessel, the *Bella,* remained at the service of the new colony. Even this vessel was finally lost, so that the colony was without the means of leaving the country by water.

After landing, a little search soon revealed the fact that the bay which they had entered had no connection with the Father of Waters. This was indeed a tremendous disappointment to La Salle, but he was not yet downhearted. In order to find a suitable site for a camp until the Mississippi could be located, a voyage was made up a river emptying into the bay. The river was named La Vache, or the "river of beeves," which the Spaniards later translated into Lavaca, the name which the river

still bears. It was so named because of the great number
of buffaloes. The fort which he built was named Saint
Louis, in honour of the sovereign who financed his expedition. La Salle gave the same name to the bay, but the
Spaniards named it Espiritu Santo, and sometimes called
it San Bernardo.

Bad luck continued to follow the La Salle expedition,
even after Fort St. Louis was established. Two of the
members deserted almost immediately, one was hung for
a crime, and one of his best men died as the result of a
snake bite. Before the first summer had passed, thirty
had succumbed to disease. Treacherous Indians on all
sides threatened the security of those remaining. Let the
imagination of the reader fill out this scene on the shores
of Matagorda Bay. An unhealthy shore, provisions
scarce, fear of the natives, no way of returning home,
exact location unknown—these were only a few of the
troubles. It was enough to daunt the staunch heart of
the most fearless explorer. Some of his men became
mutinous and clamorous. A weaker man would have
yielded to despair. It was not so with La Salle. In
October, 1683, La Salle set out to find the Mississippi,
but returned a few months later unsuccessful. In 1686,
he began a second attempt, but only reached the Trinity
River. Here he was attacked by a fever, which delayed
him two months, and again he found it necessary to return
to Fort St. Louis. He started on a third overland journey in January, 1687, in an attempt to reach the French
settlements in Canada for succour. He had not proceeded
far when he was assassinated by some of his own men.
A couple of shots rang out from the tall grass of the
prairie, and La Salle dropped dead with a bullet in his
brain.

Thus ended the career of one of the most intrepid ex-

RICE READY FOR HARVESTING

plorers of the days of great discoveries in the New World, at the early age of forty-three. His only reward for adding an empire to the realm of his sovereign master was the bullet of an assassin. He was a lonely and un-communicative man, who made no confidants. His tem-perament was gloomy and unsocial, and this, combined with a fierce temper, undoubtedly angered some of his followers, many of whom were of the scum of Paris, and led to the death of the only man who might have brought succour. But he was a knight of spotless purity, of daunt-less courage and of unbounded self-reliance, so we are told. His loyalty to his sovereign was of the nature of a religious sentiment, while his devotion to his church would have stood the test of martyrdom. The exact place where this tragedy took place is unknown, and several sites are claimed, but a recent authority says it was near the present site of Navasota.

Fort St. Louis survived a couple of years longer. The colony on the Gulf was left to its fate by the "Grande Monarque," Louis XIV. In his gorgeous palace at Ver-sailles he turned a deaf ear to the account that reached him concerning the unfortunates at Fort St. Louis. Sev-eral expeditions were sent both by sea and by land by the Spaniards, to locate and destroy the French settlement, all of which were unsuccessful. One day a Spanish ship, said to have been guided by deserters from La Salle, sought out the spot where the colony had been, intent on its destruction. But the destroyers found the place silent as the tomb. The weather-beaten palisade was dilapi-dated, and the roof of the storehouse had tumbled in. The dismounted cannon lay scattered around in the mire. The whole place had fallen into decay. Looking a little farther the Spaniards came upon a cluster of human skele-tons, lying as if they had fallen there in death.

Awed by the mystery of the place, the strangers were about to leave when two men, looking like Indians, came up. They said that many of the colony had died from small-pox, and the rest had been murdered by the Indians. They were the sole survivors of the colony. They were made prisoners of war and sentenced to life imprisonment. Thus disappeared the colony established by the intrepid La Salle in Texas. Thus ended the first attempt to establish a settlement of Europeans on the soil of Texas. But it was the French attempt that did finally lead to the Spanish settlement and development.

Although the Spaniards took possession of this Gulf Coast, the title of Spain was in dispute for more than a century. France at all times laid claim to it by reason of the discovery and settlement by La Salle. With the Louisiana Purchase this claim was passed on to the United States in 1803. It was not until the general settlement made with Spain by Uncle Sam in 1819, which was a part of the general bargain by which Florida was acquired, that the right of Spain to this part of the Gulf Coast was recognized. This was only two years before the title was again lost as a result of the successful revolution of Mexico.

It is doubtless true, however, that the Spaniards first set foot on Texas soil. In the year 1532, three white men and a negro arrived in Mexico. They related one of the strangest and almost unbelievable stories of shipwreck, suffering, captivity, and ultimate escape ever spoken by mortal lips. Cabeza de Vaca was the leader of this party, all of whom were survivors of an expedition led by Narvaez, which had been sent out by Spain to subdue Florida, the name then applied to the entire coast. They had been shipwrecked somewhere along the Texas coast, and had been held in slavery for several years by the

Indians. From all the accounts that we have these men were the first to tread the soil of Texas.

Matagorda Bay and its adjacent waters which indent the coast have been the scene of many later historical incidents. These include Lavaca Bay and River, Espiritu Santo Bay, and the San Antonio and Colorado rivers. The shores have been the seat of many ambitious towns and seaports, but the locations of some of them can be found with difficulty. Prince Solius Braunfels selected a site here, which he called Carl's Haven, as the landing-place for his immigrants. Large numbers of these unfortunate Germans succumbed to a pestilence while awaiting transportation to the interior. Indianola was once an important town and the second seaport in Texas, but it is now a "lost town." Other towns at one time promising were Cox's Point and Dimitt's Landing. A great storm in 1875 destroyed the old port, and a majority of the inhabitants were drowned. At the present time hardly a building indicates the site of this once flourishing seaport. Matagorda was formerly the leading town here, but Port Lavaca is much larger to-day. The bottom lands at the mouth of the Colorado are among the richest in the State, but the lack of drainage long prevented development. The level land and abundance of water, however, were just the necessary conditions for rice cultivation, and this has been developed on a large scale.

There are many other places of historical and general interest on the Gulf Coast. It is claimed that the site of Corpus Christi (Body of Christ) was discovered by La Salle, and was named Corpus Christi Bay because it was discovered on the day of that celebration of the Roman Catholic Church. The news that Texas had accepted the proffered terms of annexation, which was to be the signal for General Taylor to land his troops on the fron-

tier of Texas reached New Orleans on July 21, 1845.
On the following day the "Army of Occupation" embarked for Texas with explicit instructions to limit its
activities "to the defense of the territory of Texas," now
"an integral part of our country." Ten days later General Taylor established his camp on the site of the present
city of Corpus Christi, where he remained wholly inactive
for seven months awaiting Mexico's offensive. At the
end of that time the army began its weary march across
one hundred and fifty miles of plains to the mouth of the
Rio Grande. The country was almost wholly depopulated, for the Mexicans had fled. The food problem was
easy, for wild cattle and wild horses roamed these plains
in almost countless numbers. It was not until several
years later that the rehabilitation of the country began.

At the time of General Taylor's arrival at Corpus
Christi Bay there was a little town on the hill which was
called Bluff City, said to be the highest land on the coast
within Texas. Corpus Christi is directly on the shores
of the bay, which is landlocked and twenty-five miles
across, but about forty feet above the water. After the
Mexican War Corpus Christi soon became the leading
port between the Rio Grande and Galveston. In 1822 it
was captured by Lieutenant Kittridge, who seized several
Confederate boats lying in port and destroyed others.

For years Corpus Christi was a sleepy and dreary sort
of place with a noticeable air of old Spain, and it still has
a considerable Mexican population. But it has developed
into the most attractive and most important city on the
Gulf coast south of Galveston. The bay is both broad
and beautiful, which affords a magnificent setting, and it
has a sweeping water front of several miles. The lack
of a deep harbour was for a long time a serious drawback,
but this was overcome about ten years ago when the Port

of Corpus Christi was officially opened. To-day many
steamship lines maintain offices here and the foreign commerce runs into big figures. A great causeway has been
built across the bayou, which affords better access to the
mainland. Like Galveston it is rapidly becoming a favourite playground both winter and summer, for surf bathing can be indulged in almost every month in the year and
it is said to be without undertow. There are good hotels
and plenty of amusement. The population numbers
about thirty-five thousand, and the growth is steady.

The development of the natural resources of the country round about Corpus Christi has been very rapid within
the past twenty years. Thousands of acres are now devoted to the raising of early vegetables for eastern
markets until it has become quite a competitor of the
Brownsville and Laredo districts. Another remarkable
development has been in the oil industry. Many fields
have been discovered and are being exploited within the
territory that is necessarily contributory to Corpus Christi.
This new source of wealth, together with the products of
the farms and ranches, is certain to ensure prosperity to
this city at the mouth of the Nueces River. The lover of
fishing will never grow stale, for every kind of game fish
found in the teeming waters of the Gulf of Mexico may
be caught in the surrounding waters, including the fighting tarpon, which is exciting enough sport to satisfy any
fisherman.

Three trunk line railways now serve Corpus Christi,
so that the transportation problem has been solved. One
of these, a branch of the National Railways of Mexico,
was first built as a narrow gauge and called the Corpus
Christi, San Diego and Rio Grande Railway, crossing the
river at Laredo. The railroad was completed in 1879 and
was a very important factor in bringing about settled

conditions throughout the territory traversed by it. It also helped to develop and bring prosperity to Corpus Christi.

Just a short distance north of Corpus Christi is another harbour, or bay, known as Aransas Pass, which has been navigated from the very beginning of Texas colonization. Here was also the historic Copano Landing, which was of great importance for the landing of supplies during the Texas Revolution. After the war Rockport and Fulton arose, and both became important shipping ports as well as commercial centres. Cattle were driven here from the back country for shipment or for slaughter. In recent years the Government has expended considerable money in deepening harbours and the construction of jetties so that vessels of deeper draught can enter the bay.

The territory all about here, now represented by Refugio, Aransas and San Patricio Counties, was included in the concession granted for Irish colonists to Hewitson and Power, or McMullen and McGloin. The capital of the former was at Mission del Refugio, and the latter at San Patricio. The mission at Refugio was destroyed not so very many years later, and only a little settlement remained at the time of the Revolution. Near San Patricio there was a Mexican fort, called Fort Lipantitlan, which was captured early in the Revolution. These Irish settlers came in from 1829 to 1833. San Patricio is one of the original counties of Texas. The boundaries have been changed several times, and the thriving town of Sinton has succeeded San Patricio as the county seat. The Irish are now only a very small proportion of the population.

Artesian water assured life and prosperity to a large section of the Gulf Coast. A great drought of 1901 brought it about. The death of thousands of cattle had made the ranchers desperate. A geologist had reported that a sheet of water underlay the whole coast country, and it was determined to find it or prove the report false. When a stream of limpid and clear water spouted out of the hole, and spread over the browned and parched prairie, there was great rejoicing. The discovery added another empire to Texas. It brought about the railroad extension to Brownsville. Towns arose along the route like mushrooms.

Until the artesian belt was discovered this land between the Nueces and the Rio Grande was considered worthless, except to the big ranchers. It is said that there were only a half-dozen houses in which white people lived in the last one hundred and fifty miles toward Brownsville. Now it is becoming a populous region of farmers as well as ranchmen. Other wells were put down. The flow of clear and sparkling water continued to come to the surface. The wells are generally from five hundred to twelve hundred feet in depth. The water comes up from this great underground river quite warm, and must be cooled to make it palatable to drink. No man can put down more than one well on his farm, and the well must be properly made. In this way the future water supply is husbanded.

One of the most interesting features of the development of the Gulf Coast is the inner waterway. The entire coast is lined with a series of lagoons, as a glance at a good map will show. The Laguna del Madre extends from within a mile of the Rio Grande to Corpus Christi Bay, a distance of a hundred miles, with a natural depth of three feet of water. From there there is little solid digging to Matagorda Bay. The route to Galveston involves several miles of solid excavation. But the bottom of the lagoons is generally soft mud, which is easily deepened by means of dredges. It is planned to connect these lagoons

with a series of canals and to deepen the lagoons where
necessary, so that there will be a storm-free route for
small vessels and barges from the mouth of the Mississippi to the Rio Grande. The official name of this project
is the Intracoastal Waterway of Louisiana and Texas.
It is now completed and in operation with a uniform
nine-foot depth and one hundred-foot bottom width, to
Galveston Bay and the Houston Canal, a distance of three
hundred and sixty-three miles. Considerable progress
has been in excavation south of Galveston, but it may
be several years before it reaches Corpus Christi, two
hundred miles away. It is already used a great deal,
although not officially opened until 1934, and it is believed that it will eventually be an important highway of
commerce, for it will connect at the one end with thousands of miles of navigable waterways in the Mississippi
Valley, and the saving in transportation cost will be considerable. Mexico also has plans to continue the improvement along her own long coast line as soon as
internal conditions warrant the expense.

The Gulf coast of Texas became very troublesome for
shipping in the early part of the nineteenth century, because of the many buccaneers and filibusters. For the
motley crowd engaged in this occupation, who were recruited from practically all the nations of the world, Galveston Island became the chosen rendezvous. It was not
only a good harbour, but it was within easy striking distance of several of the Spanish colonies. The first known
occupation of the island was when Commodore Louis de
Aury set up an organized government there in opposition
to Spain. To him came Xavier Mina with a couple of
hundred men and several ships. These leaders devoted
themselves mostly to plundering Spanish commerce and
the slave trade. The aim was to capture slaves and smug-

gle the blacks into Louisiana, as the customary price of a slave was a dollar a pound. Several hundred men were soon attracted to this island, among whom, it is said, were many citizens of the United States.

While the forces of Aury and his associates were engaged in an expedition against Mexico, Jean Lafitte quietly took possession of Galveston Island. It was simply one pirate stepping into the shoes of another. Lafitte has been called the Pirate of the Gulf. In a duel in Charleston, South Carolina, about an affair of the heart, he killed his antagonist, after which he adopted the life of a buccaneer. For his services in the War of 1812, Lafitte was granted an unconditional pardon. But after peace with England was declared, he returned to his old calling. Thus it is that we find him at Galveston. For a time previous to this, Lafitte had been engaged in operating near the mouth of the Mississippi until it became too warm for sea rovers there. His establishment in Barratavia had been broken up in 1814. Once established on this island, Lafitte erected buildings, built a fort, and organized a complete government with heads of several departments.

Lafitte claimed that it was only Spanish vessels which he attacked, and justified this course by saying that he had once suffered from the Spaniards, so that he had declared eternal war on Spain. It is said, however, that his men showed a remarkable degree of impartiality in their unlawful enterprise. It was indeed their willingness to make captives of United States vessels that hastened their downfall. The fortification built by Lafitte on the site of the present city of Galveston, and the flourishing town established by him, was named Campeachy. His own house was the most conspicuous building, and it was painted red—an appropriate colour. By his men he was known as Lord of Galveston, and he exercised almost absolute authority.

In 1821, after the attention of the authorities at Washington had been attracted to the work of Lafitte, an expedition was sent to the island with orders to break up this nest of pirates. Lafitte received the commanding officer and entertained him with princely hospitality. When he found that the Lieutenant's orders were imperative, he took his favourite ship, the *Pride,* a foretopsail schooner that mounted fourteen guns, and sailed out of the harbour with a hundred picked men. He never returned to the Texas coast, but died a few years later in Yucatan. The rule of pirates on the island of Galveston was then at an end.

If there always seems to be something romantic about an island, Galveston has her full share of romance. It was named "Galveston" after Count Bernardo de Galvez, who was Spanish viceroy to Mexico when this island was a part of that country.[1] The Mexican Government established a miltary post and custom-house here in 1830, and the "Port of Galveston" came into official existence. It still remains, and includes a much greater territory than the island itself. The City of Galveston secured its first charter from General Sam Houston, when that famous warrior was President of the Republic of Texas.

Like Houston, Galveston was promoted by a private company. But its very situation destined it for a great port. Here is the largest and safest harbour along the

[1] Galvez was one of the most enlightened and liberal rulers that ever occupied the vice-regal throne in Spanish-America. He introduced many reforms. He had been a friend of the American revolutionists. The Mexicans, many of them at least, wanted to throw off the Spanish yoke and make Galvez king. He declined to consider the subject. He died suddenly in 1794, as a result, so his friends believed, of poison administered by enemies.

coast of Texas, and near it are some of the richest and
most populous counties. Before the time of railroads,
water provided the only outlet, and Galveston had assumed great importance even before the war of the rebellion. For four years during that conflict, however, business was at a standstill. The only boats in the harbour
were the gunboats of the opposing forces. In 1862 a
force of federal marines landed and remained several
months. It was then recaptured by the Confederates.
Nevertheless a close blockade was maintained by the Federal fleet until the close of the war, and it was finally
occupied by the troops of the Union again in 1865.
Hence it is that one is treading on historic ground when
walking about the city of Galveston.

Galveston is probably better known to-day because
of her calamity than any other single incident in her
history. It frequently requires misfortune to bring out
the best that there is in man, and so it seems to be with
a municipality. Galveston was a growing and prosperous
town prior to the great disaster which befell it on the 8th
of September, 1900, when approximately five thousand
lives were lost and a third of the property destroyed.
Within a few short years it has arisen above this disaster,
and the Galveston of to-day is a far greater city than it
ever was before. There is no finer example of real spirit
and pluck existent in America to-day than Galveston.
History might perhaps overlook the storm of 1900, if it
were not for the fact that out of that calamity arose new
forces, whose influence is significant not only in this city
but throughout the entire United States.

The night of terror in the opening year of the twentieth
century, during which great damage was wrought to
Galveston, was enough to crush the spirit of the strongest
man. Wind and wave together devastated almost the

entire area on the eastern and southern sides of the city. Frame buildings were swept from their unsubstantial foundations; they were tossed about like small boats upon a reef. Thousands left their homes and waded the swift current in the streets to find security in the schools and other solid buildings. But many failed to realize the danger until it was too late. They remained in their frail houses, and in the final wreck were either drowned or crushed among the falling timbers.

The tidal wave occurred on Saturday, and, when Sunday morning opened, the flood had withdrawn almost as quickly as it came; but the city was a ruin. Fully half of the improvement values had been destroyed. Even to one whose immediate family did not suffer, the scenes of wreck and death were enough to unnerve him. This, and the fear of another similar occurrence, caused thousands to leave Galveston and seek new homes elsewhere, and only a very small percentage ever returned to the city. But those who remained were stout-hearted. The great majority had no thought other than to restore their homes and institutions. Sparta is now nothing but a memory, but Spartan courage has not been forgotten. Galveston is still with us, and its courage in the face of disaster is still a living remembrance.

I brought all the forces of imagination to play in an effort to picture in my mind the Galveston following the great tidal wave. One gentleman, who had lived there at that time, drove me over the city in an automobile, pointing out to me on the way the line where the destruction of houses ended. He gave me a vivid picture of the scene that he had witnessed, in which his own family had suffered greatly. But words alone could not depicture the terrible fury of the winds, the terrific lashings of the waves, the ominous crackling of the heavy timbers as they yielded to the destructive forces of wave and wind.

The majority of the inhabitants of Galveston met the situation brought on by the disaster bravely. Public meetings were held and committees were appointed; plans were immediately initiated to rebuild the city, and to provide reasonable assurance that a similar disaster might never occur. All petty differences among the various factions in the city, which existed there just as they do everywhere, were forgotten, and the entire populace seemed to work as a unit in the upbuilding of their stricken city. An unofficial body of fifteen business men, without real political authority, known as the Deep Water Commission, assumed the direction of affairs until the reorganization of the city government was effected. This committee was in almost continuous service for many weeks following the storm. It was to this spirit of co-operation, and the common desire for uplift, that was due the birth of the commission form of government which has spread so rapidly over the country.

There had been so much politics in the previous administration of Galveston that every one was anxious to eliminate this problem for the future. Business men and professional men alike dedicated their best thought and endeavour toward solving this question which has troubled all our American municipalities. Hence the commission plan was adopted to eradicate the evils of partisanship in municipal affairs, and the success was so great that the "Galveston Plan," as it is everywhere called, has been adopted in several hundred municipalities throughout the United States. By this system the mayor and four commissioners conduct business in the same way as do the heads of a great business enterprise. Notwithstanding the heavy municipal debt inherited from previous administrations, and the necessity of unusually heavy expenditures immediately, this body of business men accomplished wonders.

Galveston is situated on the east end of Galveston Island, which is on one side of Galveston Bay and in Galveston County. The island is thirty-six miles long, and from two to two and a half miles wide. The total area is about thirteen square miles. It is an island of sand, and before the disaster was only a few feet above the level of the sea at its highest point. The tidal wave, impelled by tempestuous winds, poured its waters over the island, while wind and water together spread destruction everywhere. It was decided to raise the level of the city an average of about seven feet. The total area to be thus elevated was about three square miles. It does not necessitate much calculation to realize that the amount of sand required to cover a surface of three square miles to a depth of seven feet, is almost incalculable. It runs into the millions of cubic yards. A canal two hundred feet wide and a mile and a half long was cut into the centre of the city to facilitate the filling process. The work was done by sections. In each section the owners of the houses were obliged to raise their homes on stilts to the required height, and the city then filled in the lot at public expense.

At the completion of this work of filling, the average level of the island on the side facing the sea was seventeen feet above sea level. To protect this filling a concrete wall was built, which follows the contour of the island for a distance of five and a half miles. This wall is sixteen feet wide at the base, seventeen feet high, and five feet wide at the top, with a concave outward face to break and turn back the force of the waves. The entire structure rests on a foundation of piles driven forty feet in the sand. Adjoining the wall is a splendid boulevard throughout the entire length, with concrete benches placed at regular intervals where people may sit and enjoy the seaward outlook to their hearts' content.

The stretch of open water between the island and mainland has always presented a serious obstacle; the first bridge was destroyed in 1867. Before the disaster there were several bridges for railroads and one for vehicular traffic, but all were destroyed by the mad waters. A concrete roadway was then constructed to accommodate all traffic. It is two and one-half miles long and one hundred and fifty-four feet in width, with a lift-bridge to permit boats to sail through. The amount of traffic passing over this causeway is enormous.

In August, 1915, the new and reinforced Galveston experienced its first great test against the storm king. It is claimed that the wind reached an even greater velocity than fifteen years earlier, but the rebuilt city resisted the destructive elements nobly. A few buildings were wrecked and communication on the causeway was interrupted for a time, but the great concrete wall withstood all the attacks and counter-attacks of wind and wave. The loss of life was small. The wisdom of those engineers who planned the defense was fully demonstrated.

Galveston is strategically located for a seaport and, since the removal of the treacherous bars, the largest ocean liner can reach the wharves. There is space sufficient to dock over one hundred steamers at the same time. The flag of every carrying nation in the world may be seen at the docks, and sailors of every nationality parade the streets. Several foreign nations maintain consulates in Galveston. A walk along the wharves, where boats are constantly loading and discharging cargoes, with the smell of tarred rope that always seems to be present at an ocean port permeating the air, is an interesting experience for one unfamiliar with such sights and smells.

Galveston is not a large city, for it has dropped far behind younger places in the race for population. The unfortunate calamity probably contributed in a measure to this. But it is a vigorous municipality of some fifty thousand people. Lofty skyscrapers are conspicuously absent. New buildings and residences are constantly being erected, the city has an air of prosperity and there is still plenty of room on the island for expansion. One of the most interesting buildings is the old City Hall. Here the "Galveston Plan" of city government was born and here it had its first trial.

The visitor to Galveston is close to the sea at all times. He is breathing the salt air constantly. He can take a dip in the sea or try his luck with the finny tribe whenever the spirit moves him. If he is content with the "smaller fry," such as mackerel, redfish, trout, red snapper and sheephead, they can be found near the shore. But if he is ambitious to catch the gamy kingfish or great silvery tarpon, he must journey out farther into the open sea in a motor boat; but success will bring a real thrill, a thrill that all deep-sea fishermen crave.

Galveston is blessed with an almost semi-tropical climate and there is an abundance of rainfall. Every month is a growing season, but the only crop carefully cultivated is the winter visitor. The municipal authorities and citizens work together in the effort to beautify the city. The rose now blooms everywhere, but it has been called the "City of Oleanders." This beautiful flowering bush here grows to gigantic size and contributes an indefinable charm. One should remember that before anything could be grown on the island it was necessary to bring in soil from the mainland and mix it with the sand that had been superim-

A SKYLINE IN THE DAVIS MOUNTAINS

posed. The streets are lined with palms, and many yards are brightened with these same graceful plants. They give a charming aspect to the place which attracts many winter visitors. Galveston is generally a city of balmy breezes, and it is possible to bathe in the surf even in midwinter. It is the most popular bathing resort in the State of Texas. It has been looked upon as a resort both winter and summer, and much enterprise has been manifested to improve the attractions and facilities of the city for this purpose. The Gulf breezes usually temper the summer heat, and the winters have only occasional chilly spells of short duration. A magnificent hotel was built by public subscription to take care of the resort seekers, which is only another instance of the public spirit to be found here in Galveston.

Everywhere in Galveston one encounters reminders of one of her famous citizens. Few cities of the size have so many examples of private munificence. In 1843 a poor Swiss immigrant came to that city and began to peddle notions on the streets. A little later he embarked in the mercantile business, in which he seemed to be successful from the very start. He realized, however, the obligation that a successful business man owes to his community, and began his benefactions before life had closed in for him. We find there a handsome public school as one of his benefactions. He also built the Young Men's Christian Association, with gymnasium, baths, reading-rooms and dormitories; the Grace Episcopal Church, a fine stone structure, is one of his monuments. A Home for Old Women, where aged and homeless old ladies may live, and an Orphans' Home were also erected with money left by him. He established a Public Library, with an endowment of four hundred thousand dollars, which is one of the finest libraries for a town of its size that I have ever seen.   On the most prominent street in the city stands a notable monument to the heroes of Texan independence, which, we are informed by an inscription, was built by Henry Rosenberg.   It is no wonder that the memory of Henry Rosenberg is ever green in the hearts of his fellow townsmen.

A little way up the Bay of Galveston one will find the old port of Anahuac.   Under the Mexican rule the collector of the "port of Galveston" resided near the mouth of the Trinity.   A fort was built there in 1831 and was given the name of Anahuac, the ancient title of the City of Mexico.   This fort, constructed of brick, was on the bay shore, and the outline could be traced until recently. It played a conspicuous part in the early history of Texas, and the name is almost as familiar as Goliad and Nacogdoches.   Just a short distance away is Turtle Bayou, where the famous "Turtle Bayou Resolutions" were promulgated.   In 1836 as many as thirty houses in addition to barracks for the soldiers were seen there by a traveller. It is now the county seat of Chambers County, and has again become of some importance.   The greater city of Galveston, however, overshadows Anahuac, and few travellers ever take the time to visit this historic old landmark.

CHAPTER XI

ALONG THE RIO GRANDE

SOME inspired poet ought to arise and compose "The Watch on the Rio Grande." Such a song would be based on fact, and it would not require a very vivid imagination to supply the requisite romance. Along the Rio Grande there has been more or less necessity for a guard or patrol ever since Texas joined the federation of states. It existed during the time of the Republic, although the boundaries were not at that time clearly defined.

For fifteen troublous years following the downfall of Porfirio Diaz, the dictator who had guided the destinies of our neighbouring republic for more than thirty years with a hand of steel, in 1910, thousands of our khaki-clad boys paced their solitary beats along this lonely river all the way from El Paso to Point Isabel, at its mouth. At one time President Taft mobilized the greater part of the regular army within easy reach of the Texas-Mexican border. On several occasions withdrawals had hardly taken place before reinforcements were hurried forth as fresh outbreaks of violence occurred. State militia were called into service to supplement Uncle Sam's regular troops. During these long years parts of the border were patrolled at all times, and there is scarcely a mile along this famous river which has not at some time echoed to the steady tramp of the advance sentry of the United States. For a goodly number of these boys the patrol along the Rio Grande was the last beat, and "taps" was

181

sounded. A flash in the night, and an American boy was no more. Sometimes the bullets were fired purposely by some sombreroed son of Mexico, and again the tragedy has been the result of a stray shot across the border. The contending forces on the Mexican side have not been particular about the direction in which their guns were aimed. In either event the result was the same— mourning in some home on this side of the international boundary; a freshly-made grave for the victim of an untimely death.

I had a little personal experience with the recklessness of the Mexican revolutionary troops. In company with three newspaper correspondents, I was exploring the American side of the Rio Grande near Brownsville and directly opposite where a desperate battle had been fought a few days before. Many bodies of dead horses on the river bank, and in the fields adjoining, marked the scene of the skirmish, in which three hundred Villistas were slain. The whole scene was plainly visible from our point of observation, for the river is not very wide at this point.

Some fresh marks in the sand near us prompted our curiosity, since they looked as if something had entered the sand from the direction of the Mexican shore. In each case we would find a bullet imbedded only a few inches in the sand. They had undoubtedly landed there at the time of the battle. At least two of the bullets were of the dum-dum (soft-nosed) variety, so condemned in modern warfare. All this time rifles were cracking from the trenches, which were not more than four hundred yards distant. Occasionally the peculiar sound of the Mauser bullet was heard. We could see a couple of scouts of the enemy concealed in some corn at which they were evidently shooting. Finally one bullet sounded as if it

HARVESTING THE COTTON

exploded almost over us. It startled but did not alarm me.

"It is time for us to skip," said the New York man, who had followed the Villa forces for two years, and had witnessed many a skirmish. "I know that sound, and that bullet was too near for comfort."

"You are right," said the San Antonio representative, who had served three years in the United States Army, and knew something about bullets. I knew nothing about bullets, but I was willing to accept the advice of those who were wiser than I, and I followed the others up the bank and back into the cane. It was interesting enough finding the bullets in the sand on the bank of the Rio Grande, for they were perfectly harmless there.

During the late summer and early autumn of 1915, up to the time of the recognition of Carranza, the disturbances along the Rio Grande reached their climax. Organized bands composed of Mexican soldiers and refugees terrorized a large section in and around Brownsville, and reaching almost to Laredo. Some of their raids extended from fifty to seventy-five miles north of Brownsville. This has not been a difficult feat because of the thinly settled character of the country, while the mesquite and chaparral furnished abundant cover. Furthermore, the fact that at least two-thirds of the inhabitants were of the same race, promised additional security, for they were reluctant to betray those of the same blood. The most audacious act of the Mexican desperadoes was the wrecking of a passenger train just a few miles north of Brownsville, by which lawless act and the shooting that followed, a couple of Americans were killed and several severely wounded. Almost every home of Americans in that section became an armed camp. The anti-arms law of the State was openly violated, and people went about armed and ready for any trouble. They formulated themselves into walking arsenals. Cattle and horses were stolen by the raiders and driven across the river.

It was claimed, and some proof was adduced, that an organized movement had arisen to win back a section of the country for Mexico. The invaders evidently believed that the entire Mexican population would welcome them with open arms. Several hundred United States troops were again despatched to Brownsville and other points to stop the depredations and capture the depredators. In this work the small body of rangers assisted, and special deputies were sworn in by the county sheriffs. Several United States troopers, and a still greater number of Texans lost their lives. Several pitched battles occurred between small bodies of Mexicans and the Americans, but as usual the Mexicans fired wildly, while the Texans and troopers were more deliberate and their aim was better. The number of Mexicans who were slain has never been made known, but it must have been many score.

It was a strange looking body of revolutionists that I visited opposite Brownsville at the time of these troubles. You would have thought them bandits, or guerillas. Their uniforms were all shades of khaki, and tan. Some wore fatigue hats; in other cases hats inclosed the wearers. All were "armed to the teeth" with guns, pistols, knives, and cartridge-belts. Are these soldiers, or has a boy scout troop been turned loose here? This was the thought that occurred to me, as I saw some of the "soldiers" walking about the camp.

"How many years have you?" I asked a boy in the idiomatic Spanish.

"Fourteen years, señor," he said in a boyish voice.

But he had already seen two years of service in the revolutionary armies.

Seated on their horses, these boys were almost hidden by their big hats, and they were so small that they seemed entirely out of place in the big Mexican saddles. These are the kind of soldiers that filled the ranks of all the contending parties. Few commands carried a commissary department, but the soldiers were compelled to forage for themselves. As forage became scarce on the Mexican side, these men had no scruples against crossing the Rio Grande into a land of plenty and helping themselves. Having been accustomed for months, and even several years, to taking private property on the Mexican side without questioning ownership, it was an easy matter to stifle any scruples that might yet remain when necessity arose and only a river lay between want and abundance.

When there has been no revolutionary disturbance in the years past, the border patrol has been obliged to look out for smugglers, of whom there were many. The smugglers were as likely to be Americans as Mexicans. Sometimes a venturesome stockman would attempt to drive an entire herd of cattle, or a bunch of horses, across the Rio Grande in order to evade the duty. It might only be a little tobacco. It was the revenue officers' duty to prevent all smuggling of every sort. The barrier was not without its loopholes, but they did very well considering the paucity of men and the hundreds of miles of border. Uncle Sam may well be proud of his officers.

In descending the Rio Grande from El Paso there is no really important port until Eagle Pass is reached. Presidio, in the county of the same name, is an old settlement and has long been a port of entry and the seat

of a custom house. It is opposite the Mexican town of
Presidio del Norte. Upon the completion of the railroad
headed this way, Presidio will undoubtedly become a
town of much greater importance. Some of the scenery
along the Rio Grande between El Paso and Eagle Pass
is beautiful, and its loneliness is seldom disturbed by the
traveller. One of the grandest and most imposing sights
is where the Pecos River pours its waters into the Rio
Grande, a short distance above Del Rio. The Pecos
approaches the larger stream through a canyon which it
has carved out to a depth of several hundred feet. The
Rio Grande, formerly the Rio Bravo, also runs between
walls of garnet and grey rocks which are hollowed out
into natural caves. Above the Pecos the waters of the
Rio Grande are clearer than below, for the yellow and
turbid flood of the Pecos colours it.

"O vale of Rio Bravo! Let thy simple children weep;
Close watch about their holy fire let maids of Pecos keep;
Let Taos send her cry across Sierra Madre's pines,
And Algodones toll her bells amidst her corn and vines;
For Lo! the pale land seekers come, with eager eyes of gain,
Wide scattering, like the bison herds, on broad Salada's plain."

Eagle Pass has become quite an important border city
in recent years. Here a branch of the Southern Pacific
meets the Mexican National and forms what is called
the International Railroad. Eagle Pass is one of the
natural outlets for Mexican trade, as it lies at the entrance
to one of the most fertile regions of the Mexican border.
It has now developed into a prosperous little city, far sur-
passing the town of Piedras Negras, or Ciudad Porfirio
Diaz, on the other side of the Rio Grande. Near Eagle
Pass is old Fort Duncan, which, for many years, was
one of the most important military posts of the border.

This fort had its beginning soon after the Mexican War when a company of soldiers established Camp Duncan here in March, 1849. A little later the site was acquired by the United States, and eventually a modern fort with substantial stone buildings was constructed. It was abandoned in 1905 and remained unoccupied for almost five years, when the troubles across the border caused it to be occupied once more. The first settlement established here was called California Camp, as so many California immigrants were stranded here during the gold excitement. Many of these afterwards became gamblers and highwaymen, so it is said by local authorities. During the Civil War, and for a few years afterwards, there were no soldiers here and the conditions were almost unsafe for a law-abiding white man. For almost a decade it was abandoned to the Indians, a few renegade white men, and unscrupulous Mexicans.

Through Eagle Pass formerly ran a great trade route from Durango and Chihuahua northward to San Antonio and St. Louis. This was carried on by means of caravans, and was an active competitor of the famous Santa Fé Trail. It took a merchant about forty days to go from Chihuahua to New York by way of New Orleans, and he was lucky to receive his purchases within ten months from the time he left his home city. One will still see relics of that age in the *carretas,* or wooden-wheeled carts, without a particle of iron in their construction, across the border. The wheels are hewn from a single block of wood, and they are yoked to the patient oxen by a rigid cross-bar lashed to their horns.

The most important border point in Southern Texas is Laredo. This city is generally reached by travellers over the International and Great Northern Railway from San Antonio, about one hundred and fifty miles almost directly north. The route traverses a country of ranches covered with mesquite and the prickly pear, not greatly unlike the territory west of San Antonio. There are immense tracts almost immediately tributary to the railroad that are practically unoccupied. The trouble is that it is owned in large tracts by wealthy men, who have never attempted any intensive improvement of their holdings.

Laredo is one of the oldest settlements in Texas, since its history covers more than a century and a half. For a long time it was the only permanent settlement on the north side of the Rio Grande. It was founded in 1755 by one Don Thomas Sanchez, to whom liberal concessions were made. Its founding differed from the older settlements of Texas in that there was neither mission nor presidio, and there was not even a resident priest. It was simply an armed camp of settlers like those early settlements of Anglo-Americans. As the settlement was not bothered by Indians, it became quite prosperous. It proved to be the only permanent settlement of Spaniards on the lower Rio Grande.

Ranches and haciendas gradually extended over the country toward the Nueces, and in the early part of the last century extensive herds of cattle were pastured between those rivers. The remains of the stone buildings, wells and water-tanks may still be seen. During the troublous times following the attempts of the Mexican people to separate themselves from Spain, however, the savage tribes again made raids upon this country and caused much devastation. The war of the Texas Revolution disturbed the peaceful security of the inhabitants but little. In 1842 Laredo was occupied by Texas troops, and again during the Mexican War the soldiers of the United States took possession and a military post was established. This border post was called Fort McIntosh.

Until the construction of railroads Laredo was isolated from the rest of Texas and was in much closer touch with Mexico, and there are still reminders of its early years. One will find many houses built of sun-dried adobe brick and roofed with thatch, where dwell the Mexican labourers who constitute the majority of the inhabitants. As international trade developed Laredo became increasingly important because it is the shortest route between the Mexican capital and eastern markets. Millions of dollars worth of our industrial products and Mexican raw materials pass through here yearly. For a number of years trade was stagnated and tourist travel absolutely at a standstill, because of the protracted revolutionary disturbances, but in the last dozen years there has been a revival of both, and Laredoans hail their thriving city as the "Gateway to Mexico." The city has grown to thirty thousand and been so thoroughly modernized that it will compare with other cities of its size. A fine new million-dollar international bridge now spans the Rio Grande. With the completion of the Pan American Highway to the old capital of Montezuma, some seven hundred miles away, Laredo will become of still greater importance, for the automobile traffic is certain to be large. Just across the river is Nuevo (New) Laredo, much smaller and less progressive, but which always interests the American visitor.

A number of years ago some enterprising citizen discovered that this region was adapted to truck farming and that the river would provide the necessary moisture. Since then about ten thousand acres have been brought under cultivation and thousands of cars are shipped annually, the producers specializing in Bermuda onions, so pleasing to many palates. Also other vegetables are grown.

Below Laredo there is a large triangular section

of country bounded by the river on one side and the Gulf of Mexico on the other. This forms what might with truth be called Uttermost Texas. It is also Southernmost United States, for the lowest point is nearer to the Equator than the mainland of Florida. A map of Texas, published a little more than half a century ago, designated it as "a wilderness occupied only by droves of wild horses." On a map published in 1839, which I examined, the following explanation was printed across this great section: "Of this section of country very little is known. From the fact that the Nueces on the south side and the Rio Grande on the north side are without any considerable tributaries, it is inferred that it is mostly a dry elevated prairie." This is all the information that was vouchsafed about that section of Texas, larger than our Middle West States, lying between those two rivers and as far west as Laredo, and on a line drawn northeast from that city to its junction with the Nueces.

It would be a surprise to that cartographer to visit to-day some parts of this vast domain, which he dismissed with a single paragraph. This territory between the Nueces and Rio Grande was always a subject of contest between the Texans and Mexicans, which was only settled after the Mexican War. When the question of sovereignty was adjudicated, the territory was divided into a number of counties and the name Cameron given to the most southerly one. It remained a scene of disturbance for a period even subsequent to our own Civil War. As late as 1867 it was said to be "subject to occasional raids from Indians and Mexicans, and only suited to those who are willing to live where they are subject to such occurrences." Mexican revolutionists freely crossed back and forth and added to the turmoil. At that time fully four-fifths of the population were Mexican, but

OATS READY FOR THE THRESHER

now the proportion as a whole is about half. In some sections the proportion is much greater. With the exception of Brownsville, the whole region was practically uninhabited up to 1890, save for herdsmen with their thousands and tens of thousands of cattle, horses and sheep. One realizes in travelling down here that although Texas has been occupied by the white man to some extent for almost four centuries, it is still somewhat new in spots, and big spots at that.

Proceeding down the Rio Grande towards its mouth from Laredo, there are no towns of great importance until Brownsville is reached. The population is sparse and scattered. Large regions are still not provided with railroad service. Stock raising is the principal industry, and large numbers of cattle feed on the range. Even though it does require ten acres to feed one steer, there are so many acres that the number of cattle mounts into the hundreds of thousands. Although tin cans may not be superabundant, goats seem to thrive on the prickly pear and other cacti, and may be found by the tens of thousands. The old settlement of Carriza has been renamed Zapata, and is the county seat of the county of the same name. Rio Grande City is the county seat of Starr County. Both of these towns are on the river. Opposite Roma is the old Mexican town of Mier, which was the objective point of the disastrous Texas expedition in 1842. The Texas Almanac of 1857, in speaking of this section of the country, says that the population are said to be nine-tenths Mexican, engaged in agriculture and stock raising. Three-fourths of the Americans were reported to be teachers and merchants, and the other fourth gamblers and blacklegs. The writer may have made the latter proportion a little too small from a natural prejudice in favour of his State.

Up to 1905, when the railroad was completed into Brownsville, this lower section of the great State of Texas was absolutely isolated. It was necessary for the people to travel more than one hundred miles by stage to Alice, the county seat of the new Jim Wells County, a journey of almost two days, to reach the nearest railroad connection, if they wished to go to the capital or any other section of the State. As a result they did not go visiting very often. It is probably for that reason that this district has remained the most backward section of the State, and one will find still in existence the most primitive methods of agriculture. You might easily imagine yourself in Mexico, for the Mexican characteristics seem to prevail. You will see many a Mexican ploughing with a yoke of oxen which are yoked by the horns in the cruel way characteristic of Mexico. Wagons and carts are also drawn in the same way. The great eyes of the poor beasts bulge out as though ready to fall from their sockets when travelling over a rough road. I saw many thatched and reed huts, which are exactly the same as one will find in the tropical parts of Mexico and Central America as well. They look anything rather than American, and one is surprised to find such dwelling-places within our own borders. One or two rooms will accommodate a very large family.

The city of Brownsville had its origin just prior to the Mexican War, when General Zachary Taylor established a fort on the Rio Grande not far from its mouth. It was on the 25th day of March, 1846, that the "Army of Occupation," under the command of General Taylor, reached Point Isabel, on the Gulf near the mouth of the Rio Grande, which Taylor intended to use as a base of operations and a depot of supplies. Leaving a garrison here, he advanced up the Rio Grande to a point almost opposite the Mexican town of Matamoras. Here he erected Fort Brown, which was named after Major Brown, whom he left in charge. During a month spent in the construction of defensive works numerous communications came to him from the Mexican commanders. As his instructions were to do nothing aggressive until an "open act of hostility" occurred, General Taylor remained inactive. Hearing that the Mexicans were crossing the river, however, both above and below the fort, he despatched a small reconnoitring party under Captain Thornton. Just how the engagement began is not settled, but the Mexicans were victorious and captured all of this party who were not killed.

This was the "open act of hostility" for which Taylor waited. He reported the occurrence to Washington, and President Polk sent the memorable message to Congress, in which he said: "Mexico has invaded our territory and shed American blood upon American soil." This message led to a declaration by Congress that a state of war existed between Mexico and the United States.

Taylor returned to Point Isabel, after leaving a garrison of five hundred men with some artillery to defend Fort Brown. On May 3rd the Mexicans began an attack upon Fort Brown which continued for six days, with inconsequential losses to the Americans. One of them, however, was Major Brown, after whom the fort had been named. Taylor could hear the cannonading from Point Isabel, and he turned his face again toward Fort Brown. In the afternoon of May 8th, at a point almost midway between Point Isabel and Fort Brown, and known as Palo Alto, he encountered the Mexicans blocking his way. It was a head-on collision between hostile forces, for dense thickets lined the road on either side. The Mexicans greatly outnumbered the American troops, but the latter had better guns and were more accurate gunners. When night fell, the field was in the possession of General Taylor's army, the enemy having been gradually forced back from their successive positions. Such was the battle of Palo Alto, which was an indecisive engagement and fought almost entirely by artillery. The enemies' casualties were over six hundred, while Taylor's loss amounted to but fifty-six men.

At dawn of the following day General Taylor resumed his march toward Fort Brown, although he was fully aware that another battle must be fought before he could reach that fortress now under siege. Strong reinforcements joined the Mexicans, who occupied a strong position upon a great ravine called Resaca de la Palma. The Mexican General Arista had selected this position with care, and he had his cannon strategically placed. A fierce charge of the American cavalry and a succession of bayonet charges, however, won the day. As the Mexicans fled, the Rio Grande became filled with the corpses of those who had ventured to swim its current in an attempt to reach the other shore. By this battle the boundary line between Mexico and the United States was definitely fixed at the Rio Grande for the first time. With odds against him of fully three to one, and with a paltry loss of one hundred and thirty-seven men, Taylor had won an important victory. Fort Brown was relieved, and a few weeks afterward Taylor started on his victorious march down into the interior of Mexico.

Following the Mexican War a settlement grew up at one side of Fort Brown. The original fort has disappeared, but a later one still stands, although it has been abandoned as a permanent fort. Brownsville has now become a considerable place. Until recent years it was chiefly important for its military post. During the Civil

Courtesy Brownsville Chamber of Commerce
A GIANT TARPON CAUGHT NEAR POINT ISABEL

War it was captured by the Federalists and held for a time, which crippled the Confederates because they were securing cotton and food from here. In August, 1906, the notorious "Brownsville Raid" by turbulent coloured troops occurred on the Fort Brown reservation. As a result the post was abandoned for several years until the Mexican disturbances necessitated the dispatch of troops to the border.

Brownsville is the undisputed metropolis of the lower Rio Grande, with a population of about twenty-seven thousand, whereas a quarter of a century ago it was only a sleepy, lethargic town, peopled mostly by Mexicans. The Anglo-Saxon element has brought in greater progressiveness. Scores of new buildings, hotels, schools, business blocks, have been erected, streets have been paved and beautiful homes have arisen until the Brownsville of to-day is an up-to-date city. Four railroads now provide transportation, including the National Lines of Mexico. A ship canal with a depth of twenty-five feet to the Gulf makes the city an ocean port. This work was done under federal supervision and largely with federal funds. The municipal airport is one of the best in the United States, for this is the jumping-off place for Mexico and Central America. Mexico maintains a customs office here to facilitate the international traffic.

In spite of the changes Brownsville has managed to retain some of the old atmosphere. Home builders have copied the Spanish or Mission style of architecture. The Spanish tongue is heard on every side. Mexican candy vendors are stationed on many corners selling "dulces," and women offer for sale exquisite pieces of drawnwork which have doubtless been smuggled across the border. The city market maintains a Mexican atmosphere where tortillas, tamales, chile con carne, frijoles and other characteristic foods are sold. And bargaining is not unknown, although less animated than across the river. Big-hatted loafers lounge about. On Sunday morning women wend their way to church with faces enshrouded in black shawls after the Spanish custom. The men prefer to go across the river to see the bull-fight forbidden on this side.

Matamoras is a typical Mexican town. Once an important city of forty thousand souls, it now numbers only a few thousand, although happier days are no doubt coming. A fine new automobile bridge now crosses the river. It is a walk of only two or three miles and will afford the visitor an insight into old Mexico. Most Americans go across to enjoy an occasional Mexican meal in one of the restaurants, or see some other characteristic sight—even the bull-fight. It used to be, in the days of drought, that they went across to satisfy their thirst, but that is no longer necessary. Matamoras boasts considerable history, for a number of bloody battles have been fought in and around the city. It will soon be possible to motor from here to Monterey and the City of Mexico over good highways.

Brownsville used to be the home of many bad men—men who habitually wore their guns in plain sight. But those days are past. If you see anyone carrying a revolver he is sure to be an officer, deputy sheriff or policeman. The revolver is the Texas officer's insignia of office. A Texas ranger may occasionally be encountered, but calls for their services have been few in recent years.

There are several points of interest on the Gulf that afford a pleasant motor journey. One of these is Point Isabel, or Port Isabel, about thirty miles distant. It is to-day a popular seaside resort and a good place from which to make a fishing excursion. At certain seasons of the year tarpon abound in these waters. If anyone has

a longing to add one of these splendid silvery ocean deni-
zens to his list of trophies, here is a good place to come
before their nomadic instincts lead them to migrate toward
the Atlantic. In addition to these the waters abound
with kingfish, Spanish mackerel, redfish, speckled trout,
red snapper, flounder, jackfish and many other finny
tribes. Boca Chica, south of Point Isabel, is easily
reached by a hard surfaced road from Brownsville. Here
is an extensive beach where surf bathing is enjoyed the
year around on one of the best beaches to be found on
the Gulf. It has developed into a popular resort.

The hunter need not go very far away from the irrigated district to find an abundance of game. It will remain so as long as there are great stretches of uncleared
brush land. Agricultural development has driven the
wild life back, but a large area still remains. The deer
is naturally the first choice of the hunter, and they are
quite plentiful. Both jack rabbits and cottontails are
common, and an occasional mountain lion is killed. Of
the birds the wild turkey is doubtless the most popular.
There are half a dozen species of wild geese and a score
of ducks, coots, gallinules, plover, rails and other water
birds. Quail abound and both white-winged and mourning doves may be shot in Texas. The chacalaca, a Mexican bird, is regarded as gamy. The only thing to be
careful about is to keep within the game laws.

When you are told that the Brownsville region is only
about one hundred and fifty miles north of the tropics, you
will better understand the reason for the magical development. With only about twenty-seven inches of natural
rainfall it needed the stimulus of irrigation to bring out
the latent possibilities. The soil is black, brown or choco-
late loam of remarkable fertility in which almost any kind
of plant life thrives. I rode through one jungle along the

Rio Grande which could be photographed and labelled
Central America.   The trees are covered with vines, moss
and all kinds of parasitic growths.   Bamboo and other
canes and hundreds of palms contribute to the tropical
setting.   There was a regular village of thatched huts,
occupied by Mexicans,, which could be duplicated in
almost any tropical land.

Irrigation was experimented with several decades ago
and for a time the country went promotion mad.   But the
men behind this movement were promoters simply and not
developers.   Millions were poured into irrigation plants
and digging leagues upon leagues of irrigation canals.
Great sugar plants were erected before there was any real
prospect of a sufficient supply of cane to operate them.
Settlers were lured there by lurid literature which was sent
out by the ton.   But they were the wrong kind of settlers,
for they had not the patience to wait.   As a result of
miscalculation in crops and soil and the shifting channel
of the river, which left their pumping plants high and dry,
several of these projects were abandoned.   Such pranks
are not uncommon on the part of this uncertain river.   A
lack of transportation and inability to get their products
to market when the prices were right were also a contributing factor.   One in particular attracted my attention, for it had been laid out on an elaborate scale.   But
the pumping plant was idle, the canal dry, and the beautiful ranch house was falling into decay.   It was a sad relic.

The later irrigation projects have been more successful,
for they were conceived by men of vision and backed by
sufficient capital to carry the well-laid plans to a successful
conclusion.   The greatest success has been achieved above
Brownsville and spreading out for some distance beyond
the river.   What was a waste tract of mesquite-covered
land has been transformed into a vast garden.   The level

land lends itself readily to irrigation by gravity with a minimum of pumping. All kinds of truck farming have been experimented with, and it has been found that almost every garden vegetable can be grown successfully. Thousands of carloads of onions, cabbages, lettuce, beans, tomatoes, celery, asparagus, summer squash, sweet corn, broccoli and cantaloupes are shipped to the northern city markets each year. The railroads now provide excellent transportation, and the future has a rosy aspect. The original development paralleled the river toward Samfordyce and Rio Grande City, but when the Southern Pacific built their line farther back a decade ago, it was immediately followed by new towns which sprang up like magic. To-day there are more than a score of thriving little cities scattered over this region. This lower Rio Grande, with almost half a million acres under irrigation, now ranks with the Imperial Valley of California and the Salt River Valley of Arizona in importance. It has been found that cotton can be grown profitably on these irrigated lands and the output is constantly increasing. It matures here earlier than anywhere else in the U. S.

The lower Rio Grande valley is destined to be a great fruit-growing region. Among these are figs and dates, grapes and papaya, a fruit growing in popularity. The papaya is something like a melon, with pinkish meat, and grows on small trees near the top. Olives are being experimented with. But the real magical development has been in the growth and spread of the citrus industry.

A score of years ago the commercial growing of oranges and grapefruit was almost unknown. Soon afterwards a few small orchards were planted and their success encouraged the planting of additional orchards. It required considerable experimentation to find the kind of trees best adapted to soil and climate. To-day there are several million citrus trees already producing and millions more growing. Thousands of boxes are shipped each year, and Texas bids fair to become one of our greatest producers of oranges and grapefruit. The sweetness and flavor of Texas oranges are equal to any. Some success has been had even on unirrigated land, which of course makes the cost of production much less.

Under an old treaty with Mexico the Rio Grande was recognized as a navigable stream. With the Elephant Butte Dam above El Paso and the many local projects along the Pecos River and the Rio Grande itself, it begins to look as though there would not be enough water to float a good-sized canoe during the dry season. Even the Mexicans will doubtless recognize eventually, when the political disturbances end, that the water is immensely more valuable for irrigation than the floating of small boats; if so, they will probably claim their share of the water. It is predicted that little of the water from the upper Rio Grande will reach the lower river, so that the supply for these projects must come from the streams emptying into it below El Paso. As a number of these feeders come from the Mexican side, our neighbours will have an especially strong claim for their share of the muddy current. But the producers would be compelled to find their market in the United States.

CHAPTER XII

EAST TEXAS

THE history of East Texas centres around and about the town of Nacogdoches. Up to the period that American settlers began to pour into Texas under the leadership of the various concessionaires, Nacogdoches was the only settlement of any considerable importance north and east of San Antonio. It exercised jurisdiction over all East Texas practically down to the time of the Revolution. Almost an equal distance across the Sabine River, in what is now the State of Louisiana, and what was then the old Spanish and French province of the same name, was the town of Natchitoches, which was the westernmost outpost of French, and then American settlements. Between these two frontier stations there was constant intercourse and contraband trade, in spite of the rigid royal decree interdicting commerce between the inhabitants of Texas and Louisiana. After the United States had acquired the territory of Louisiana in 1803, and as a result of the many filibustering and revolutionary expeditions organized for the purpose of conquering Texas, Nacogdoches became a frontier military post, or presidio, and a garrison of Spanish soldiers was maintained there for a number of years.

Nacogdoches was the usual terminus of the Old San Antonio Road, as was San Antonio the end of the western journey for the greater part of the traffic. This famous highway was a noted trail in the early days, which

is often called for in the early prairie surveys of many
counties. It started originally from a mission church in
Louisiana and had been travelled for over a hundred
years by mission priests, led by an "Intendant," and protected by an escort of Spanish cavalry in their annual
visitations of the missions of San José, Concepcion and
San Juan, near San Antonio; then they visited the mission
on the San Saba, until after the priests there were massacred by the Indians. The annual visitations continued
to the missions at El Paso, on the Gila River in Arizona,
and terminated at the missions in California. In later
years a perpetual stream of ox-carts laden with produce
of all kinds, and carrying the effects of incoming immigrants, passed along the rough, and, at times, almost impassable highway.

The Old San Antonio Road crossed the Colorado River
eighteen miles below Austin, before the town of Bastrop
was built. After Bastrop was located it intersected the
Colorado at that point. Its location could be traced
across Texas in many places as late as 1852. The first
station east of the Sabine on the old San Antonio Road
was the historic old town of San Augustine, which was
long known as "The Gateway to Texas." It was also
distinguished as the Athens of the State, because it actually possessed a three-story university and another
smaller college. After the old highway ceased to be the
main artery of traffic, San Augustine remained isolated,
difficult of access, and became secondary to the many
newer centres of population.

The name of Nacogdoches is derived from that of a
body of Indians, whose principal village was somewhere
within the present county of the same name. The principal centre of Spanish missionary and colonization enterprise in Eastern Texas was at Nacogdoches. The in-

itial work began with the closing years of the seventeenth century, and, in 1716, one of the group of missions and military garrisons (presidios), designed to protect the authority of Spain in Eastern Texas, was established in the vicinity of the present town. Within half a century numerous Spanish and French traders, as well as many friendly Indians, had settled in and about Nacogdoches, where there were many opportunities for trade with Louisiana. When the royal order, issued in 1772, for the abandonment of all the missions and settlements in Eastern Texas arrived, there was naturally much dissatisfaction and resentment among the inhabitants. The removal of the sacred vestments and the insignia was made to San Antonio under the escort of a military guard, but many of the inhabitants remained behind. They preferred to remain and take a hazard rather than abandon lucrative business and seek a new location. This marks the real beginning of the history of Nacogdoches as a commercial settlement rather than a mission outpost.

Until the adjustment of the Texas-Louisiana boundary in 1819, Nacogdoches suffered a great deal. It was occupied on several occasions by American revolutionary expeditions, and again by the Spanish forces. Spain enacted retribution divers times upon the inhabitants because of the supposed sympathy for Americans. When Stephen Austin passed through Nacogdoches in 1821, he found the town in ruins, with only one church and seven houses standing around the public square. The stone house was the only relic of the early days left, and it unfortunately has disappeared at the present time in the onward march of improvement. This town was the central point of the Fredonian War in 1826, and was again the scene of what is known as the Nacogdoches Rebellion of 1838, in which the Mexican population, which had always been numerous, disclaimed their allegiance to the new Republic.

An old account of Nacogdoches (1856) speaks of it as follows: "The town is compact, the houses framed and boarded. One or two Mexican stone houses remain, and, like the Aztec structures in more southern cities, have been put to the uses of the invading race. One of these, fronting, with an arcade, on the square, is converted into a bar-room. About Nacogdoches there are many Mexicans still living. Two or three of them, wrapped in blankets and *serapes,* we saw leaning against posts, and looking on in grand decay. They preserve their exclusiveness, their priests, and their customs, intermarrying only among themselves, and are considered lawless vagabonds."

Poor Lo has almost disappeared from Texas, his old-time happy terrestrial hunting ground. In Polk County, however, still linger some of the Alabama Indians, as they are called, the sole surviving aborigines in Texas with the exception of those at Isleta, mentioned elsewhere. For this reason they are of interest in a book upon a State once overrun by that people. They number about two hundred. These Indians have been stripped of their buckskins, and now wear "hickory" shirts, cotton overalls, and brogans. From nomadic followers of the chase they have taken to more peaceful pursuits. They occupy a reservation of two square miles granted them by Texas in 1854, and it is about as unproductive land as could be found in that section of the commonwealth. For that reason, and possibly for others as well, the tribe has not greatly prospered. The typical home is a one-room log house with a porch in front. One or more hungry dogs generally have possession of the front yard. The furniture is home-made. In every yard will be found a corn mortar, made of a hollowed-out log. The wooden pestle is about four or five feet long. With this they make the food called sotki, which is just a variety of hominy, and is their principal sustenance. The Indians are very hospitable, and they will share the last crust with the others.

These Alabama Indians deserve better treatment by both State and National Governments. They are absolutely self-supporting, but ought to be granted more fertile land and more modern implements with which to cultivate it. The Presbyterian Church has maintained a missionary among them since 1881, and nearly all the tribe are professed members of that denomination. Their character has been greatly improved through this religious work, as the Indians have taken very kindly to it. The majority of the younger ones now possess some education, and are able to both read and write. In 1913, Chief John Scott died at the age of one hundred and nine years. He migrated with his tribe to Texas in the early years of the last century, and had been a witness to all the political changes through which Texas has evolved. He remembered Sam Houston well, and recalled with pleasure his efforts to help the red men.

It is a revelation to that misinformed person, who harbours the idea that Texas is all treeless prairie, to travel through East Texas. This section is included in what is known as the timber belt of Texas. This is a broad belt of land extending from near the coast to the border of Oklahoma. Even at Nacogdoches, the oldest settled portion of Eastern Texas, the lumber industry still constitutes one of the chief resources. The country was originally heavily forested with the long-leaf and other pines, and with a great variety of hardwoods. Numerous rivers and creeks traverse East Texas, many of which are navigable and provide the means of transporting the timber to market. The land, except along the coast, is generally undulating and slightly hilly. The streams are sluggish and discoloured, and are engirded by broad bottom lands which are subject to overflow. The soil is generally very rich, although much of it is sandy.

The long-leaf pine district extends about half the way up the State from the Gulf. Then comes the region of the short-leaf pine, and the various hardwoods, of which oak is one of the most important. In some of these counties the cleared land has proved wonderfully well adapted for the cultivation of fruits. The growing of peaches on a commercial basis for northern markets has been followed for a considerable time, and their development has greatly spread. To-day thousands of refrigerator cars filled with peaches are shipped from this section each year. Cherokee County and the territory immediately surrounding is in the very heart of this fruit section. The fruit trees are numbered by the hundreds of thousands. The soil is of a sandy nature which is superimposed upon a porous red clay and is loose enough to afford good drainage. The cultivation of peaches has been followed by pears, plums, apples and almost all other fruits of the temperate zone, not excluding the luscious strawberry.

This timber belt of Texas, generally speaking, lies between the Trinity River and the eastern State line. To the west it reaches almost to a line with Dallas in some places, for Henderson County is one of the heavily timbered districts. In Bowie County, the extreme northeastern county, it was estimated thirty years ago that nine-tenths of the county was covered with dense forests of oak and yellow pine. Only about five per cent of the land was then enclosed in farms, although there were small settlements here that antedated the Texas Revolution. To-day more than half the county is included in farms, which demonstrates how industriously the sawmills have been at work. As the lumberman has cleared off the forests, the agriculturist has followed, and the "cut-over" lands are being cultivated in increasing amounts each year. Almost as much corn is planted in this district as cotton. The same natural conditions apply to the other counties in this section. They are all in the timbered sections, although in some there may be a little more prairie than others, and again the hardwoods may predominate over pine, or vice versa. In some, more of the original timber is still standing than elsewhere. They were all in the slaveholding part of the State, and the negro population to-day will enumerate from one-fourth to one-third of the entire inhabitants.

The post-oak is a prominent feature in Texas scenery. It is a somewhat small, broad-leaved oak of symmetrical shape, and appears where the soil is light and sandy. It is an open forest growth, and grows in a sort of island in the large prairies. It is frequently not even eradicated before cultivating the soil, and in the districts farther west, where timber is scarce, an island of post-oak adds much to the value of the tract for sale, since it furnishes material for buildings and fences.

A far more attractive tree than the post-oak is the live-oak, which here reaches its complete vigour and full foliage. The live-oaks are almost invariably garlanded with festoons of the ornamental Spanish moss. Farther west they are more meagrely furnished with leaves, and on barren hills they remind one very much of the olive both in the shape and size of the tree, and in the hue of the leaves. On rocky ledges the tree will cling with its distorted roots, disputing the scanty nourishment with the stunted grass. The Spanish moss swings in the breeze with slow and pendulous motion, and seems to harmonize with the tree itself.

The most important city in Northeastern Texas, and also one of the peculiar cities of the Union, is Texarkana, Tex-Ark. This is the formal method of addressing mail to this city, which is about equally divided between the States of Texas and Arkansas. At one time the Arkansas side of the city was the most populous, but the majority of the population now resides on the Texas side. To prevent friction and jealousy, the common postoffice has been built exactly on the State line. But there are two separate city, county, and State governments. It even has two Federal courts, one for each State, a distinction probably shared by no other city in the Republic. Likewise separate schools are maintained. There are two mayors and two city councils, but they get along quite harmoniously with one fire department, one waterworks, and one street railway system. This little city already celebrated its fortieth anniversary in 1913, and has become quite an important commercial town.

The real development of the timber industry began in the neighbourhood of Beaumont. Here the waters of the Neches and the Sabine furnished convenient transportation to transport the lumber and other products to the various outside markets. For the same reason the merchantable timber in that neighbourhood disappeared earliest, so that by the beginning of the present century the cutting of lumber was already a failing business. Railroads have been extended up into the timber country, however, and Beaumont still retains a position of primary importance in the lumber industry of the State.

The earliest mention of Beaumont is found in 1836, when the following paragraph appeared in a newspaper: "A town has lately been laid out on the tide water of the river Neches at a place known by the name of Tevis's Bluff. It has received the name of Beaumont." At the time of the Battle of San Jacinto this town was portrayed by a traveller as a hamlet of three or four houses. At a later period it developed into one of the flourishing small cities of Texas, but to the outside world it was an unknown and obscure town.

Beaumont is probably best known to-day because of the almost unprecedented excitement caused by the discovery of remarkable gushing oil wells at what is known as Spindle Top, four miles south of Beaumont. This was in January, 1901, and in a few days the name of Beaumont was sounded familiarly in the streets and offices and even in the homes of the Americas and Europe. Because of the great publicity given to this discovery, one is inclined to think of Beaumont as a city dotted with oil derricks. As a matter of fact the entire Spindle Top pool was beneath an area of only about two hundred acres, and there is not a single oil derrick dotting the landscape within several miles of the city of Beaumont. The original well, called the Lucas, began to flow at the rate of seventy thousand barrels per day, which was unparalleled in this country.

Within a period of six years upwards of forty million barrels of oil were marketed from that group of wells, notwithstanding the large amount wasted and consumed by fire. Hundreds of wells were put down at a great cost all around the Spindle Top pocket, but they were "dry holes." Within the narrow limits more than twelve hundred wells were sunk, and hundreds of derricks still stand, but the production of to-day is only a fraction of what it was in the days of the remarkable boom.

As a result of the discovery of the petroleum, Beaumont experienced an inflation such as has befallen few municipalities. Speculators from everywhere made a mad rush to get there. They bribed freight conductors and brakemen to save a few hours of time. Everybody wanted to be ahead of everybody else. Land was leased on all sides for drilling. Stock companies were promoted, wells were contracted for, oil stock was hawked on every street corner almost. Twenty thousand strangers arrived within a week after the first "gusher" was struck, twice as many as the population. Buildings were contracted for so rapidly that the streets were rendered almost impassable by the accumulation of building material. When the frenzy of speculation subsided Beaumont had the good sense to take advantage of the opportunities presented and begin the work of building up a substantial city. To-day it is a busy city of sixty-five thousand and presents a thoroughly modern appearance.

Encouraged by the success of Houston, Beaumont decided to become a seaport. The distance from the Gulf was just about the same—forty-nine miles, and the conditions not very different. The Neches River was already there and only needed dredging. The country was flat. A channel to the depth of twenty-five feet was completed in 1916, but this has been increased to thirty feet, with a width of one hundred and fifty feet at the bottom. With a large turning basin close to the heart of the city and splendid terminals of the latest design, Beaumont is now a port of the first class. And the enterprising citizens are not going to be satisfied until a uniform depth of thirty-four feet has been reached. The annual tonnage runs into millions of tons and several hundred ocean-going vessels sail up the canal each year. And, to the credit of Beaumont, all of this was a municipal enterprise.

On the shores of Lake Sabine, in the southeast corner of Texas, below Beaumont and only a few miles from the

THE "DEVIL'S TOMBSTONE" IN PALO DURO CANYON

Gulf, is a thriving little city, which did not have an existence until 1898, when it was made the ocean terminal of the Kansas City Southern Railroad, which had just been completed. It was named Port Arthur, in honor of Arthur E. Stilwell, its promoter. The port grew rapidly. Within a decade waterworks, street railways and other modern improvements that go with a city had been completed. The growth and development have continued until to-day fifty thousand inhabitants dwell in the municipality.

Beaumont and Port Arthur, and the intervening territory, have become probably the largest concentration points for the oil industry in the Southwest. Evidences of this are visible on every side. Nearly every one of the major oil companies are represented here. Great steel storage tanks stretch out in unending monotony over thousands of acres. There are large oil refineries in both cities, some of the largest in the country. Pipe lines from Oklahoma and other Texas fields bring in an unfailing supply of the liquid wealth. Crude oil, kerosene and gasoline are poured into tank steamers and transported to all parts of the world. Lubricating oil, greases and other by-products of petroleum, manufactured in Beaumont or Port Arthur, will be found for sale wherever motor cars are used. It is claimed that one tenth of all gasoline used in the United States is produced in this area. There is no doubt but that the output is tremendous.

On the coastal prairies of southeastern Texas rice has become as important as is cotton in much of the South, wheat in the Dakotas, or corn to the farmers of Illinois and Iowa. As the traveller passes along the coast between Beaumont and Houston, he will see great fields stretching out on either side of the railroad track or highway, through which irrigation canals run. Some of these fields are hundreds of acres in extent. This land is very flat, but there are occasionally diminutive ridges on which the main canal is placed. This plan is followed in order that the water may stand slightly above the general level of the land to be inundated.

It is a mistaken idea that rice can only be produced on marsh land, for none of this soil could properly be classed as such. It is planted on elevated land, exactly the same as the wheat and oats of our Northern States, except that it is absolutely necessary for the land to be flooded during the growing season. This Texas rice land has an advantage over the rice lands in the Orient, because it can be ploughed and harrowed while it is yet dry, and when it is much easier to perform that work than after the water has been turned on. On the large farms it is broken by tractors pulling gangs of eight or ten ploughs.

The cultivation of rice along the Gulf Coast began shortly after the Civil War. A small colony of Germans settled along that coast of Louisiana, in the Parish of Arcadia, and began to raise rice in a small way. The land was irrigated in the simplest method by means of a levee thrown up with a shovel; the grain was harvested with sickles, and threshed out with flails. The results of the labour of these Teutons demonstrated that the raising of rice along this coast was a profitable undertaking, and other settlers began to take up the work. Starting from such a small beginning, the march forward of this industry has been one of continued triumph.

It was not until 1887 that the rice culture was taken up after modern methods, and with a larger outlay of capital. The industry responded to these new conditions and methods. Then it was that irrigation on a larger scale was attempted. Incorporated companies were formed to furnish the necessary water. Small ravines and gulleys were dammed up, and allowed to fill with water during the rainy months in order to provide an unfailing supply of water for irrigation during the period necessary. Small pumps operated by engines of five or six horse power were used to elevate the water to the fields in the growing season. The broadcast seeder attached to the farm wagon rapidly superseded the human planter carrying a bucket of rice and sowing the seed broadcast by hand. The self-binding harvester supplanted the old-fashioned sickle and the cradle, just as it did in the grain fields of the North. The man who used to flail out a few sacks of rice in a day, when the wind blew enough to winnow it properly, was out of a job. The steam thresher could do more than a hundred times as much, and do it better. Sulky ploughs and gang ploughs replaced the implements formerly in use, and modern discs usurped the duties of the old-fashioned drag.

Rice culture soon radiated from Louisiana to the coast of Texas, where the land was found equally suited to the cultivation of this important food product. The first effort of any magnitude was made near Port Arthur in Jefferson County, in 1897. After the Port Arthur Canal was installed, each year saw the number of acres sown to rice increased, and it was not long until a quarter of a million acres were thus employed. The yearly value of the crop ran up into the millions of dollars. The industry gradually extended to Houston, and even beyond that city, and to-day the rice fields may be seen almost to the Nueces River.

This coastal plain in Texas, which is as level as it is possible for land to be, is crossed by a number of streams which afford a large water supply, and the elevation is sufficient to provide good drainage. The surface of the streams is generally lower than the lands to be irrigated, and it is frequently necessary to pump the water twenty-five or thirty feet into the irrigation canals. The canals are built by throwing up parallel levees over the prairie. For a main canal they are sometimes one hundred feet apart. The main canal is located on the highest ridge, so that all the land will be beneath the level of the water. Lateral canals branch off as frequently as are necessary. When the farmer wishes water, he simply lifts the flood-gates and permits the water to pour over his land. The period of irrigation generally continues about seventy days.

It has also been found that an abundant supply of water could be reached at a comparatively slight depth, and many of the wells flowed; with others, it was necessary to pump only a few feet. Thousands of these wells have been sunk all over this rice belt of Texas, and the flow from one well is frequently sufficient to irrigate from one hundred to one hundred and fifty acres.

It does not require a deep soil for rice, so we are told, and in fact it is better that a clay strata should be at a depth of twelve or fifteen inches under the surface. The ground in that variety of soil will dry much more quickly, and the harvesting is very much easier. One requisite, however, is that the surface must be nearly level, so that the water will stand evenly on the land. The ground is ploughed during the winter. The seed is usually sown in April and May. Soon afterward the fields are flooded, since the rice derives a large percentage of its nourishment from water. For that same reason it does not exhaust the soil so quickly as other cereals, and many successive crops can be raised from the same land without any appreciable injury to the soil. When the plants begin to mature the water is turned off, and it requires from twelve to fifteen days for the soil to dry. The rice is then cut with self-binders, which differ very little from the binders used to harvest wheat and oats, and it is threshed with the same thresher employed for oats. The only noticeable difference in the machine is the broad wheels that are used to prevent sinking into the soft ground, which has not yet thoroughly dried. The rice is shocked much like wheat, and is allowed to dry for two or three weeks before it is threshed. Quite a number of Japanese will be found engaged in raising rice here in Texas.

The Government reports the average yield of rice at twelve barrels per acre, but a farmer will frequently obtain fifteen and occasionally as much as twenty-five barrels of one hundred and sixty-two pounds each from a single acre. This will sell in the field for from three to four dollars per barrel. In all the principal towns rice warehouses will be found, just as grain elevators are located at the principal towns in our Northern States. The rice, as it comes from the field, however, is far different from that which is sold over the counters of the corner grocery. I doubt if many people would be tempted by a dish of rice in its natural state, for it has a brownish colour. Before it is placed on the market all of the grain is sent to a rice mill, where it is thoroughly polished, which gives it the attractive whiteness that we find in the commercial rice. It probably does not add anything more to the nutritive value of the rice than does the whitening process through which flour passes. It may, in fact, detract from its nutritive value, but it does render the rice more attractive and palatable.

There is no grain that fills so important a part in the feeding of the world as does rice. It is the leading, and in some cases almost the only food, of from one-third to one-half of the entire human race. Rice constitutes the principal food of the teeming millions of China, who number one-quarter of the population of the globe. In Japan statistics show that rice forms half of the total sustenance of the many millions of that island. And yet the Japanese are credited with a great deal of endurance. The same may be said of India, with its population of a quarter of a billion. In Java, in the Philippines, and many of the islands of the Pacific, with their millions upon millions of population, the people would starve were it not for the sustenance given them by rice. We can probably never supply more than a small proportion of the rice used in our country, but it is fortunate that such excellent rice lands have been discovered down here along the Gulf Coast.

CHAPTER XIII

THE BLACK WAXY BELT

ROBERT E. LEE and some friends, who likewise became famous during the Civil War, were standing together out on the Texas prairie. The time was in the early fifties, so the story goes, and Lee was then an officer in the United States Army. Lee became pensive, and gazed out upon the boundless plain without uttering a word.

"What do you see?" asked one of his companions.

"I am listening to the footsteps of oncoming millions," was the answer.

This prediction of the great Confederate leader has come true in a measure, and the process is continuing. One by one, two by two, score by score, they infiltrate across the boarder and increase the work of the next census taker. But there is no jostling as yet. Only in the vicinity of Dallas is the settling up of the State noticeable. One-third of the entire population will be found within one hundred miles of that city. Dallas and Fort Worth are growing rapidly, while many other prosperous towns and villages are scattered over this rich territory, which is known as the Black Waxy Belt. Even in the country a farmer can enumerate several neighbours within his horizon.

The richest section of all Texas from an agricultural standpoint is the Black Waxy Belt, which has its centre at the northern metropolis of Dallas. Dallas is situated more than two hundred miles north and a little west of

217

Houston, with which city it is connected by several rail-roads. Here it is that cotton is supreme, and the term King Cotton is not a misnomer. The prosperity of the great community is determined each year by the yield and price of that commodity. If you should travel through here when cotton is ready for the pickers, your astonished gaze would fall upon heaping mounds of the "Texas snow" which does not melt on every hand.

Cotton is a New World product. Long before the white man was aware that such a plant existed, the native brown man was apparelled in clothes made from cotton. The Spanish explorers discovered Montezuma's follow-ers wearing garments woven from the fibre of the cotton plant, which was cultivated by them. Cortez, in his re-ports to the crown of Spain, dwells upon the skill dis-played by the natives in the spinning of cotton and manu-facturing it into cloth. This proves conclusively that this plant was indigenous to America.

When the bolls have unfolded, and the pure white floss of the bursted pods greets the eye everywhere, the cotton fields of the Black Waxy Belt are a beautiful sight. In places they spread out almost as far as the vision reaches. Old white-haired negroes, looking like "Old Black Joe," and the comical little pickaninnies toil side by side all day long in the burning sun. The ripened fields are picked over time and time again, as the pods unfold at irregular times, and it is not advisable to leave the opened pods exposed to the weather long after being ready for the pickers. The capacious wagon boxes are loaded with the white harvest and hauled to the "gin"; there the seed is separated from the fibre, and the cotton is incased in bales of about five hundred pounds each. The bales are then loaded on cars and taken to the "com-press," where they are squeezed into less than half their

FIRST HOEING OF COTTON

original size by the application of tremendous pressure.

The boll-weevil worm has inflicted great damage in the cotton belt of Texas, along with other cotton States— the loss in a single year climbing up into the millions. Through scientific investigation and experiment, however, the ravages of this costly pest have been greatly reduced in the last few years. One successful method has been the introduction of early maturing varieties of the cotton plant, together with other means of hastening the harvesting of the crop.

The Houston and Texas Central is one of the oldest railroads in the State, and for quite a distance after leaving Houston traverses the region where many of the land grants of the early *empresarios* were located. For that reason it is one of the oldest centres of American occupation. The negro population is very large in many sections, for these colonists brought slaves with them. Before the war the slave population almost equalled the white in many places. To-day they will number a third outside of the large cities. The simple cabins of the Ethiopians dot the fields, and the ebony faces of the inhabitants enliven the landscape. At Prairie View there is a large educational institution for the negroes that is supported by the State. It is primarily intended as a training-school for negro teachers.

About a third of the way toward Dallas the railroad intersects the old San Antonio Road, over which most of the early immigrants to Texas came. This road was the connecting link between the upper and lower settlements of the Spaniards. Indian hostilities prevented the spread of American settlements north of this highway until after statehood. Most of these settlers established themselves as near as they could to this road for fear of the marauding Indians. At the opening of the

Revolution there were settlements every five or ten miles from here to Nacogdoches.

The San Antonio Road continued to be an important highway until long after the admission of Texas as a State. There was a continuous succession of teams and horsemen along the highway because it was the great artery of traffic between the United States and Texas, and the Mexican provinces as well. Caldwell and Bastrop were both stations on the San Antonio Road between here and San Antonio. The north line of Brazos County also follows this old highway for some distance. Near it, on the Brazos, was established in 1830 the old Mexican fort of Tenoxtitlan. This was done for the double purpose of protecting the frontier against Indians and of enforcing the laws of Mexico among the American settlers. A small town grew up, which was little more than a name after the Revolution, and its identity has since been lost in Texas geography.

A recent historian positively asserts that the death of La Salle occurred near the site of Navasota. Not far distant from this city is the once noted town of Washington on the Brazos, which was, until the Civil War, one of the political and business centres of Texas, as well as a seat of civilization and culture. The municipality was organized in 1835, and the municipality later became Washington County. The town of Washington was the first county seat, but that distinction has disappeared. It now dwells in the past. As the place where the Texas Declaration of Independence was promulgated, and as the one-time capital of the Republic, the old town of the Brazos merits more than casual notice. It acquired prestige as the leading market town of the upper Brazos, for steamboat navigation was then maintained on this river.

In the forties and fifties Washington reached the zenith of her glory, with a population of at least fifteen hundred, and was one of the largest towns of the State. But the citizens haughtily refused a bonus to the Houston and Texas Central Railroad, then being projected, because they believed it would interfere with the river traffic. One man, possessed of wisdom beyond his fellows, walked the streets and almost tearfully entreated the inhabitants to accede to the demand. But they were obdurate. In his resulting wrath, it is said that he cursed the town, and prayed that he might survive to see the day when the site of old Washington would be planted with cotton. The result was that the people vanished, Washington is still without a railroad, and another town is the county capital. The prayer of the outraged citizen has been almost realized. It is now a small town, with a single store to supply the wants of the neighbourhood. Old foundations, brick cisterns, and debris, now indicate the site of the town as it once stood. Nothing remains but shadowy memories, and a shaft of grey Texas granite, erected by the school children of the county in 1900, on which is this inscription: "Here a nation was born."

Near Corsicana was discovered and produced the first oil and natural gas of commercial volume in Texas. Up to this time the country had been purely agricultural. This was in 1896, several years before the Beaumont boom. It still remains an important producing point for petroleum. The oil boom started the town on the up grade, until to-day it is a prosperous little city and is the county seat of Navarro County. This county is in the richest agricultural district, for more than half the land is actually cultivated. Cotton is the principal crop, and far more land is devoted to the cultivation of this plant than all others together. It is not an old section of the country, for there were no settlements within it until after Texas was admitted to the Union.

In the northern part of Texas, and a little east of the centre, are located the "Twin Cities" of Texas, which are the Minneapolis and the St. Paul of that State. There is considerable rivalry between these two municipalities, and it is rather interesting, and frequently amusing, to listen to the citizen of one city express his opinion of its rival.

"Fort Worth is the largest of our suburban towns; you really ought to see it," says the citizen of Dallas, speaking in a sort of disparaging way about the other city.

"Dallas is nothing more than a big wholesale town," says the man who lives in Fort Worth. "There is little real manufacturing in Dallas, and it is manufacturing that makes solid city growth."

The two cities are connected by a splendid interurban line, and at the most they are but thirty miles apart. If both cities should continue to increase, as the inhabitants of each one predict, and should grow toward each other, then it might be that at some future time the two cities will make one great Southwestern metropolis. As any rate, there are many who look forward to the day when this intervening distance will be a continuous succession of pretty and thriving villages, country clubs, homes, and outing resorts. This, however, is looking quite a ways into the future.

At the time of the Texas Revolution this fertile country was the roving ground of Indians. When a white man, in 1841, erected a tiny hut on the banks of the Trinity River, occurred the first invasion of this primeval wilderness by that race. The nearest court at that time was at Nacogdoches, two hundred miles away. Five years later the little settlement had increased to an even half dozen families. It was named Dallas in honour of George Mifflin Dallas, Vice-president under President Polk. The pioneer log cabin of John Neely Bryan, the first settler, now may be seen on the court house grounds.

"Life in Dallas," says a contemporary writer, "in the early fifties moved on primitive lines. An old-fashioned hand mill, brought by one of the settlers in 1852 to grind the corn with, was in such demand that it was allotted to the applicants one day at a time. One sewing machine served the village for years." The first court house was a rough structure of cedar logs, with a puncheon floor and with split logs for seats; all the merchandise and supplies of every kind were hauled from Houston with ox-teams. Even when the roads were passable, it required about four weeks to make the trip.

It was not unusual advantage in topography or opportunities for transportation that dictated the choice of the site of Dallas, nor are they responsible for its prosperity. The only asset was the rich black loam of the surrounding prairie. As settlers came in and agriculture spread, a great distributing centre became necessary, and the enterprise of her citizens directed that development to Dallas. The municipality was incorporated in 1856, when still only a village. With the advent of railroads in the early seventies, the city began to grow and improvements rapidly followed. The streets were thronged with great lumbering freighting wagons, drawn by oxen or mules, which were ready to haul supplies to any section of Texas or beyond. One contemporary writer says that "a special police force was required to keep from congestion the immense concourse of wagons." Maybe that was the beginning of the traffic officer. It is quite certain that speed was not one of the menaces.

We read frequently about the personality of great cities,

and it is a recognizable quality in Dallas. Primarily it impresses one as being a Northern city beneath a Southern sun. It is essentially a commercial city and has the same air of business activity that one will find in Kansas City or Indianapolis. Its leaders have largely come from that section of the country. The characteristics may not be so pronounced as in San Antonio or Quebec, Boston or New Orleans, but Dallas certainly does possess an individuality. San Antonio is reminiscent of the Don, and even Houston is softer and more suave. But in Dallas money talks and mere bigness impresses. Dallas citizens like to talk of big things, colossal enterprises, wealthy residents, lofty buildings, the magnitude of her wholesale trade, her unique annual fair. The outstanding characteristics are those of Chicago, only in a lesser degree as a matter of course. You drive along the streets and come upon a palace fit for a prince to live in.

"Whose home is that?" you ask, as you admire its magnificence.

"Oh, that house belongs to a rich rancher," is the reply. "He bought land when it could be had for a trifle and then sold it to farmers. Probably is a multi-millionaire."

You pass on to another mansion which, you are informed, is the residence of a retired cattleman, "who has so many cattle he can't count them." Still another houses a rich oil man who has made his pile and is now intent on enjoying life. And so your host continues until you begin to realize that Dallas is actually the home of great wealth. It is the financial centre of the State and the home of strong financial institutions.

It is now almost thirty years since I first visited Dallas, and I have revisited it at intervals of only a few years ever since. At that time it was little more than an overgrown county seat and far from impressive. But at each return

I have marvelled at the rapid transformation, until to-day it has a real metropolitan air. The rich black loam and the abundant rainfall have attracted a large population into the contributing territory, which reaches up into the grain belt of southern Oklahoma. There are now many thriving little cities of from eight to fifteen thousand inhabitants within a radius of one hundred and fifty miles, each one thoroughly modernized, and a still greater number of smaller places. These towns are supplied by the half a thousand establishments of Dallas, the combined trade amounting to many millions each year.

Lofty skyscrapers dominate the horizon of Dallas. Capacious hotels await the visitor with a warm welcome. The public buildings are built on a generous scale. The parks and playgrounds are many and attractive. The residential districts have spread out on every side. The streets have been laid out with an eye to beauty. The population has already passed the quarter of a million, so that Dallas is the second city in Texas, being outnumbered only by Houston.

One of the really unique institutions of Dallas is the Dallas State Fair. Although called a State fair, this exposition is purely a local affair, but it has been exceedingly profitable. Several hundred thousand people pass through the stiles each year, and it has been of infinite advantage in promoting the business of Dallas. Initiated as a purely private enterprise the stockholders, a number of years ago, generously transferred the property to the city for fair grounds and park purposes, reserving only four weeks in the autumn for their exposition. Many commodious buildings of attractive architecture and permanent in construction have been erected and are now owned by the municipality. Among these is the Coliseum, which will seat several thousand people. This and the unusual hotel capacity have made Dallas a favourite convention city, and led to its selection as the central exposition city of the Texas Centennial of 1936.

Dallas is not only famous for its public school facilities but also for a noted educational institution. Although its doors were not opened to students until 1915, the Southern Methodist University, located on a spacious site in the northern part of the city, has already become one of the greatest colleges in the South.

The ambition of the Dallasites is absolutely unlimited, and the energy with which they attack problems is commendable. They thoroughly believe in the old adage that in union there is strength. Nothing whatsoever daunts them. A great concrete viaduct exceeding a mile in length was constructed across the lowland through which flows Trinity River a number of years ago, in order to connect the city with the suburb of Oak Cliff. Still more recently the river itself was picked up and moved several hundred yards, its channel straightened and confined between levees. By this project the danger of floods was eliminated and several thousand acres of land in the heart of the city were reclaimed for improvement. Although the cost ran into the millions, it was cheerfully paid.

Because of high freight rates, which places Dallas at a great disadvantage over the Gulf ports in the cotton market, the enterprising citizens decided to make inland Dallas, five hundred and fifty miles distant from the Gulf of Mexico by the nearest waterway, into a port. They succeeded in getting the national government at Washington to make liberal appropriations to develop Trinity River into a waterway deep enough for barges carrying cotton and other bulk freight to navigate between Dallas and the Gulf, and now it is proposed to extend the improvement to Fort Worth. Unlike most similar projects the work was begun near Dallas and not at the mouth of the stream. The channel was deepened and locks constructed on the upper reaches of the Trinity.

For a number of years the project made little progress, but another intensive campaign has been initiated, especially since the government has been making heavy appropriations to provide labour for the unemployed. It is true that in early days flat-boats were occasionally used to float cargoes down the Trinity to the Gulf. But that was before the days of the railroads. The main purpose undoubtedly is to reduce the freight rate on cotton and thus divert some of the business that goes to Houston, Galveston and Beaumont. Whether the project will ever be completed or not, the future alone will reveal. If it does not, it will not be because the Dallasites lack energy and resourcefulness. They will fight to the last ditch for what they want, and I admire them for these very qualities.

It is rather unusual to find two large cities so close together as Dallas and Forth Worth, except in congested centres, each growing, expanding and prospering without any appreciable effect upon the other. As a rule one succumbs sooner or later to the other. But these twin cities continue their friendly rivalry, each being among the fastest growing cities in the United States. Fort Worth, with a population only one hundred thousand less than its rival, is the fourth city in Texas. And it is a very lively competitor for its enterprising neighbour. Fort Worth lies at the very edge of the black earth belt, for one does not travel many miles toward the setting sun before a broken region is entered, which extends for a hundred and fifty miles or more. The motorist is continually going either up or down and around. The population is sparser. Agriculture is less general and less intensive. Cattle are more numerous.

At the close of the Mexican War General Winfield
Scott dispatched a troop of dragoons to this section to
establish a post for the protection of the scattered settlers
from the ravages of Indian war parties, who were then
in an ugly mood.   Major Arnold, who was in charge of
the dragoons, selected a site where Fort Worth now stands
and named it Camp Worth after Brigadier-General
William Worth, who had become a popular hero through
his brilliant exploits in the war just ended. This was
on June 6, 1849. A few months later the name was
changed to Fort Worth, but only four years later it was
abandoned as a military post. It was never really a fort
in the modern understanding of that term, the barracks
for the soldiers being the only buildings and they were
located in the very heart of the modern city.

As a result of the protection afforded by the presence
of soldiers a little settlement gradually grew up in the
vicinity of the fort. A very meagre population was scattered here and there throughout the surrounding country.
A supply train now and then was about the limit of the
trade in that day.   Perhaps a few covered wagons passed
through on their way farther south or west.   Cattle trails
were not yet established.   In fact, the cattle business was
still in its infancy.   There was no promise that the little
settlement would ever become of importance.   It did not
grow a great deal until the close of the war between the
states when many confederate veterans settled here.   By
that time Fort Worth had become an important station
on one of the leading cattle trails to the North.

When Tarrant County was created by the Legislature
the county seat was at first located at Birdsville, about
seven miles northeast. This move did not suit the ambitious inhabitants of Fort Worth, who immediately began to scheme for a change. When this was accom-

plished, they were wild with joy. The official records were placed in a wagon, three fiddlers mounted on top, who played stirring tunes, and the county seat thus transported to the little village perched on the bluffs above the Trinity. Little now remains in Birdsville to remind one of its heroic struggle to become the county capital and seat of justice. Until about 1870 Fort Worth was on the real western frontier, and the motto of the present city is "Where the West begins." It was not incorporated until 1873.

Although another railroad had been completed into the city a few years earlier, the real growth of Fort Worth did not begin until the completion, after several years of financial tribulation, of the Texas and Pacific Railroad in 1876. The succeeding boom brought with it a host of rough-and-ready characters who were never without their six-shooters, and many of whom were of the type known as two-gun men. They could shoot from the hip as well as the waist and were almost as accurate with the left hand as the right. It thus became a sort of clearing house between the regulated customs of the East and the free and untrammelled life of the West. Thus the railroad introduced its measure of evils as well as benefits. Cattlemen at once made Fort Worth their headquarters and drew their supplies therefrom. Those were the days when buffalo robes were in great demand in the North, and it soon developed into a great market for these skins. Every farmer prided himself on the possession of one of these warm leg coverings. More than two hundred thousand hides of these shaggy animals were received there in a single season. The warehouses were oftentimes filled to overflowing and the vacant ground was utilized. With such prodigal slaughter, it is not surprising that the great herds rapidly diminished and finally disappeared.

To-day the warm and snug buffalo robe is rarely seen. It has gone the way of sleighs and sleighbells.

When the meat barons of Chicago began to search for a desirable location for the establishment of packing houses in the Southwest, they chose Fort Worth. This decision decided the fate of the city, and for a time the meat industry dominated everything else. It is still the greatest cattle market in the South, and one of the largest horse and mule markets as well. The amount of meat products sent forth runs into imposing figures. The slaughtering and packing houses were all located in one section of the city, which was called Niles City. But to-day the industries of Fort Worth are very diversified. They include oil refineries, railroad shops, flour mills, grain elevators, factories for the manufacture of materials and articles made from cotton, leather goods, etc. It does not require an expert to see that Fort Worth is more of a manufacturing centre than its near-by rival, although the haze of smoke once so noticeable has largely disappeared because of the almost universal use of oil and gas as fuel. A regular army of factory workers will be seen on every side. One of the great events of the year is the South-western Exposition and Fat Stock Show held annually in March. This always brings many thousands of visitors.

Fort Worth is well supplied with educational institutions. The Texas Christian College, the largest of these, is an institution of the highest class, has a large enrollment and is liberally endowed. The Southwestern Baptist Theological Seminary is one of the largest theological schools in the United States. The Texas Women's College and Our Lady of Victory College and Academy, a Catholic institution, are two other schools of high rating.

One of the attractive sights of Fort Worth is the municipal rose garden in Rock Springs Park, where thousands of roses of every species known here are grown. The many parks are attractive, for flowers bloom out of doors from late February until early December, because of the mildness of the climate. The reservoirs for the water supply have been developed into popular municipal playgrounds. Lake Worth, five miles northwest of the city, covers a water area of over five thousand acres. On its shores is a good bathing beach, a board walk and a fine casino and dancing pavilion where the visitors at all times may find diversion. On its waters sail many boats and fishermen find recreation. Above Lake Worth two other lakes have been created by dams, called respectively Eagle Mountain Lake and Bridgeport Lake, which will add still more to the recreational facilities of Fort Worth.

CHAPTER XIV

AROUND AND ABOUT THE CAPITAL

THE proximate cause leading to the selection of the site of Austin for the Republic's capital was a buffalo hunt indulged in by General Lamar, accompanied by an escort of rangers from a frontier fort which stood a few miles below the present city. Halting on the hill where now stands the magnificent capitol, and gazing across the valley covered with wild rye, he was fascinated with the outlook. When Lamar became President shortly afterwards, he approved of the act of Congress, which provided that the location of the capital "should be selected at some point between the rivers Trinidad and Colorado," and above the San Antonio Road. He called the attention of the commissioners appointed by him to this situation, and it is believed that his admiration for this locality had much to do with the report of the commissioners.

That great central section of modern Texas was almost a *terra incognita* at the time of the Texas Revolution. The old San Antonio Road, which passed through Bastrop and Caldwell, was practically the line of demarcation. At that time there was not a house between Austin and San Antonio. Before statehood a few settlements had arisen between those two cities. But settlers beyond there did not arrive until after annexation. The members of the Santa Fé Expedition of 1842 brought back practically the only reliable information concerning a large

232

part of it. By the time of the Civil War, however, the white man had established his habitation out as far as Coleman and Brownwood, and the cattlemen had ventured to drive their herds out upon the luscious grasses for a considerable distance west of the capital. Some of the counties were not fully organized until after that great event, and other counties have been subdivided into smaller divisions.

A diminutive settlement, consisting of a few cabins, was already here when the new capital was established, and was called Waterloo. The act of Congress had provided that the capital should be called "The City of Austin," a recognition of the exalted character and patriotic service of Stephen F. Austin. Henceforth Waterloo disappeared from the map. Austin has one of the pleasantest and most inviting sites of any of the cities of Texas. The county was afterwards named Travis to commemorate the heroism of the commander of the Alamo garrison.

The selection of Austin showed a farsightedness on the part of the commissioners, and of President Lamar as well. It was almost at the extreme limit of settlement, and was near the theatre of Indian depredations. So exposed was Austin to Indian attacks that the members of the Government were sometimes obliged to take their turn at standing guard. The commissioners laid out the town on the bank of the Colorado River. About a dozen square miles of land were included in the purchase by the commissioners. The price was a little less than three dollars per acre, which probably meant a good profit to the original owners for wild land on the frontier sandwiched between the white settlements and Indian domain.

After choosing the ground for the capital, the commissioners surveyed one square mile, laying it off in blocks and lots, and designated the locations for the various public buildings. Their report was rendered to Congress in April, 1839, and, so rapidly was the work hastened, that by October houses for the accommodation of most of the governmental departments had been completed. The town enlarged slowly because of its exposure to Indian forays. A few hundred was the maximum of its population during the days of the Republic. The early houses were mostly constructed of hewed logs, generally double houses with a passage between. The public buildings were covered with boards split by hand.

The natural advantages of Austin have always commended the wisdom of its selection. Although the administrative offices were removed for a while and Congress convened elsewhere, it has remained the practical seat of government ever since the choice fell upon it. President Lamar removed his residence to Austin within the same year that the capital was established there. An ordinary double log house at the intersection of Congress and Eighth Streets became his office, as well as that of Presidents Houston and Jones and the governors of Texas for the ten years succeeding its admission as a State. Similar log houses housed the other departments of the Republic. All of these have now disappeared. The residence of the President was a little more pretentious, being two stories in height. The first capitol was a large one-story frame building. As late as 1846, the year of the transfer of government, this building was encompassed by a stockade fort for protection against the Indians, whose raids were still not infrequent. A few years later a traveller wrote of Austin: "There is a remarkable number of drinking and gambling shops, but not one bookstore."

BRIDGE OVER THE COLORADO RIVER, AUSTIN

Sam Houston, after the close of his first presidential term, was elected to the Congress, and was obliged to attend the sessions of that body at Austin. In a private letter, dated December 10th, 1839, recently published for the first time, he expressed his contempt for the new capital as follows: "This is the most unfortunate site upon earth for the seat of government. Bad water, cold region—indifferent and sparse timber. It is removed outside the settlement and not a house between this and Santa Fé. Our eating is very plain, and no society to enjoy in this place, for I do not visit 'court' (President Lamar). It is said to be rather fine—so it should be from what appears on our financial records. The expenses of this year are appalling to those who do not wish to be buried by taxation. Without some change in our affairs, the Government must cease, because the situation of the people is not such as will enable them to pay an exorbitant contribution. . . . I might have been happy at home had I known the full extent of Lamar's stupidity."

When Sam Houston again became President, he objected to this site, because it was exposed to attack from the Mexicans, who had become troublesome, but remained there until San Antonio was actually captured. Indian raids and massacres occurred within what is now the corporation limits. It is little wonder that Austin did not flourish. A special session of Congress was called at the city of Houston by President Houston, in 1842. This action aroused intense indignation among the people of Austin, who would not surrender the government archives. Houston sent special messengers for these necessary documents, but the citizens shaved the manes and tails of their horses and drove them off in contumely and disgrace.

On the 20th day of December, 1842, Houston despatched a company of armed men with wagons to recover
the archives. While these men were loading the boxes
on wagons, a six-pound cannon, loaded with grape, was
trained upon the building. This was touched off by a
woman, but fortunately no one was injured. Houston's
men succeeded in securing three wagon-loads of books
and papers, and then started in haste for Houston. But
the cannon-shot had aroused the citizens. The infuriated
Austonians followed, and about eighteen miles from
Austin overtook the "thieves." They forcibly took the
documents, which were returned to Austin. And there
they have remained to this day. The archives were
sealed up in tin boxes, and jealously guarded by the citizens for several months in an old log stock-house. Some
of them were afterwards buried in the ground as a precaution against future raids either by Mexicans or the
Government.

Thus did the sturdy pioneers of Austin boldly and
defiantly resist the head of the Republic and retain the
archives. Houston complained to Congress about the
insubordination and justified his action, but nothing
was ever done by that body in the matter. In 1842,
Austin became the permanent capital of the Republic of
Texas. Upon the admission of Texas as a State of the
Union, Austin was retained by a vote of the people as
the seat of government. It was still a sparsely settled
region, and remained a hunter's paradise almost until
the outbreak of the Civil War.

Austin is almost in the centre of the State from north
to south, and for that reason it is well situated to be
the seat of government. Many Mexicans dwell there, but
it is near the northern demarcation line of that race.
Beyond that there are few Mexicans, except track la-

bourers on the railroads. It has a pleasant location on the Colorado River, which is here quite an impressive stream. A long and imposing concrete bridge connects the two sections of the city. The main street, called Congress, leading from the bridge to the capitol, is a broad and spacious thoroughfare. The Texas pioneers displayed their wisdom in planning their new capital. If some of our congested eastern cities had such an avenue for their main artery, it would be an asset worth millions of dollars. Those who planned Boston, Lower New York and other cities lacked vision even when the land could be purchased for almost nothing. To-day the widening is too costly.

Although it has attracted manufacturers and wholesalers, Austin has retained the essential character of a capital city, the seat of institutions rather than business and industry. It has long been noted for its churches and schools, and is to-day a city exceeding fifty thousand people. Politics thrive here and there are frequently exciting scenes when the Legislature is in session, for Texans take their politics seriously. They removed one governor, and then, as if in a repentant mood, turned around and elected his wife to that high office on two occasions. But they are learning to scratch their ballots, for in 1928 the State's electoral votes were cast for the republican candidate.

Austin possesses one of the most imposing capitol buildings in our country. It is the only state that can boast of a three-million-acre capital. Half a century ago the State possessed much land but little money, and it felt a great desire for and need of a new building. Negotiations were entered into with a syndicate which was willing to construct the building and accept the only commodity Texas had to offer—land. The new capitol cost approximately three and one-half millions of dollars, and the syndicate re-

ceived a trifle over three million acres of land. The building itself, exclusive of porticoes, is more than five hundred
feet in length. The State acquired a good building, and
the syndicate received land equal to a principality. This
land was situated in the counties of the Panhandle and
Llano Estacado bordering on New Mexico. The act
of the Legislature making this appropriation was enacted in 1879, long before there had been any development in this section. It was then considered simply as
arid land, and the State believed it had made a good
bargain. The syndicate initiated work, however, to develop its land, and now its value is several times what
it cost. The members of the syndicate made millions of
money, but it was a legitimate profit. No one appeared
to foresee the development that has transformed the
Panhandle.

The great dome of the capitol dominates the horizon
for several miles before the train reaches Austin, for
the imposing red sandstone building stands slightly above
the rest of the city. Looking at it from the opposite end
of Congress Street, it gives very much the same effect
as Pennsylvania Avenue in Washington from the Treasury. The dome is surmounted by a statue of the blind
goddess of Justice upholding the lone star of Texas more
than three hundred feet above the level of Capitol Hill.
It is built of Texas material. The stone was secured
from what is termed a mountain of granite near Marble
Falls, about forty or fifty miles northwest of the capital.
At this place an almost unlimited amount of this red
sandstone is available, and it is a splendid material for
building.

The grounds about the capitol are dotted with trees
and shrubbery, which makes an artistic setting. There
are a number of monuments, including one to the Texas

heroes who sacrificed their lives in the massacre of the
Alamo.   Among the most striking features are two
small cannon, at the principal entrance, one on either
side.   The coat of arms of Texas, with the single star
prominent, ornaments each one.   The following inscription also appears: "This gun was used in the Texas
Revolution and in the Civil War."   It is not strange
that these two small pieces, which would be of absolutely no efficiency to-day, are treasured by the people of
Texas.   By the side of a forty-two centimetre gun of
the Teutons they would be mere pygmies.   The whole
gun could be put inside such a monster.

The most imposing room in the capitol is the House of
Representatives.   It is a splendid assembling room for
this body, for it is capacious and inviting, with a gallery
encircling three sides, and is lighted both from a skylight
above and side windows.   The Senate is not so large a
room, for that body is much less numerous.   In these two
rooms, and the entrance corridors, is assembled a gallery of Texas history on canvas.   The famous picture
of the "Surrender of Santa Anna" at San Jacinto is in the
corridor.   It depictures General Houston reclining on a
blanket, with his foot bandaged, and gesticulating with
his hand.   "Deaf" Smith, in the uniform of a frontier
scout and with a long rifle over his arm, holds one hand
to his ear while listening to what is being said.   The
surgeon, who has just been dressing Houston's foot,
has not relinquished his instruments.   In the group are
many of the historic characters of the Revolution.   Santa
Anna is pleading with head bared before his captor.   In
the Senate is hung a painting of the "Battle of San Jacinto" by McArdle.   Some of the flags borne by the Texans bear the inscription "Liberty or Death."   These were
the words of Travis.   It is a picture of frightful carnage.

There is another painting here of the "Siege of the Alamo." The Texas flags in this picture all have "1824" on them, which refers to the Convention and Constitution of that year.

I was interested in studying the face of Lorenzo de Zavala, Vice-President of Texas under the Provisional Government. He migrated to that new country from Mexico, because he would not submit to the tyranny of Santa Anna after that general had proclaimed himself dictator. He had been a member of the Cortez of Spain, and both houses of the Mexican Congress, having served as presiding officer of each, and governor of one of the Mexican States before coming to Texas. He resigned the office of Minister to France in order to establish a new home in Texas, where he had purchased lands. The Texans welcomed with joy the arrival of this distinguished representative of Mexican republicanism, and his advice was eagerly sought. It was only a few months after his incoming that the Consultation was called, and Zavala was commissioned a delegate from Harris county. He only survived a year longer—long enough, however, to see Santa Anna humiliated and Texas freed. Although a Mexican, this true friend of liberty was highly esteemed by the Texas leaders for his integrity, sagacity and courage. He entered heartily into the struggle for independence, and his descendants still dwell in the State.

There is exhibited a portrait of Alphonzo Steele, the last survivor of the Battle of San Jacinto, who was ninety-two years of age at the time the picture was made. A painting of Sam Houston shows him as he looked when an exile among the Cherokee Indians. The leading canvas in the House of Representatives is the Settlement of Austin's Colony. In it is a portraiture of Stephen F.

Austin, accoutred with rifle, hatchet, knife, and powder flask, all of them indispensable friends of the frontiersman. Sam Houston is represented in another portrait seated in the chair of office and enveloped in a robe which resembles a blanket. This was only one of the many eccentric costumes worn by that hero.

Of the monuments around the capitol, the one that impressed me most is that erected to the memory of the men who fell in the Alamo. The names of those heroes are arranged in alphabetical order. One reads these patronymics reverentially for the lesson they offer of sublime self-sacrifice and of lives offered up willingly for their adopted country. The most striking memorial is dedicated to the Confederate soldiers in the War of the Rebellion. It reveals the spirit that animated the soldiers who wore the grey. It bears this inscription: "Died for State rights guaranteed under the Constitution. The people of the South, animated by the spirit of 1776, to preserve their rights, withdrew from the Federal compact in 1861. The North resorted to coercion. The South, against overwhelming numbers and resources, fought until exhausted. During the war, there were twenty-two hundred and fifty-seven engagements; in eighteen hundred and eighty-two of these, at least one regiment took part. Number of men enlisted: Confederate armies, 600,000; Federal armies, 2,857,132. Losses from all causes: Confederate, 437,000; Federal, 485,-216.

"Erected A. D. 1901, by surviving comrades."

The State of Texas has provided a home for her Confederate veterans in Austin, which is said to be the best-conducted home anywhere in the South. It is an institution to which the Austonians point with pride. It also has more inmates than any similar institution in the

Southern States.   It does not compare with the homes for those who wore the blue in the north, for they had the resources of the National Government back of them.   It is indeed commendable that states of the Confederacy should thus care for those who fought so valiantly for what they believed was right.   In a few years there will not be a survivor.

Austin has a number of state educational institutions, military schools for the deaf, blind and mental defectives, but the greatest of all is the University of Texas, the largest in the South.   Its most grievous trouble has been growing pains, for the attendance has frequently outstripped its equipment.   In 1905 there were only fifteen hundred students.   Thirty years later there are more than five times that number.

The library of the University, housed in a fine new building, contains several notable collections of books. In addition to its extensive Texas historical material, it owns what is known as the Garcia Library, which is said to be the most complete collection of books on Mexico in existence, covering every phase of Mexican life and history.   They were collected by Genaro Garcia and purchased from his heirs.   The Wrenn Library of six thousand volumes, all first editions or manuscripts of English and American literature, was made by John Henry Wrenn of Chicago.   Then there are two other collections of rare books and manuscripts and de luxe editions, known as the Aitken and Stark collections, which are very valuable.

The site of the University of Texas is well chosen with a magnificent view from and toward the capitol.   It is approached by the broad parked University Avenue, which affords a fine setting for the main building.   The chief difficulty for the State has been to give the institution as generous support as it deserves.   The in-

UNIVERSITY OF TEXAS, AUSTIN

come from the permanent funds has not been sufficient to meet the needs of rapid growth. But the work of turning out educated young men and women goes on, and the constant accretions in attendance speak well for the aspirations of the youth of this great State.

A short distance out from Austin is a dam on the Colorado River, which furnishes the water supply of the capital, and power for the electric plant as well. A number of years ago a lofty dam was constructed on this same site, which formed a body of water called Lake McDonald. It was destroyed during a flood on the 7th of April, 1900. The present dam, which is almost eleven hundred feet long and sixty-five feet high, was completed in the spring of 1915. The impeded water backs up between the low hills, which encompass the river, and has formed a lake twenty-four miles long. This new body of water has been christened Lake Austin, and has been developed into a beautiful inland pleasure resort. The Colorado River is a clear stream, and the water in the lake is as pure and sparkling as in any of our great lakes. Many private launches and pleasure boats sail over the bosom of this new lake. In this way are the people of Austin, and other cities as well, making up for the lack of natural lakes as pleasure resorts. The cliffs of the river become higher and grander the farther up one goes. Between the dam and the city is a charming stretch of rocky cliff, which has been named Deep Eddy.

German settlers have had an important influence in the settlement of Central Texas. In fact the Germanic element in Texas has been very influential in many sections. To these immigrants is due the founding and growth of a number of splendid towns. Even in San Antonio for a long period the Germans were the largest national group, excepting the Mexicans themselves. A dozen years after the admission of Texas as a State, the number of Germans in a few counties of what is now termed Central Texas, numbered as many as twenty-five thousand.

The general wave of German immigration to Texas began about 1848 at the climax to the revolutionary troubles in the German states. The trend toward Texas, however, had been initiated a little earlier. A number of German nobles had interested themselves in directing the immigration of German people to Texas, and this organization became known as the "Mainzer Adelsverein." It was one of the many schemes evolved about that time as a result of the agitation for social amelioration, and the diminution of pauperism. Because of its isolation, and the possible opening of a new source of wealth and power, Texas appealed to the nobility. A German dependency or new Teutonic nation might result, so they reasoned.

Prince Carl Solms-Braunfels, the general agent for this association, came to Texas in 1844 to select the land for the colonists, and prepare the way for the immigrants to follow. To each immigrant subscribing one hundred and twenty dollars, a free passage and forty acres of land was assured. The association obligated itself to provide log cabins, stock, and tools at fair prices, and to construct at its expense the public buildings and roads for the settlements. The first ship docked in the same year at Matagorda Bay, and from there the immigrants journeyed overland to the place selected for them by Prince Solms on the Coman River. The land first chosen was too remote from the other settlements, so that they finally purchased a more promising site between Austin and San Antonio. There they laid out a new city to which the leader gave the name of New Braunfels, after his own home. On the hill overlooking the town a large block-house was erected, to which was given the name of "Sophienburg," and for the protection of the colonists a sort of palisade fort was built, which they called Zinkenburg.

This colony at New Braunfels survived, and was re-inforced from time to time by other German immigrants, numbering in all several thousand. The misfortunes and hardships endured by the early German colonists at New Braunfels and the other settlements were indeed numer-ous, for they were unused to the primitiveness of the wilderness. They had not the remotest idea of the toil and hardship of settling in a new country. Many of them were swindled by speculators and adventurers. Numbers of them perished from the exposure and hardships; oth-ers wandered away to other settlements. Such was the unhappy inception of New Braunfels. Nevertheless the soil and climate were good, and things soon meliorated. The settlement remained, and it has always retained its characteristics as a German town. The descendants of this German stock and later immigrants still prepon-derate in New Braunfels, and the county of which it is the capital. Another German settlement, called Fred-ericksburg, was founded shortly afterwards, almost di-rectly west of Austin and about equi-distant from that city.

One of the most important cities of Central Texas is Waco, which is named after the tribe of Indians of the same name which had its headquarters near where the present city now stands. On the early maps of Texas the only place indicated in this section of the State was Waco Village, which had for years been a permanent rendez-vous of the Waco and affiliated Indian tribes.

The late George Wilkins Kendall, in his *Santa Fé Expedition,* gives a picture of a Waco village which that party found on the Trinity River: "In a large bend of the stream the village was situated, and all around were the corn fields and pumpkin and melon patches of the inhabitants. Although the bend must have been five or six miles in length, by nearly two in breadth in the wider parts, every portion of it appeared to be in cultivation; and the land was extremely fertile. The purlieus of the village appeared to be kept clean. The wigwams, or houses rather, for they deserve that name, were built in rows and had an air of neatness and regularity about them, such as I had never before observed in an Indian village. They were of conical shape, some twenty-five feet in height, and of about the same diameter on the floor; the materials used in their construction being poles, buffalo hides and rushes. The poles were stuck in the ground, and after running up perpendicularly some ten feet, were bent over so as to converge to a point at the top, thus giving a regular dome-like roof to carry off the rains. Over these, buffalo hides in some instances were made fast, and these again were covered with long rushes —thus making thatched cottages impervious to dust and rain.

"Attached to each residence, and immediately in the rear was another building of smaller dimensions, the lower part of which was evidently used for a corn-crib and store house. In these buildings we found a quantity of corn and pumpkins, besides finely-cured venison, antelope and buffalo meat. Above the corn-crib was a species of balcony." Mr. Kendall adds: "I confess that I saw evidence of a more elevated kind of humanity than I had supposed was to be found anywhere among the original Americans."

THE CAPITOL, AUSTIN

Waco is situated on the Brazos River, along which many of the early settlements in Texas were located. As these settlements pushed north, they were exposed to Indian hostilities which resulted in fearful loss of life and property throughout the existence of the Republic and even later. Remains of Indian houses, burial grounds, and fortifications are said to have been traceable in Waco as late as 1872. It was only after Texas entered the Union that adequate protection was afforded, so that settlements might be made in this neighbourhood. There were practically no settlers in what is now McLennan County, of which Waco is the county seat, until statehood. Rangers were then despatched into the country and, in 1846, the first permanent settlement was made here by a family named McLennan, from whom the county was afterwards named.

This section of Texas was in the slave belt, and antecedent to the war there were in some places almost as many negroes as whites. The rich soil was easily cultivated, and by the aid of the slave labour development was rapid, so that it soon became one of the rich cotton centres. Waco had at that time already become an important inland city, but its real progress did not begin until railroads reached it. Lumber for building before that time had to be transported from Eastern Texas, more than one hundred miles distant, on slow trains propelled by oxen. To-day Waco is one of the leading cities of the second class in Texas. A number of years ago it became known as the Geyser City, because of the number of artesian wells of hot mineral water which were discovered within the corporate limits. These wells are utilized to-day to supply a large part of the city's water. It has also been denominated the Athens of Texas, because of educational institutions located within its limits.

It is the seat of the principal Baptist college of the South, and there are a number of other educational institutions located within its limits.

In the early days the small steamboats then in use transported a large part of the traffic up and down the Brazos River. As the size of vessels increased, however, they were not able to utilize the shallow waters of this river, and traffic by water diminished. The citizens of Waco, however, like those of Dallas, have been very energetic in endeavouring to attract government aid in deepening the waters of this river so as to make it once more a medium of navigation. The National Government has made a number of appropriations for improving this river and the construction of dams and locks sufficient to furnish navigation for vessels of light draught. The purpose is, of course, to bring freight rates down on the basis of water transportation.

The territory bordering on the Brazos below Waco was originally known as the "District of Viesca." It was important enough to be represented in the Convention of 1832. The capital of the "municipality of Viesca," and the principal seat of the settlement, was at the "falls of the Brazos," in what is now known as Falls County. This was all in what was then designated as the Nashville Colony, one of the early *empresario* grants. Two hundred families were colonized on this grant in 1830, and others arrived later. The land lay north of the San Antonio Road, lying between the Navasota River and the ridge dividing the waters of the Colorado and the Brazos. In this general way were boundary lines fixed in those days, and it is not surprising that much confusion resulted. Just prior to the Revolution it was decreed that the "town at the falls of the Brazos River in the

Nashville Colony, heretofore known by the name of Viesca," should be changed to Milam, and this was done. There is a small village, however, on this site of the old capital town, which still preserves the name of Viesca in the geography of Texas.

CHAPTER XV

THE PANHANDLE AND THE STAKED PLAIN

WAY out in Northwestern Texas, in the section designated as the Panhandle, we find a horizontal country with the sky pressing down sharply and evenly on every side. When twilight descends over the sombre flatness of the landscape, it is grey and vast with the awesome sweep of the sea. To appreciate these prairies fully one should contemplate them in the spring when the sun has wheedled the freshly moistened soil into bloom. Each day brings out some new blossom until the whole face of the country becomes radiant with colour and delicious with fragrance.· The marvellous beauty of spring out here on the prairie has never been and never will be fully described. It is indescribable. A few days suffice to transform the whole face of nature. The dreary aspect of the open country changes at once to a vivid green, and the cheering effect must be seen to be appreciated. The names of many of the blossoms are unknown to me, but there are occasions when it is far more interesting simply to behold and enjoy the beauties of nature than to attempt to analyze each plant and place it in its proper grouping.

A writer of some years ago, in a rather picturesque manner, symbolized the Panhandle as a land of ranches, rascals, rattlesnakes, and remittance men. The description was not inapt for that period; but it has changed wonderfully in this twentieth century. It is still, however, a region of bitter winds, prairie-dog holes, and little rain. The picturesque prairie-dogs, gophers, and other rodents, as well as the jack-rabbits, are doubtless a much greater evil than in former days. The wolves, lynxes, and coyotes were nature's regulators. When the white men poisoned or decimated these animals in some other way, the jack-rabbit, gopher and prairie-dog rose instantly to power. As a consequence, literally millions of these astonishingly prolific animals soon took possession of the range. The prairie-dogs not only devoured the grass, but they likewise dug up the very earth, leaving huge mounds of almost barren sand, often acres in extent. The rabbits became so troublesome that large parties of men were organized to round them up and exterminate them in great numbers.

It has been estimated that five jack-rabbits will eat as much grass as one sheep, and twenty prairie-dogs will devour and spoil more. There are regions up here where the prairie-dog villages number a population of from eight to ten thousand to the square mile. The prairie-dogs, so it is said, abandon their underground homes each autumn, turning them over to the newly-grown children. This is very thoughtful of papa and mamma. But the parents immediately excavate a new domicile for their own occupation—and this shows an absolute lack of consideration for the landlord. Poison squads are now employed by the big ranchmen to depopulate the prairie-dog towns.

Even in the days before American settlements, these prairie-dog villages were common enough and immense in area. G. W. Kendall, in his *Texan Santa Fé Expedition*, writes as follows:

"The first town we visited was much the largest seen on the entire route, being some two or three miles in length by nearly a mile in width at the widest part. In the vicinity were smaller villages—suburbs of the larger town, to all appearances. After spending some three hours in the very heart of the settlements, and until not an inhabitant could be seen in any direction, we re-saddled our horses and set off in search of the command. Thus ended my first visit to one of the numerous prairie-dog commonwealths of the Far West.

"If a person is fortunate enough to gain the immediate vicinity of one of their villages unobserved—a very difficult matter, for their sentinels are always on the alert—he will discover the inhabitants gambolling, frisking, and running about the well-trodden paths, occasionally stopping a moment as if to exchange a word with a neighbour, and then hurrying back to their own lodges. Should he chance to discover some quiet citizen, sitting gravely at his doorway, he has but to watch him for a short time ere he will notice some eccentricity of conduct. His manner of entering his hole will remind the spectator of the antics of Pantaloon in a pantomime; for, instead of walking quietly in, he does it with an eccentric bound and half somerset, his hind feet knocking together as he pitches into the darkness below; and before the aforesaid spectator has yet fairly recovered from the half laugh caused by the drollery of the movement, he will see the dog slowly thrust his head from his burrow, and with a pert and impudent expression of countenance peer cunningly about, as if to ascertain the effect his recent antic had caused."

The Panhandle reminds me vividly of the endless pampas of Argentina, the only dissimilar feature being the forests of mesquite which cover the prairie in many parts, for the Argentine pampas are absolutely treeless in their natural state. The land reaches out in every direction as far as the vision extends, with scarcely an observable deviation in the elevation; and one knows that beyond this meeting-place of earth and sky the same unending monotony continues. It can best be characterized as an ocean of land spreading out like an unruffled sea from horizon to horizon. There is a fascination about the very vastness of these plains.

These vast stretches of level land may produce a certain sense of irritation upon one newly arrived in the Panhandle. He may ride for league upon league on his horse, or travel hour after hour by train, awaiting that change of scenery which his experience leads him to believe must inevitably occur. And yet there is a fascination about the very vastness of these prairies—in these leagues upon leagues of rich soil which here hold themselves in readiness to receive the seed from the hand of the farmer. The scene superinduces retrospection also. In imagination one can behold countless numbers of the shaggy buffaloes feeding here while migrating to or from their northern pastures. The herds were at one time so vast that the undulations of their moving bodies were like the waves of a choppy sea.

Here in the Panhandle, a territory almost as large as Pennsylvania, there is, in the words of the late Joaquin Miller:

> "Room! Room to turn round in, to breathe and be free,
> To grow to be giant, to sail as at sea
> With the speed of the wind on a steed with his mane
> To the wind, without pathway or route or a rein.
> Room! Room to be free where the white-bordered sea
> Blows a kiss to a brother as boundless as he,
> Where the buffalo come like a cloud on the plain,
> Pouring on like the tide of a storm-driven main,
> And the lodge of the hunter to friend or to foe
> Offers rest; and unquestioned you come or you go."

Sometimes there would come, with the suddenness of a volcanic eruption, one of those terrible prairie fires, which terrified man and beast alike. A rumble as of distant thunder might be the first warning. All knew there was not a moment to spare. Spurred on by the impetuous winds of a "norther," which sometimes sweeps across these prairies in uncontrollable fury, the crackling flames would travel faster over the parched sward than the legs of animals could carry them. All animosity and all hatred of one animal for another or toward the human was forgotten. All realized that safety rested only in flight, and joined in one frenzied rush away from the onrushing fiery flood. None paused for another; the laggard and the feeble were overwhelmed and trampled beneath a thousand callous hoofs. Mingled together were—

"The howling of beasts and a sound as of thunder—
Beasts burning and blind and forced onward and over.

Till they died with a wild and a desolate moan,
As a sea heart-broken on the hard brown stone—"

It was during the decade of the seventies that the Indians and buffalo made their last stand against the onward march of civilization. Organized bands of buffalo hunters roamed these plains chiefly for the sake of the profit derived from the hides of the slain animals. The centre of this trade was old Fort Griffin, and a small army of hunters rendezvoused there. Thither they brought their wagons piled high with the bales of hides, and at the fort they purchased supplies of food and ammunition for the next trip into the buffalo country. It was about the "wildest and woolliest" place in Texas. Professional gamblers and whiskey sellers mingled with cattlemen, soldiers and skin-hunters. Its fame and even existence were transitory. It is now scarcely recognized

A NEW TOWN IN THE PANHANDLE

as a place in Texas geography.   Here is a description of
Fort Griffin in 1877:

"The post, on a hill a quarter of a mile south, is almost depopulated, one company of negro soldiers keeping garrison.   F. E. Conrad's storerooms, near the post,
are the most extensive establishment in the place.   There
hunters procure supplies and deliver most of their hides.
To give an idea of the immensity of his business, imagine
a huge, rambling house, of several different rooms,
crowded with merchandise; with forty or fifty wagons to
be loaded, and perhaps one hundred hunters purchasing
supplies. . . . This is a frontier town, with all the usual
characteristics, but is orderly. . . . The picket houses
are giving way to rock and shingle-roofed frame buildings, the lumber being hauled from Fort Worth.   The
buffalo hide industry has reached large proportions, two
hundred thousand having been received here last season.
. . . It is a gay and festive place; night is turned into
day; the dance and flowing bowl are indulged in freely,
while hilarity and glee range supreme from eve until
morning hours.   Lager beer is twenty-five cents a glass."

The Panhandle is mostly tableland from thirty-five
hundred to four thousand feet above sea level.   In area
it will equal Ohio.   There are whole counties where there
is not a river, or a creek, or a watercourse of any kind.
There are sometimes depressions into which the surplus
rainfall drains, and some of the basins, or saucers, retain
water the greater part of the year.   In other sections,
water is very near the surface, so that sufficient water
can be obtained for stock and even for irrigation on quite
an extensive scale by means of power pumps.   Where
irrigation has been employed some remarkable crops have
been produced.

In some places there are depressions which furnish the

winter range for cattle, giving them a natural shelter from the storms of winter. A wise rancher always aims to include some of this kind of land, for it would be a great undertaking to build shelter for the vast herds of stock which still wander over the Panhandle. These canyons are encountered most unexpectedly, for there may not be a tree or a bush to mark the location. In places the sides will be nearly perpendicular for a distance of several hundred feet. The rains of centuries have carved these great excavations, and the little stream at the bottom has carried away the debris. The working of the water upon the different strata of earth and rock has formed many strange and fanciful shapes. There will be pillars and columns such as might have been carved by the artists of Greece or Rome, and dedicated to a god; frowning turrets like unto those on some old mediæval castle; breastworks as of forts will also be distinguished.

The Palo Duro Canyon in Armstrong County is the most picturesque feature of the Panhandle topography. It has frequently been proposed that this canyon should be set aside as a national park. It is as much as eight hundred feet deep in places. One is lost in admiration of the strange and fanciful figures made by the washing of the waters in the rainy season in Palo Duro. Even Niagara sinks into insignificance when compared with the wild grandeur of this great chasm with its deep abysmal solitude.

One must not understand that this prairie is really smooth like an even, well-kept lawn, for so it may appear from a distance. On the contrary the smoothest of this western Texas prairie has an uneven surface, and is filled with the holes of the mole and field-mouse and prairie-dog. Through the slight thickness of earth which covers these holes, the feet of the horse frequently sink, and, unless a horse has been brought up on the prairies, he can never be taught to run upon them with that confidence which develops his full powers.

This part of Texas was not laid out into counties until the United States was celebrating the centennial of its independence, thirty years after the admission of Texas into the federation. In that year this immense region of the State was subdivided into fifty-six counties. Names were bestowed upon these new subdivisions to commemorate revolutionary heroes, Alamo victims, early pioneers, and colony promoters. Yoakum, the diligent historian of the State, was likewise honoured. At that time there were not enough settlers in many of these to make a working corps of necessary officials, so that they remained unorganized for a number of years afterwards.

The Panhandle used to be, and still is in a modified degree, a region of princely ranches. In the western part, along the western tier of counties, will be found the famous three-million-acre tract given to the Capitol Syndicate. Thousands of acres have already been alienated, but it still is an enormous tract of land to be under one management. It is a short grass country, and the shimmering stretches of grassy tableland reach out to the distant edge of the sky. It is doubtless true that the cattlemen of old spread discouraging reports concerning these lands, in order to intimidate prospective settlers because of the wealth which they were reaping from the grazing of cattle on herbage which cost them nothing. With the development of dry farming, however, there arose a demand for this land of little rain. It was found possible to raise corn, oats, wheat, alfalfa, Kafir corn and milo maize, even though the rainfall did not exceed ten or twenty inches in every twelve months   Land values advanced so high that the ranchers became willing to alienate their possessions in small tracts.

To a person from one of the Eastern States, unfamiliar with the West, to journey through the rapidly developing Panhandle, the surprise comes when one discovers that the prairies, which were the favourite grazing lands of the buffalo, and over which the red men hunted not many decades ago, are now besprinkled here and there with the little dwellings of the homesteaders, and the primeval sward has yielded to the destructive plough of the farmer.   Development has everywhere followed the construction of the railroads, for the iron highways introduced settlers along with transportation facilities.

It was my good fortune, not so very long ago, to peragrate through this section over a new railroad, which had just been opened to traffic.   In some places the little houses of the settlers dotted the prairie at regular intervals as far as the eye could reach.   Occasionally one would stumble upon a genuine sod house, or some other improvised habitation, but these were infrequent.   The shingles on the roofs had not been darkened by exposure to the weather, and the unpainted siding still appeared as if it had just come from a lumber yard.   The surface that was as yet untouched by the destroyer was covered with the short bushlike mesquite; but this was rapidly disappearing in order to plant the cotton which has proved to be such a profitable crop.   Populous villages of the prairie-dogs, with the occupants standing at perpendicular near the entrance, ready to tumble in at the first alarm, were a common sight.   Many rabbits of the excessively long-eared variety were visible from the train, and an occasional coyote could be seen leisurely running away from the track, as if inviting a chase.   The mirage

THE SPANISH BAYONET

would frequently deceive us, and some one would point out what was apparently a great shimmering lake. But we all knew that no water was there—it was all a delusion like many of our ideas in real life.

Towns were everywhere springing up along this new railroad, some of them almost in a night. One twelve-months-old infant municipality boasted a population of nearly two thousand. There were a number of two-story business blocks, and a fine stone bank building was nearly completed. The town had electric lights, and was already planning for a water-works plant. Nearly every town had a newspaper, and some of them boasted more than one. Real estate offices were numerous. As this train carried the president and a number of officials of the new road, reception committees met us at the stations with true Western hospitality. At one station the entire population, headed by the town band and a party of cowboys on horseback, greeted the party. Everybody was boosting his own town, and had at his tongue's end all the good points of that place and all the advantages of the soil in the neighbourhood. No one was finding fault or trying to destroy what others were building up. This characteristic will be recognized throughout all the newer sections of Texas, and in the older ones as well.

The Panhandle has passed through severe crises. The first settlers were not of the most stable kind. They began farming as they would at home, where the annual precipitation of moisture was twice or three times as great. Forty years' time on the principal sum and five per cent interest on the deferred payments had drawn them. A few lean years wiped out their funds, and they quietly vanished. Since then the limitations as well as the possibilities of the Panhandle have been better realized. Agriculture has been conformed to suit the conditions; crops have been adapted to the soil and climate. The later settlers are informed about the country and a great improvement over the early boomers. They understand that agricultural conditions in a country where the annual rainfall is only twenty inches is different from where it is forty inches or more.

It is doubtful if there has been as great a transformation in any other part of the United States in the last thirty years as in the Panhandle. The person who visited this region in the early years of this century and comes back to-day can hardly believe his own eyes. The wilderness has disappeared. Half a million people now dwell here. Each year several hundred thousand additional acres are reduced to cultivation. Wheat in the northern part and cotton in the southern part are the principal crops. But most cereals also thrive there. One of the largest oil and gas fields in Texas lies just north and east of Amarillo. Hard surfaced roads are rapidly replacing the red clay highways, so that motoring is a pleasure. Good hotels and comfortable camps await the tourist everywhere.

Practically every town in the Panhandle has an appearance of newness. The county seats possess an imposing court house and jail, although there is less need for the latter than formerly. "Bad men" are just as numerous in Chicago and New York, if not more so. They are as different from the old trading-places as the country now dotted with homesteads has changed from the old cattle range. The public schools are strictly up to date. The business and residence sections are attractive. The streets are generally wide, and hundreds of miles are now paved. The wide-open saloons and dance halls are conspicuous by their absence. The cowboys are constrained in their behaviour when they make their periodical visits. Tascosa, the wildest of the old towns, is now in a peaceful apple-growing community. To it came cowboys and rustlers alike to quench their thirst and find diversion. Seven saloons once catered to the wild mob. Its "Boot Hill," where those who met violent death were hastily interred with their boots on, is almost forgotten.

The motorist travelling either east or west across the rather monotonous level of the Panhandle, and especially one who has come across the desert region of New Mexico, will be astonished as he approaches Amarillo, whose tall skyscrapers are visible in the clear atmosphere for many miles. One does not expect to find such a delightful city way out here where cattlemen ruled and fought only a few decades ago. It might be described as an old western town gone modern in dress, without losing its spirit of pioneering. It is a city made by cattle, oil and agriculture. Three decades ago Amarillo was only a good county seat town; to-day it is a prosperous city exceeding fifty thousand people. Palatial hotels, tall office buildings, great department stores, splended public buildings, fine schools, beautiful churches, gives it the appearance of a small metropolis, which it really is. It is strategically located almost in the centre of the thirty-two counties comprising the Panhandle and, as agriculture has increased and the oil industry grown, Amarillo has expanded to supply the wants of the oncoming thousands. Three trunk-line railroads and their branches, each of which maintains shops here, employing thousands of workers, together with many truck and bus lines give it unusually good transportation facilities, and it is becoming an important airport in the transcontinental systems.

It seems like only yesterday that the newly born Amarillo was the scene of a town-site war. The original town was located a short distance away, but there was one wealthy rancher who vigorously objected to the location. Undaunted by the fact that a courthouse had already been voted and a thousand people had arrived, he continued his opposition, for he had selected a site on his own ranch, which he deemed more desirable. He erected a hotel, laid out streets and built buildings. The result was that the old town was gradually deserted until nothing but the courthouse remained. Even the officials preferred to live in the new city. The old rancher's aggressive spirit must have passed on to the city he founded, for it is one of the wonder towns of modern Texas. The name Amarillo (pronounced Am-ar-eey-o) is the Spanish word for yellow, but there is no such streak in its progressive citizens.

Let me suggest to the unhurried motorist—and it is only he who enjoys to the maximum a transcontinental trip—that he make a little detour to Palo Duro Canyon, mentioned above, which is only twenty-seven miles southeast of Amarillo. Here is a great gash in the earth's surface which makes it a miniature Grand Canyon. You may enjoy it even more, for the very magnitude of Arizona's wonder sometimes appalls the onlooker. It is so vast that the finite mind has difficulty grasping it. Here the mind can comprehend the details. The formations are quite similar and the coloring equally wonderful, for each canyon is the result of erosion. Water seeking an outlet, aided by wind and frost, gradually deepened the gash and carved the fantastic outlines of the rocks throughout millions of years of activity for your enjoyment and mine. Until very recently it was not possible to drive down into the canyon, but a good easy-grade trail has been constructed, since Palo Duro is now a state park. There are thirty miles of foot and horse trails, fantastic rocks and caves waiting to thrill the visitor. In all, the park area exceeds fifteen thousand acres. There are free camp sites, cabins are cheap and El Coronado has been erected for those who seek greater comfort. The little stream at the bottom is the beginning of the Red River, which courses its tortuous way across Texas, Oklahoma and Louisiana to empty its muddy waters into the Gulf of Mexico.

In the western part of the Panhandle and extending over into New Mexico is a vast region once widely known as the *Llano Estacado,* or Staked Plain. To the youthful student of geography half a century ago this was a land of mystery and romance. The tales of thirsty travellers being overcome on its limitless stretches and of the wandering herds of camels stimulated the imagination of youths everywhere. It was then generally looked upon as a desert as inhospitable as the Sahara Itself. The legendary account of the name *Llano Estacado* added to the fascination. It is said that the mission fathers when they crossed this high plateau set up stakes with buffalo heads upon them so that others might follow their route. Hence the name "Staked Plain."

A map published in 1856 gave only this meagre information concerning the *Llano Estacado:* "From the headwaters of the Red, Brazos and Colorado Rivers to the Rio Pecos is a desolate and sterile plain from one hundred and fifty to two hundred miles in width, elevated about four thousand five hundred feet above the Gulf of Mexico, without water or timber, and with a scanty vegetation." No further details were vouchsafed. But to-day we know more about this great grazing land. To be sure it requires more acres to the animal than the rich Gulf Coast, but any of the forty counties into which it has been divided will inventory from ten to forty thousand head of cattle, besides many sheep, goats, horses

and mules. Human beings have increased greatly also.
Whereas Cochran County, Texas, only enumerated sixty-
five persons in 1920, after a diligent search, the census
to-day shows a population of two thousand. The adjoining county of Hockley has increased in the same period
from one hundred and thirty-seven to nine thousand.
How is this for the American Sahara?

We are accustomed to read so many horrible tales of
suffering upon the desert and see the fearful agonies
of the thirsty portrayed upon the screen that the idea of
anything attractive about "the land that God forgot"
seems entirely foreign. I want to speak a good word for
this much-maligned portion of our country. To-day we
can travel across the desert by railroad or bus, or drive
our own automobile over hard surfaced roads and find
stations at convenient intervals where there is an abundant supply of water. Each transcontinental railroad left
a trail of green spots wherever a water-tank is located.
If water is not found, water trains bring it in. The fool-
hardy traveller can still encounter danger from thirst, but
it will be his own fault. The wise traveller will forget
the dust and discomfort and admire the freakish desert
growth, the strange colourings of rocks and sand, the remarkable clearness of the atmosphere, the radiance of
sunrise and sunset.

Cacti abound in innumerable varieties, from tiny
prickly balls covered with long gray hairs to giants that
tower fifty feet in the air. They are not only the most
numerous, but they are the most beautiful of all the forms
of desert vegetation, and all species flower at some season
of the year. Then there are also the sage, mesquite, palo
verde, chaparral and greasewood. And a little rain in
spring will carpet the desert with delicate flowers of every
hue.

Almost all the cacti have their use for those who are versed in the lore of the desert. In them the Indians find material for their homes, food, drink, medicine and raiment. One of the most common species in Texas is the prickly pear. The yellow blossoms are very pretty and the fruit is much prized by both Mexicans and Indians. When the spines are burned off cattle eat it with avidity, and it is nourishing. A spineless variety was developed by the late Luther Burbank, and hundreds of acres of it are now cultivated for stock food.

One species of the yucca, which grows over a much more extended area than the parent plant, is the Spanish Bayonet. It will be found from California to the middle of Texas, and a close relative reaches to Georgia and Florida. Each one of the leaves terminates in a spine. When ready to flower, it shoots up a stem several feet high, which bears myriads of showy white flowers almost lily-like in appearance. As many as six thousand blossoms have been enumerated upon a single plant. It also yields a yellow fruit, which ripens in August and September, and is pulpy and sweet as well as nourishing.

CHAPTER XVI

THE HERO OF SAN JACINTO

In the beautiful capitol building at Austin are preserved many of the documents and old State papers of the Republic of Texas. Among these archives one will find scores of documents bearing the signature of the most remarkable man produced by that Republic. This signature always reads Sam Houston. The given name is so written that one can easily give it the interpretation which people were wont to say he meant, and that is, "I am Houston."

Herein is illustrated one characteristic, which was always attributed to the man who was twice president of the nine-year Republic, and that is an exaggerated ingredient of egotism; but the man who is always called by an abbreviated given name, or by a nickname, has already attained an element of popularity that signifies a great deal to any one who seeks political preferment. This statement is well illustrated in the life of Sam Houston, who, during a remarkable political career, served as Governor of Tennessee, Representative in the United States Congress, President of Texas, Senator of the United States, Governor of the State of Texas, and Commander-in-Chief of the Texas Army, in addition to many inferior political and military offices in two Republics.

In the House of Representatives of the State capitol, there hangs a picture of Houston seated in a chair and clothed in a brilliantly coloured blanket, or *serape,* as it is called. This depictures another essential characteristic of Sam Houston. He always endeavoured to dress in the height of fashion, but with a certain peculiar and personal idiosyncrasy. This appears even in his earlier political career. When Houston was inaugurated Governor of Tennessee, he wore a costume which is described as follows: "A tall bell-crowned, medium-brimmed, shining black beaver hat, shining black patent leather military stock or cravat incased by a standing collar, ruffled shirt, black satin vest, shining black silk pants gathered to the waistband with legs full, same size from seat to ankle, and a gorgeous red-ground, many-coloured gown or Indian hunting shirt, fastened at the waist by a huge red sash covered with fancy bead-work, with an immense silver buckle, embroidered silk stockings, and pumps with large silver buckles." In such toggery he must have been a picture wonderful to behold.

A description of Houston as he appeared at the grand San Jacinto Ball, just one year after that momentous victory of the Texans, is as follows: "Being the President-elect, he was, of course, the hero of the day, and his dress on this occasion was unique and somewhat striking. His ruffled shirt, scarlet cassimere waistcoat and suit of black silk velvet, corded with gold, was admirably adapted to set off his fine, tall figure; his boots, with short red tops, were laced and folded down in such a way as to reach but little above the ankles, and were finished at the heels with silver spurs." When Houston was a United States Senator, and performing his duty as such in the city of Washington, it was his habit to wear, in addition to the ordinary clothing of the gentlemen of those times, an immense Mexican sombrero, as well as a blanket with red lining, such as the one shown in the portrait described above. It is not surprising that his presence on the street in the national capital naturally attracted attention.

In the State Senate of Texas is exhibited a painting of Sam Houston, which portrays him as he appeared when an exile among the Cherokee Indians. This painting reveals a third introspective view of the character of this many-sided man, which is not well known except to those who have made a study of his life.

When a young man in the adolescent period, Houston decided to abandon the civilization of Western Tennessee, where his family lived, and cast his lot with the Cherokee Indians, whose territory lay contiguous to his home. The reason for this decision is variously stated. One explanation is that his older brothers refused him permission to study Latin, and the other is that he was unwilling to clerk in a country store. It is quite probable that his older brothers exercised a tyranny over him. A simpler and more plausible explanation is that this move was doubtless that breaking out of the wild blood and longing for the free life of the wilderness which characterizes most boys, but which in the youthful Houston existed in an even greater intensity. In other words, it was the call of the wild. To use his own expression, he preferred "measuring deer tracks to measuring tape."

Whether the reasons given are correct or not, it is an historic fact that Sam Houston spent several years in all following a wild and primitive life. He was adopted in the family of one of the under chiefs of the Cherokee tribe. "Houston had many of the characteristics of the red man in his nature," says Williams in his biography; "among these were his hot blood, his strong passions and appetites, his fondness for adventure and the untrammelled freedom of the wilderness, his solemnly childish vanity and turn for histrionic effect, . . . an eloquence of original power and impressiveness, a loftiness of spirit and the dominant quality of determination and courage." He thoroughly mastered the Cherokee language, and lived as one of his adopted people.

Samuel Houston, as he was named, was a descendant of a Scotch-Irish family from Northern Ireland. His father was an officer of the famous brigade of riflemen that Morgan led to the assistance of General Washington from the right bank of the Potomac. His mother was a pioneer woman of splendid physique, with the strength of mind and courage to equal her physical strength. Sam was introduced to this—for him—world of romance and adventure on the 2nd of March, 1793, at a place called Timber Ridge Church, near Lexington, Virginia. At the age of thirteen he journeyed with his mother, who was already a widow, and numerous brothers and sisters over the Allegheny Mountains, the entire family settling in the wilds of Western Tennessee. They constructed a rude cabin, and lived in the same primitive fashion as other pioneers.

The schooling of the youthful Houston was very limited, but in after years he overcame to some extent this lack in his early education by reading. Throughout his entire life, however, Houston was a man of few books, but these few he studied deeply. His literary gifts and his power of vigorous expression seem to have been a natural gift. And yet we ascertain that after he returned from his first exile among the Indians, he opened up a country school at the early age of eighteen. His intellectual attainments would hardly seem suited to such a vocation, but it is quite likely that the average school pedagogue of that period was not much better qualified than Sam Houston. The school was a private one, each family paying its own tuition, of which one-third was corn, one-third in cotton and other goods, and the remaining one-third in cash.

There were few public positions which Houston did not at some time fill. He himself once said that he had performed the functions of almost every elective position, except that of President of the United States. He was as much at home seated on a store box and telling stories as he was in a parlour. Add to this a dignity of manner, an impressive physique, and a natural friendliness of disposition, and you have the secret of his political success.

"No person," says F. R. Lubbock, the War Governor of Texas, "ever met Sam Houston in the early days of the Republic without being impressed with his greatness. He was then about forty-two years of age, just the prime of life. Standing largely over six feet in height, with a massive, well-formed hand, a most remarkable foot, measuring more around the instep than in length, a large head, a piercing grey eye, a mouth and nose indicating character, of fine proportions, and as straight as a majestic Indian, he was a most perfect specimen of physical manhood. With such a presence we can well understand that upon state occasions his manner was graceful and courtly. But more to be admired than this, among his friends he was social and agreeable, with the ladies most suave and deferential, and towards the young always kind, interesting, and assuring. Often while in conversation with ladies and children he would carve a perfectly shaped ring, heart, chain, cross, or other emblem, and tender it to some of the party. He was

quite fond of whittling, keeping in his pocket soft pine
or cedar and a good sharp knife for that purpose; and
the making of these little presents was a pastime for
himself, and by those who received them they were
treasured mementoes."

Houston studied law for six months, and then was admitted to the bar of Tennessee. This was not extraordinary at that period, for "Old Hickory" was made a
district attorney without knowing how to spell. A sten-
torian voice and the "gift of gab" signified more in the
prospective lawyer than technical knowledge in those
days, and Houston was abundantly supplied with both.
His caustic tongue brought him many challenges to duels,
although he never fought but one. He always had a
ready response for the challenging party. To a friend
who had challenged him, he said: "Well, I should like
to know if a man can't abuse his friends, who in h—— he
can abuse." This rejoinder brought a laugh, and the
incident was ended. On another occasion, Houston is
said to have handed the written challenge over to his
secretary with the instruction to number it fourteen and
file it away. He then turned to the messenger and informed him that this affair must be held in abeyance until
the other thirteen had been disposed of.

Houston enlisted in the Army of the United States, in
1813, to serve against England. His principal fighting
was in the conflict with the Creek Indians. After the
massacre at Fort Mims, Houston's regiment joined General Jackson in his campaign to crush that recalcitrant
nation. He greatly distinguished himself for personal
feats of bravery at To-ho-pe-ka, a bend on the Tallaposa
River. This battle was one of the most desperate and
most hotly contested engagements ever fought by the
Indians against white troops. He was wounded several

times in that victorious engagement, nearly losing his life as a result of these wounds. He gained the good will of Jackson, however, and ever afterwards retained that general's friendship and confidence. He was promoted to a lieutenancy for gallantry, and remained in this service five years.

Toward the close of his period of enlistment Houston was appointed a sub-agent of the Cherokees, because of his knowledge of their character and language, and at the direct suggestion of General Jackson. Going to Washington with a delegation of this tribe, he was rebuked by the Secretary of War because of appearing before that official garbed like a wild Indian. This led to his resignation. Whether this incident is true or not, it would be entirely characteristic of the man in his youthful days to do just such a thing. We know that on other occasions, when pleading for the red man, he did clothe himself in their garments.

The characteristics and personal habits of the youthful Houston were not altogether without fault. While a candidate for a second term as Governor of Tennessee he abandoned the woman who had been his wife for only a few weeks, resigned the Governorship, and again sought asylum with the Cherokee Indians. The cause for this trouble was never made public by either of the principals. The best explanation appears to be that when he discovered his wife did not reciprocate his own affection, his sensitive nature was wounded and his pride revolted. It is to his credit that he never would allow an unkind or slighting remark to be made about her in his presence. She afterwards secured a divorce from him and married again.

During his second and last sojourn with the Cherokees the Indians commonly designated this white man as the

"Big Drunk," because of his convivial habits. These relapses occurred during periods of great depression to which he was subject; possibly, in part, from a sense of degradation. At this time the tribe of Cherokees he joined lived in Western Arkansas. He was formally admitted into the tribe as the adopted son of the chief, Oo-loo-tee-kah, or John Jolly, and resumed his Indian name of Co-lon-neh, or the Raven. He dressed in Indian clothes, and wore his hair in a queue down his back after the manner of the tribe. He also married after the Indian fashion a Cherokee girl. The period of this self-exile lasted more than a year.

Houston ever remained a friend of the red men, and always retained wonderful influence with them. His communications to them are almost as picturesque as their own writings. Here is a little example from a letter sent with a Texan commission to Red Bear in 1842:

"My Brothers: . . . My red brothers, who know me, will tell you that my counsel has always been for peace; that I have eaten bread and drank water with the red men. They listened to my voice and were not troubled. . . . Bad men make trouble; they cannot be at peace, but when the water is clear they will disturb it, and make it muddy. . . . Let the war-whoops be heard no more upon the prairies. Let songs of joy be heard upon our hills. In our valleys let there be laughter, and in our wigwams let the voices of our women and children be heard. Let trouble be taken away far from us; and when our warriors meet together, let them smoke the pipe of peace and be happy.

"Your brother,

"SAM HOUSTON."

It was not possible for a man like Houston, supremely conscious of his own abilities, to remain content for any considerable time in the seclusion of the wilderness, with no companions but the half-civilized aborigines. A visit to Washington, and his cordial reception there, turned the tide. The greatest and most notable part of the career of Sam Houston was subsequent to his second voluntary exile. It is quite natural to believe, as has been testified to, that Houston had in his mind the idea and possibility of a new Republic in which he would have a leading place. Like many other restless and ambitious spirits, he doubtless dreamed of wresting this expansive empire from turbulent Mexico. His first trip there was as a government commissioner to arrange treaties with the Comanches and other nomadic Indian tribes. This was in 1832, and on this trip he first met Austin and others who afterwards became prominent. At the request of James Bowie he made a trip to San Antonio to have a "talk" with some of the Comanche chiefs.

Under date of February 13, 1833, Houston wrote to President Jackson: "I have travelled nearly five hundred miles across Texas, and am now enabled to judge pretty correctly of the soil and the resources of the country. And I have no hesitation in pronouncing it the finest country, to its extent, upon the globe; for the greater portion of it is richer and more healthy, in my opinion, than West Tennessee. There can be no doubt but the country east of the Rio Grande would sustain a population of ten millions of souls. My opinion is, that Texas will, by her members in convention, on the first of April, declare all that country as Texas proper, and form a State Constitution. I expect to be present at the convention, and will apprise you of the course adopted so

GUADALUPE PEAK (9000 FEET) THE HIGHEST MOUNTAIN IN TEXAS

soon as its members have taken a final action. It is probable I may make Texas my abiding place; in adopting this course, I will *never forget* the country of my birth."

From this time he did make this "richer and more healthy country than West Tennessee . . . his abiding place." He soon afterwards returned to Nacogdoches, and, in a convention summoned to demand organization as a separate territory, held at San Felipe on the 1st of April, 1833, Houston was a delegate from that municipality. Because of his political experience, Houston occupied a prominent place in its deliberations. He was chairman of the committee to frame a constitution. Thus we find his lot cast with Texas. We also find that he was among the first to openly advocate the independence of the territory. Austin was far more conservative on this subject.

The greater part of Texas at this time was still in the primitive condition in which La Salle discovered it when he disembarked on the shores of Matagorda Bay. These regions were inhabited only by marauding tribes of aborigines who knew no restraint. Among them were a few white hunters and trappers scarcely less primordial in their habits than the savages themselves. Texas at that time contained only a small white population of the general character of pioneers. It is only natural that a man of such an imposing figure as Houston, and one who had already enjoyed political prominence in a State of the United States, commanded consideration.

Houston had not been in Texas long until he was made commander-in-chief of the Texan army. He issued a proclamation calling for recruits. He is said at this period to have read with eagerness Cæsar's *Com-*

mentaries for the military lessons to be learned therein. His active military experience prior to that time had been limited, but he was resourceful, and must have had some military talent. It is doubtful that he can be called a military genius, however, any more than he can be placed on a pedestal with our greatest statesmen. His great retreat before the Mexicans, immediately preceding the Battle of San Jacinto, almost wholly disintegrated his army. But the armies were made up of independent-minded pioneers who enlisted for no particular term, and there was little discipline. Each soldier appeared and vanished as he pleased. After this battle he was taken to New Orleans for medical treatment. His wound had not received proper attention, and mortification had set in before he arrived there. His recovery was slow and painful. A score of pieces of bone were removed from the wound.

When Houston was first suggested for the presidency of Texas he professed a great unwillingness to be a candidate. It was doubtless only a little discreet coyness. He was inaugurated on the 22nd of October, 1836, and delivered an extemporaneous inaugural address. He displayed on this occasion one of his histrionic effects, of which there were many during his career. Removing his sword with a dramatic movement, and pausing for a moment, as if struggling with his emotions, he extended it to the presiding officer with these words: "It now, sir, becomes my duty to make a presentation of this sword, the emblem of my past office. I have worn it with some humble pretensions in the defence of my country, and should the danger of my country again call for my services, I expect to resume it, and respond to that call, if needful, with my blood and my life."

The responsibilities of the meteoric Republic thus interjected among the nations were onerous. With little actual money in prospect, it was absolutely necessary to maintain an army for defence against invasion, to equip a navy to patrol the coast, and to guard against hostile Indians, in addition to the ordinary functions of the government. Signing the resolution recognizing the independence of Texas was the last official act of President Andrew Jackson, the friend of Houston. This placed the Republic on a little better basis, and officials breathed a little more freely.

"We now occupy the proud attitude of a sovereign and independent Republic," said Houston in a message to Congress, after recognition by the United States, "which will impose upon us the obligation of evincing to the world that we are worthy to be free. This will only be accomplished by wise legislation, the maintenance of our integrity, and the faithful and just redemption of our plighted faith wherever it has been pledged. Nothing can be better calculated to advance our interests and character than the establishment of a liberal and disinterested policy, enlighted by patriotism, and guided by wisdom."

The Constitution of Texas prohibited a second consecutive term, and Mirabeau Lamar was elected to succeed Houston. At the end of his term, however, the financial condition was so hopeless that the voters rallied to their first president and he was again elected. The voters were all either Houstonites or Anti-Houstonites. By his measures of economy, Houston established greater claim to the name of statesman during his second term than he did during his previous administration. It was difficult for him to restrain the people from declaring war against Mexico, because of the latter's aggressions. During the three years of this term all bills were paid from revenues, and there was a small balance in the treasury ready to be transferred to his successor.

While President, Houston's life was a singular mixture of frontier primitiveness and ceremonial dignity. His home was in a log cabin of only two rooms, which, we are told, would not always have been approved by a sanitary inspector. On ceremonial occasions he could assume all the airs of state, and is reported to have worn a sort of velvet robe which was certainly in great contrast to his primitive surroundings. He had not yet abandoned his convivial habits, and did not, in fact, until his second marriage in 1840. At the age of forty-seven he took a bride of twenty-one, but they lived happily and her influence almost transformed his personal character. During his second term he established a better house, and relegated many of his reckless habits. Among these were both drinking and swearing. He also united with the Baptist Church. A little later he dramatically said in the United States Senate: "I am a disciple of the advocates of temperance. I needed the discipline of the advocates of temperance, and I embraced it, sir. I would enforce the example upon every American heart that influences or is influenced by filial affection, conjugal love, or parental tenderness."

During all of his public career, Houston was constantly a friend of the United States; he was desirous for the annexation of Texas to the greater Republic on her border. But his patience was at one time nearly exhausted over the procrastination, as an incident related by an intimate friend illustrates. It also reveals another disconformity of this eccentric man, for, when he wished to be emphatic, he always referred to himself in the third person. Late in February, says this friend, "He (Houston) came into my room, booted, spurred, whip in hand. Said he, 'Saxe Weimar (his saddle horse) is at the door saddled. I have come to leave Houston's last words with you. If the Congress of the United States shall not by the fourth of March pass some measure of annexation which Texas can with honour accede to, Houston will take the stump against annexation for all time to come.' Without another word, embracing after his fashion, he mounted and left." But this contingency did not arise.

After the annexation Houston was made a Senator of the United States, and served a number of years in that body. He took his seat on the 30th of March, 1846. This was in the days of Webster, Calhoun, Clay, Thomas N. Benton, and many other giants. Houston naturally became conspicuous. A contemporaneous writer (1848) speaks of him in Washington as follows: "He (Houston) was large of frame, of stately carriage and dignified demeanour, and had a lion-like countenance, capable of expressing the fiercest passions. His dress was peculiar, but it was becoming to his style. The conspicuous features of it were a military cap, and a short military cloak of fine blue broadcloth with a blood-red lining. Afterward I occasionally met him when he wore a vast and picturesque sombrero and a Mexican blanket—a sort of ornamented bed-quilt—with a slit in the middle, through which the wearer's head is thrust, leaving the blanket to hang in graceful folds around the body." During the debates he continually whittled cypress shingles of which he always kept a supply. He did not keep his light under a bushel, but made his first speech two weeks after he entered that august body. As a member of the Committee of Military Affairs during the Mexican War he was consulted a great deal because of his knowledge of that country. In speeches he was always allied with the anti-slavery party, generally following the lead of Benton. He said he knew neither North nor South. He knew only the Union. After the defeat of Benton, Houston was the sole representative of the old Union Democracy from the South. This attitude finally cost Houston his seat in the Senate, for he was defeated for re-election in 1857. He was generally known in Washington as "Old San Jacinto."

In 1859 Houston was elected Governor of the State of Texas in a candidacy with the then Governor, in an election in which he ran as an independent candidate. "The Constitution and the Union embrace the principles by which I will be governed if elected," was his platform publicly enunciated. The all-absorbing question before the country at that time was slavery. Texas was a hotbed of secessionists, and Houston made an active campaign. No other man with his views could have won. He met attacks upon himself with scathing vituperation. The election of Houston was a victory for the conservatives. He assumed the office December 2nd, 1859. He refused to deliver his inaugural address before the joint assembly, according to all precedents, but delivered it from the portico of the capitol to a large audience gathered on the steps and lawn below. "Texas," said he, "will maintain the Constitution and stand by the Union. It is all that can save us as a nation. Destroy it and anarchy awaits us." The election of Lincoln to the Presidency in the following year precipitated a climax to the struggle.

South Carolina seceded on the 20th day of December, 1860, and within a month a number of the Southern States had followed her example. In Texas it was a point of honour with a great many to have the State withdraw before Lincoln was inaugurated, and thus avoid the necessity of submitting even for a day to "Black Republican rule." Houston was doing all that was possible to prevent his State from severing its ties. He said of some of the agitators: "I know some of them, who are making the most of the fuss, who would not make good negroes if they were blacked."

In the presidential election of 1860, the vote of Texas had been strongly in favour of the secession candidate. In the election the votes were three to one against Houston, but this man of iron will did not wholly despair. He was outspoken in his condemnation of the secessionists. He refused to convene the Legislature, or to call a convention for fear that it would declare in favour of secession. He was, however, practically compelled to summon an extra session of the Legislature to meet on the 21st day of January, 1861. At the meeting of this body he still endeavoured to prevent a declaration for secession, but without avail. He, nevertheless, declared that he would stand by his State, whatever its decision might be.

In his message transmitting the South Carolina Resolutions, a very lengthy document, Governor Houston declared his "unqualified protest against and dissent from the principles enunciated in the resolutions." "In becoming a State of the Union," said he, "Texas agreed 'not to enter into any treaty, alliance, or confederation, and not, without the consent of Congress, to keep troops or ships of war, enter into any agreement or compact with any other State or foreign power.' All these rights belonged to Texas as a nation. She ceased to possess them as a State." Secession won by an immense vote. Houston was summoned to appear before the convention which had been called, and swear allegiance to the Confederate States, but he refused.

"Sam Houston! Sam Houston! Sam Houston!" called out the presiding officer of the convention—but there was no response. The old Governor sat in his office whittling his pine stick. Thereupon this body declared the office of Governor vacant, and ordered the Lieutenant-Governor to assume the duties of the executive.

Houston issued an address of protest to the people, but made no attempt to retain the office by force. "I love Texas," he declared, "too well to bring civil strife and bloodshed upon her. To avert this calamity, I shall make no endeavour to maintain my authority as chief executive of the State, except by the peaceful exercise of my functions. When I can no longer do this I shall calmly withdraw from the scene, leaving the government in the hands of those who have usurped its authority, but still claiming that I am its chief executive." He then entered his formula: "I protest in the name of the people of Texas against all the acts and doings of this convention, and declare them null and void. I solemnly protest against the act of its members, who are bound by no oath themselves in declaring my office vacant, because I refuse to appear before it and take the oath prescribed."

Gathering up his personal effects, General Houston returned to his home in Huntsville. His eldest son, Sam Houston, Jr., entered the Confederate service, for which his father fitted him with arms and equipment. Although Houston had had many opportunities to amass wealth, his means were small. He owned a double log cabin and some land near Huntsville. He was accused of plotting to set up Texas again as an independent Republic. But this charge was false. His health soon began to fail very perceptibly, for old age was telling upon his rugged constitution. He suffered painful and wasting illnesses. He became melancholy and despondent. Sorrow for the miseries of his country, poverty in his own household, a broken down constitution, saddened his last days as he approached the veil that separates time from eternity.

The last speech of the old warrior was delivered in Houston on the 18th of March, 1863, and he was listened to with respectful attention. When Vicksburg fell he realized that the Confederacy was doomed. On the 26th of July, 1863, he passed away. A widow and eight children survived him. He was placed at rest in the cemetery of his home town.

The will of Sam Houston is characteristic of the man. With regard to the education of his sons, this final testament reads:

"My will is that my sons should receive solid and useful education and that no portion of their time be devoted to the study of abstract science. I greatly desire that they may possess a thorough knowledge of the English language, with a good knowledge of the Latin language. I request that they be instructed in the Holy Scriptures, and next to these that they be rendered thorough in a knowledge of geography and history. I wish my sons to be taught an entire contempt for novels and light reading, as well as for the morals and manners with whom they may be associated or instructed."

CHAPTER XVII

LIFE IN THE EARLY DAYS

Do you enjoy romance and tragedy? If so, you will luxuriate in the early annals of Texas. There is scarcely a foot of soil in Texas which could not relate its tale of heroic deed or daring adventure. When the Americans began to settle in that State, the greater part of it was nothing more than one vast wilderness. The Spanish imprint was confined to a small area. This "call of the wild" drew men of roving dispositions and devotees of adventure in large numbers. These men delighted in the wild woods and the free prairie, and gloried in all the primeval scenes of nature. The deer, the turkey, the buffalo, the wild horses, and the painted savages as well —all possessed charms for these restless spirits. Some of them were enticed by the very troubles that repelled others.

With the exception of the efforts of the *empresarios,* there was no colonizing. The immigrants came in by twos and threes. The individual, unable longer to endure the hardships of the civilization which had encroached upon him, moved out to enjoy the comforts and conveniences of the wilderness. At first he consisted of himself, his dog and his gun. A little later he probably consisted of himself, several dogs, one wife and many children. Still later a neighbour or two of precisely the same definition was added to the above-named concomitants.

After the establishment of the Republic, and following its merging with the United States, the frontier of Texas was ever a scene of disturbance. The cartographers of that period indicate all that expansive region west of San Antonio as the "Range of the Comanche Indians." This is practically the only information vouchsafed. We can scarcely realize what these early settlers were compelled to endure while attempting to subdue the wilderness. A man might start out in the morning to get his horses or oxen. Upon his failure to return a search would be made, and his body found filled with arrows and scalped. A man might leave home in the morning filled with happiness, and return in the evening only to stumble upon the bloody corpse of his wife, instead of finding a savoury supper prepared by her loving hands.

Augustine and Thaddeus Douglas, of fifteen and thirteen years respectively, were sent out on the range by their father to secure the oxen, as their father was preparing to flee before the advancing hosts of Santa Anna, a short time prior to San Jacinto. Returning in the afternoon, the flaming cabin surrounded by painted warriors met the horrified gaze of the boys. They concealed themselves in the chaparral, and succeeded in escaping the savages after many exciting adventures, for they were unarmed. They were captured and kept prisoners by the Mexican troops until after their sanguinary defeat. These boys eventually grew up to manhood and became good citizens of the State.

In addition to the numerous bands of hostile Indians, who roamed almost at will from the demarking line of New Mexico to the coastal region of Texas, there were hundreds of horse thieves, desperadoes, gamblers, and fugitives from justice in general who had escaped from other States. Out here on the limitless prairies the very vastness of the territory seemed to assure protection. If pursued too hotly from the Texan side, they would flee across the Rio Grande into Mexican territory; and likewise Mexican desperadoes would cross to the eastern side to protect themselves from Mexican justice.

It was indeed a puissant hand that was needed here to overawe this class of lawless citizens. It was for the purpose of protecting the settlers from the forays of the Indians and white outlaws, as well as for punishing Mexicans, that there came into existence a band of scouts, or bushwhackers, if you want to term them such, who were employed by the Texas Government and known as the Texas Rangers. To affiliate with this band it was absolutely necessary for a man to possess courage, to be a splendid rider and an unerring shot, and to have a horse worth at least one hundred dollars. For the utilization of all of these qualifications the ranger was remunerated with the munificent sum of one dollar per day. Many of them did not enjoy this pay very long, for they were quickly laid low by the bullet of some hostile white or red or brown man whom they were pursuing and endeavouring to bring to justice.

The ranger was usually clothed in buckskin and wore a broad-brimmed hat. For his accoutrement three or four revolvers and as many bowie knives were thrust through his belt, and a short rifle was thrown across his arm. The wide hat protected the ranger from the piercing sun in the long hikes across the prairie. The leggings of buckskin or cowskin shielded his ankles from the thorny bush and cactus. The large clanking spurs instilled new life into a tardy pony when occasion demanded. But the most important part of his equipment, outside of his own personal courage, was a horse of great speed and endurance, for upon this animal depended not

only his own effectiveness, but his safety as well. With
such an animal a ranger has been known to cover eighty
miles of rough prairie between sunrise and sunset.

The rangers carried no tents, and seldom employed
baggage wagons. Frequently they were obliged to sub-
sist solely on game. At night they enwrapped themselves
in their blankets anywhere within the lines of their sentinels. They were always ready for the chase of the red-
skins at a moment's notice. Exciting enough was such
a life for any devotee of romance and adventure. They
attired themselves practically as they chose, and they elected their own officers. Returning from a long chase
running into weeks or months, the men would enter the
settlements almost in tatters. Men and officers were on
terms of perfect equality, calling each other by their
Christian or nick-names.

"All ready, boys? Go ahead!" This was usually the
only order from the commander. Once the engagement
began, each man fought quite independently of the others.

The rangers came into existence along about 1840
in the neighbourhood of San Antonio, which was then
almost on the extreme frontier. The conditions were
anything but encouraging for one who wished to settle
in the country and enjoy a peaceful life. It was almost
impossible to keep good horses. Realizing the necessity
of an armed and active force to hold these desperadoes in
check, General Houston commissioned John Coffee Hays,
who is better known in history as Jack Hays, to raise a
company of kindred spirits to follow the horse thieves
and Indians anywhere he wished and to shoot them on
the spot if necessary. At that time he was a young surveyor, and practically unknown.

Hays was very particular as to the type of men whom
he enlisted in his company, and for that reason he prob-

ably collected the most efficient set of Indian fighters
that Texas ever produced. It was not long until a few
feet of soft earth or a few bones bleaching beneath the
sun out on the prairie marked the spot where had terminated the earthly career of some outlaw. Under Hays
the Texas Rangers achieved a name and a reputation
which was world-wide. The very name of Hays and
his rangers became a terror to evildoers. The red man
of the plains felt the weight of his mailed hand, and
learned to dread an encounter with him and his men.
When the tables were turned, and these men were taken
prisoners by the Mexicans, they drew the black beans,
which doomed them to military execution within a few
minutes, with absolute composure even if their hearts
may have thumped a little wildly.

One of the greatest encounters between rangers and
Indians was that commonly designated as the Bird Creek
Battle, in 1839. Thirty-one rangers under Captain Bird
encountered a force of hostiles near Fort Griffin, not far
from a small stream, since called Bird's Creek, and in
the vicinity of the present town of Belton. The rangers
pursued the fleeing and scattering Indians for some distance. While camping with lessened precaution, they
were almost surrounded by the wily savages, who had
received reinforcements. The rangers made a sudden
dash for a ravine, where there was also a spring. The
Indians sent up "signal smokes," which were answered
from several directions. Very quickly other bands of
Indians approached the Texans, until three hundred
painted savages, led by the noted chief, Buffalo Hump,
encompassed the little band of intrepid rangers. The
odds were fearful, but the rangers were cool, determined,
and undaunted. Few shots were wasted. Charge after
charge of the Indians was met by a hail of leaden missiles.

At length one of the rangers vowed that he would kill the chief, who led his men in the encircling charges, and he succeeded in the attempt after a few futile shots. This dénouement demoralized the savages, and they finally withdrew. Half a hundred Indians journeyed to the happy hunting grounds, while the captain and four of his rangers were killed.

The experiences that one reads in a number of books of reminiscences that have been published, and which may still be heard from a few of the later pioneers who survive, nearly surpass belief. They seem almost to transcend the power of human endurance. The rangers reached their maximum in numbers during the Mexican War. Captain Walker's company assisted General Taylor in his operations around Brownsville. "Jack" Hays himself mustered into the service three regiments of Texas Rangers, all of which did effective service during that conflict. They were employed to disperse the guerillas, who everywhere harassed the Americans in their lines of communications, and they fully demonstrated their ability to cope with that class of belligerents.

The Texas Rangers became the terror of the Mexican guerillas. Years of fierce border warfare had inured them to every hardship and prepared them for every eventuality. They remembered the wrongs which they themselves had suffered at the hands of Mexican bandits, and the deadly strife in which their friends had succumbed. Now the tables were turned, and many of them welcomed the opportunity for vengeance. Texas furnished more troops to aid the United States than she had brought into the field to achieve her own independence a decade earlier. It was a higher percentage in proportion to the population than any other State of the United States.

One of the most noted of the Texas Rangers and border fighters was William A. Wallace, who is generally
known as "Big Foot" Wallace. He was a man more than
six feet in height, large of frame, and a thorough Texan
in every way. He migrated to Texas in the year following independence, as a young man of twenty years, and
lived to pass his eightieth birthday. Because of the death
of a relative in the Fannin massacre, he had taken an
oath to go to Texas and spend his life in killing Mexicans. He settled near Austin, which was then on the
extreme frontier. He loved the wild woods; he gloried
in all the primeval scenes of nature. No sooner had
Wallace heard of the organization of the rangers than
he journeyed to San Antonio and applied to Captain
Hays for admission. He was welcomed as one of the
company.

Many horse thieves were caught and some were executed by Wallace's company, and a number of skirmishes
with Indians occurred. He was a member of the unfortunate expedition against Mier, where he was captured. Twenty-two months' confinement in the horrible Mexican prisons and the suffering of many indignities
did not mollify his sentiments towards the Mexicans.
As a result he welcomed the outbreak of the Mexican
War and enrolled with one of the bands of Texas Rangers, in which he did splendid service. Wallace died in
1899, and by an act of the Legislature was buried in the
State cemetery at Austin,—the city in which he had
dug the first well, and where he had pursued the last
herd of buffalo that ever sank a hoof on that site. In
this cemetery will be found the graves of scores of the
men who did things and made for themselves names in
the history of the Republic and State of Texas.

Wallace carried the mail from San Antonio to El

Paso for a long time. As late as 1854 there was not a settlement from Medina county to El Paso, a distance of hundreds of miles. Mails were first despatched once a month. At a later period a stage was run a little more frequently. It cost a hundred dollars to go from San Antonio to El Paso. For five hundred miles no change of teams was made. The average daily travel was about fifty miles. It was not easy work for the driver and guards, and many a brave boy was lost. On several occasions Wallace's party was attacked by the Indians with serious losses, and again Mexican bandits would waylay them. The marauding savages through that western country were generally the bloodthirsty Apaches, who created so much trouble for the United States in later years. At times there was scarcely a trip in which some one, either guard or passenger, was not killed. When "Big Foot" Wallace quit the mail service, he was commissioned by Governor P. H. Bell to collect a company of rangers for frontier defence.

The hardest fight that Wallace and his men experienced during their service was on the Todos Santos (All Saints) Creek, at a place called the Black Hills, sixteen miles from the present town of Cotulla, in La Salle County. There were eighty Indians opposed to only nineteen rangers, and one of the latter was so sick that he was forced to lie on a blanket under a mesquite tree during the combat. It was hot and dry weather, and the rangers had been three days without water. The time was in August, 1854, and the rangers were fighting to obtain possession of a water-hole which was in the hands of the Comanches. Captain Wallace knew where all the water-holes were, and had conducted his men over the hot and desolate hills and valleys, through prickly pear and catclaw bushes, to this watering place. He discovered the Indians there before him, and a desperate battle ensued for an hour or more. The Indians were finally driven away, leaving twenty-two of their number dead on the ground, among whom was the chief. Captain Wallace had killed him with a large rifle which once belonged to Colonel James Bowie. The mesquite tree behind which Wallace stood during the fight was struck by many bullets. More than one Indian had fallen under his fire. Several of the rangers were wounded, some of them severely, and they were carried on stretchers to Fort Inge. Not one of the rangers was killed.

The life of the early Texans is also well illustrated by the career of Edward D. Westfall, who entered Texas about the time of its admission as a State. Although a bright man for those days, Westfall loved the solitude and the freedom of the wilds like many another of his kind. He quickly deserted the habitations of civilized men, and built a cabin on the banks of the Leona River. He became a noted man on the frontier as an Indian fighter and a trailer for soldiers and rangers. Raids from hostile Indians were numerous throughout that territory in those days, and the experiences of Westfall would fill a book in themselves. He was a dead shot, and the Indians learned to know and fear him. As the country began to be peopled and domestic stock was introduced in greater numbers, Westfall finally sought some neighbours as a protection for himself and his stock from the marauding bands of Indians. He proceeded to San Antonio, and offered one hundred acres of land to any one who would accompany him. Several accepted and went with him, but the majority of them soon tired of the experience and quickly returned.

At one time a Frenchman, named Louie, came out and

wanted to live with Westfall. They intended to go to Fort Inge to secure the Frenchman's personal property, but postponed the trip until nightfall, as there were indications of Indians. The savages were nearer than Westfall himself dreamed, for they were then in ambush for him. After killing one Indian, Westfall was himself wounded. The Frenchman acquitted himself well, but he was struck with a fatal bullet. Although the Indians fled, Westfall remained in his cabin absolutely helpless for several days without any help reaching him. He then dragged himself and patiently made his way to the fort. It seems marvellous that such venturesome men survive even the allotted time for man, but Westfall, like his friend and boon companion, "Big Foot" Wallace, lived several years beyond the usual three score and ten and died a natural death.

The little forts scattered about the country at different times were temporary affairs. A traveller in describing Fort Inge (1856) says: "As is usually the case with our nominal Indian forts, there were no structures for defence, the only thing suggesting these being a stockade of mesquite trunks, surrounding the stables, which were open thatched sheds. There were, perhaps, a dozen buildings, of various sizes, as officers' quarters, barracks, bakery, hospital, guard-room and others. The buildings were all rough and temporary, some of the officers' lodgings being mere *jacals* of sticks and mud. But all were whitewashed, and neatly kept, by taste and discipline."

Many were the trials of the early settlers, and harrowing were their experiences. In the vicinity of the town of Gonzales there lived in the pioneer days one Michael Putnam, and another settler named Lockhart. They were industrious and thrifty men, and each had a growing family. Life ahead loomed bright and cheerful.

One bright day, however, four of their children from eight to thirteen years of age, who had gone along the river to gather pecans, were discovered by a band of wandering Comanches. With a wild shout these savages seized the children and dashed away. One can imagine the consternation in the two households when the children failed to return in the evening. A bonnet or two and little Jimmy Lockhart's hat were found, while horse tracks were numerous. A posse of neighbours was soon organized and pursuit made. Day after day the chase was maintained, and the tracks of the children were occasionally identified at the camping places. At last the quest had to be abandoned because they were entering too far into the Indian country for a small force. Another and larger expedition was quickly gathered. The children were located in an Indian camp, and an attack followed. Though greatly outnumbered, the white men struggled with a desperation almost amounting to frenzy. But valour was obliged to yield to numbers. The settlers withdrew after several of their number had been killed.

Matilda Lockhart was given up a couple of years afterwards in accordance with a treaty. James Putnam was recovered a few years later by his parents, but his eldest sister had by this time been espoused by a chief and would not abandon her adopted people. More than thirty years afterward, however, a middle-aged white woman was ransomed by an Indian agent. She was so young when captured by the Indians that she did not even remember her name. James Putnam learned of her, however, identifying her by a scar on her arm caused by a burn. This is just one of the tragedies of pioneer life that sometimes overtook the hardy early settlers of Texas.

Near where the Sunset Route crosses the Colorado,

there lived in 1837 a family named Lions, who belonged to Austin's Colony. In the morning Mr. Lions and his son Warren, a lad of thirteen, went out to milk the cows. A party of Comanche Indians were lying in wait and, after killing and scalping the father, took the boy captive. The years passed with nothing but vague and unreliable rumours of the captive boy. Every one gave him up for lost except the mother. During the Mexican War a party of Comanches appeared in San Antonio on a trading expedition. It leaked out that one of the warriors was an American. An interview through an interpreter removed all doubt. Friends resolved to take him home to his waiting mother if possible. But this was not easy, for the boy had grown to be a man enamoured of the savage life. He already had two Indian wives. At last he was induced to go for a visit, but he faithfully promised to return to his dusky spouses. He finally consented to join a band of rangers to fight Mexicans in Southwest Texas, and was thus weaned from his Indian habits and reconciled to civilization. Before his service ended he participated in several engagements with the Indians, and proved himself a valuable ranger because of his intimate knowledge of the Indian character and habits.

In what is now Limestone County, on a line between Dallas and Houston, in the early thirties, was Parker's Fort. This fruited and thickly-populated region was then a wilderness. The Fort was merely a number of cabins engirded by a stockade. At the corners were block-houses, and the outer walls were perforated with loopholes. It was built, like many others, for the purpose of being occupied by the settlers when threatened by Indians. The patriarch of the settlement was Elder John Parker, and his relatives were the most numerous. Early in the morning of a bright day in May, 1836, while most of the men were at work in their fields, several hundred Comanches and Kiowas suddenly appeared on the prairie. They claimed to be friendly, but as soon as they learned the men were away, their butchering began. The women and few men left fled and endeavoured to escape. Some did make their way to safety, but many fell. Others were borne away as captives.

Among the captives was a little girl of seven summers, named Cynthia Ann Parker, and her brother John. Many efforts were made by soldiers to trace these children. It was not until almost a quarter of a century later, after an Indian defeat at Peace River, that they were located. Cynthia Ann was then the wife of the chief to whom she had borne several children. She had forgotten the English language, and it was some time before she was reconciled to civilized life. The State extended her a pension of one hundred dollars a year. Her son became the famous Comanche Chief Quanah Parker, who was respected by whites as well as Indians. He visited his mother at her home. He died in 1911 and was buried by the side of his mother in Oklahoma. Her brother John escaped from the Indians and fled to Mexico, but later returned to Texas and served in the Confederate armies during the war between the States.

The American settlers in Texas were generally men inured to pioneer life. They were splendid shots, and entered the country of their adoption equipped and ready to endure hardships and to defend themselves. There were a few exceptions in the way of European colonies. Although a number of German settlements were established, there is a record of only one English colony. This was engineered in 1832 by Dr. Beck, a native of England. After many hardships this colony of fifty-nine men, women and children reached their concession a little below the present town of Del Rio. With much ceremony the streets and plazas of the village of Dolores (sorrows) were platted, and humble cabins were erected. A brush wall was constructed for protection against marauding Indians. But the drought arrived, the settlement was raided by the copper savages, and it gradually vanished. Some of the colonists returned to their native land, while others took up new abodes in other settlements already established.

One party of sixteen souls from Dolores started for San Patricio. On the way a band of Comanches overtook them and killed all the men. Two women, Mrs. Horn and Mrs. Harris, and some children were kept as captives. It was many months before they were ransomed from the Indians by some traders and restored to civilization. Their sufferings will not bear description. It is simply an instance of the experiences of the colonists who came to Texas. The fate of the children was never known. Many another incipient town, with even fairer prospects, shared the fate of this "City of the Sorrows." Even the sites of Tenoxtitlan and Nashville, once flourishing settlements, are scarcely known to-day.

In 1830 the celebrated James Bowie became a citizen of San Antonio and married the daughter of Don Veramendi, the Vice-Governor. On the second of November, 1831, he and his brother Rezin P. Bowie, and seven other Americans and two negro servants started to hunt for the San Saba silver mines. When in the neighbourhood of the old mission on the San Saba River, they were attacked by one hundred and sixty-four Tehuacana and Caddo Indians. The Bowies threw up temporary breastworks, which the Indians repeatedly and vigorously attacked. Failing in these assaults, the Indians next attempted to burn them out by setting fire to the long prairie grass. The Americans, however, sternly held their ground. The fight lasted from sunrise in the morning until dark, when the savages sullenly retired, having lost nearly one-half of their number. Only one of Bowie's men was killed, and three were wounded.

Near Dawson, in Navarro County, is a monument to the Heroes of Battle Creek Fight. This fight illustrates the fact that the appearance of surveyors, out on the prairie staking off lands granted to colonies, was almost invariably a signal for a new outburst of violence towards the whites. A "big talk" had been held with the Indians, and a treaty entered into in which were these words: "Peace is never to die between the parties that make this agreement, they have shaken hands upon it, and the Great Spirit has looked down and seen their actions. He will curse all the chiefs that tell a lie before his eyes. Their women and children cannot be happy." But the ink was scarcely dry before the treaty was violated. Surveying parties had initiated their work. A party of twenty-three men were sent to survey lands in what was then Robertson County. Several hundred Indians were in that neighbourhood killing buffalo for winter meat. All went well until the surveyors began their work. The Indians warned them to desist, but the surveyors refused. An ambuscade followed and the surveyors were compelled to fight for their lives. Of the entire party only seven escaped, five of whom were seriously wounded. Many other surveying parties met with similar disaster.

In 1840 a Comanche invasion advanced to Lavaca Bay on the Gulf. The savages pillaged all the stores available and their animals were loaded with booty. Linville was sacked and Victoria burned. They shot the men and kept women and children as prisoners. Several volunteer companies rallied to drive the marauders off. They rendezvoused at Plum Creek. In the early morning, as the Indians were packing their stolen mules, the Texans attacked. The Indians were panic-stricken, and shot several of their prisoners. The Texans were under General Felix Houston. The Indian chief, bedecked with high silk hat, fine boots, gloves, and a coat with brass buttons, pranced in front of the Americans shouting defiance. At first he also carried a large umbrella opened to the full. But he soon bit the dust. Beneath the fiery onslaught of the infuriated Texans the Indians finally fled in confusion. Many were killed before they reached safety in the cane brakes and hills. It is believed that this foray, probably the most formidable in Texas, was instigated by the Mexicans, who promised support. The Indians retired to their accustomed haunts to brood over their defeat and to plan revenge on their Mexican allies, who failed them at the critical time.

One of the successful settlements of foreigners was established by Henry Castro, who was descended from a prominent Portuguese family. After the fall of Napoleon he emigrated to the United States, but returned to France to negotiate a loan for the Republic of Texas. For his services he was granted immense tracts of land and became the founder of Castroville, a little west of San Antonio. In all he brought to Texas four hundred and eighty-five families and four hundred and fifty-seven single men in twenty-seven ships. He was a man of extraordinary ability and perseverance, or he could never have surmounted the many difficulties that arose.

The first settlers introduced by Castro arrived in San Antonio in 1843. At that time there were few settlers west of that city. Some of his immigrants were French, and others were Germans from Alsace, at that time a part of France. The prospect of from one hundred and sixty to three hundred and twenty acres or more of free land seemed like a godsend to the impoverished peasants of France. But they were inexperienced in frontier life. Few knew anything about firearms, and those who did possessed no guns suitable to kill game or protect from savages. They came from towns and thickly-settled districts, and knew nothing about roughing it out on the prairie or in the woods. Furthermore, they had little money.

One can only in a measure imagine the feelings of lonesomeness and disappointment when these European settlers arrived in the wilds of Western Texas. There was scarcely a trail, except that left by the surveyor. There was not even material with which to erect houses, for the mesquite was too short. Deer and smaller game were plentiful, however, so that a supply of fresh meat was easy to obtain. Many of these settlers in a short time developed into splendid hunters and effective Indian fighters. When a band of painted Comanche Indians would appear, these German and French colonists were terribly affrighted. And they had reason to be frightened. An occasional visit from rangers gave a little courage.

Henry Castro left a diary which is full of interest. From it I make a few extracts:

"July 31st, 1843.—Returned to San Antonio. Two of our rangers were taken sick with a fever.

"I have, during this excursion of seven days, seen one hundred and sixty miles of country, which can only be compared to an English park, without meeting a single settlement. No dangerous wild animals were found, but herds of deer and wild horses. With coffee, sugar, and flour, we have lived well from the product of our hunting and fishing and always had plenty of honey.

"August 25th.—Some of my colonists who had left Galveston in the early part of July will not reach this place as soon as it was expected on account of sickness. At Santitas' ranch, forty miles from San Antonio, the Indians attacked a cart which had unfortunately remained behind the convoy. A young colonist aged nineteen by the name of Z. Rhin was killed. The driver, who was an American, made his escape. The Indians burned the cart and all its contents. The driver remained in the woods the following day, and although the Indians numbered twenty he kept them at bay with his long rifle. One of the hands of poor Rhin was found nailed to a tree. He was probably the first martyr of European emigration by Indian brutality in Western Texas.

"August 26th.—To-day five or six Comanches came within two hundred yards of the house I occupy on Soledad Street and succeeded in capturing eleven mules that were grazing in the enclosure. Alarm was given in the town and the robbers were pursued, but without any result. The mules were lost. Such acts of audacity on the part of the Indians intimidate my colonists and tend to injure my enterprise.

"Four volunteers who were sent by Captain Hays to reconnoitre on the Nueces River, ninety miles from San Antonio, were surprised while bathing in the river by a large party of Indians. Two were reported killed. The other two reported that they had undressed themselves and with horses unsaddled they were bathing in the river when they were fired upon from the bank of the river. The attack was so sudden and unexpected that seeing their comrades fall and fearful of being surrounded, they fled, leaving their arms, clothing, saddles and bridles in possession of the Indians.

"In the month of July last Captain Hays with twelve of his company encountered near Corpus Christi seventy-five Comanche warriors. A fight ensued which I am told lasted fifty minutes, nearly hand to hand. Thirty Indians were killed and many others wounded and routed. This victory was greatly due to the use of Colt's revolvers that the Texans used for the first time in this engagement to the great astonishment of the Indians, who fought bravely."

It was necessity that taught these Alsatian colonists to defend themselves. Tragedies began to occur, for the Indians resented an invasion of their country. Four colonists went up the Medina, a few miles from Castroville, to establish a farm and ranch. The next day another colonist out hunting wild turkeys discovered the dead bodies stripped and their guns missing. They had evidently been killed while sleeping. The men were ignorant of camping rules, and had built their fire against a dead tree, which had blazed up and made a beacon light visible for a long distance. This had attracted the attention of the Indians.

At the time of the annexation of Texas the number of Indians in the State was estimated at twenty-nine thousand five hundred, of which twenty thousand were Comanches. The others in the order of numbers were Apaches, Kiowas, Caddoes, Delawares, Wacoes, Tonkawas, Lipans, Keechies, etc. The Comanche is the type that fills up our ideal of true savage life. He is the Bedouin of the prairie. From the earliest settlements this tribe was hostile to the Spaniards—looking upon them with contempt. Until 1836, the Comanches were on friendly terms with Americans. The Tonkawas usually lived near the American settlements because of their dread of the Comanches. They sometimes committed petty thefts, but, as a rule, were not openly hostile. The tribal existence of the Tejas (or Texas), once powerful, had already been lost, but the name is preserved in one of the most brilliant stars of the American constellation.

In 1849 it was reported that one hundred and seventy-one persons had been killed, seven wounded, and twenty-five taken into captivity by the Indians, and they had also stolen six thousand horses. Jurisdiction over these aborigines was given to the United States. During the Civil War the few who remained in Texas were comparatively quiet. Some enlisted in the Union army, and others fought with the Confederates. In order to avoid taking part in this struggle a thousand Kickapoos started through Texas for the Rio Grande. When camped at Dove Creek, they were discovered by the Texans and attacked. Both sides suffered severe losses, but the Indians reached the Mexican border. The Indians claimed that they were attacked under a flag of truce. For a number of years afterwards they would cross the border and murder outlying settlers in revenge for this fight. They were finally removed to the Indian Territory.

In the two years immediately succeeding the close of the war, one hundred and sixty-two Texans were killed in Texas by the Indians. For almost ten years there was scarcely a month in which there was not a raid on some part of the frontier. A volume might be written detailing the particulars of these raids and murders. In 1868 the Indians reached within less than a hundred miles of Austin, murdering and scalping the isolated settlers. But their raids, murders and stealing finally came to an end.

The day of the Texas Ranger is passing, but it has not yet departed. The savage Indians have disappeared from the Lone Star State, but the white and brown outlaws still necessitate the employment of a small force under this name. Scarcely a year passes that at least one does not pass to his reward while on duty. It is in the long border line with Mexico that these tragedies generally occur.

CHAPTER XVIII

RANCHES AND RANCHING

WE had been journeying for a number of miles across fine grazing land, dotted with extensive herds of splendid cattle, down in Southern Texas, between Corpus Christi and Brownsville, when the conductor passed by after a halt at one of the rather infrequent stations.

"Whose ranch is this?" I asked the train official in a casual manner.

"It is the famous King Ranch," he answered, "and we have been on this ranch now for more than an hour. The next station is Kingsville, near which is the ranch-house of Mrs. King, the owner."

After passing Kingsville, the railway traversed another splendid stretch of ranching country, similar to that on the opposite side of that station, and, as the conductor again appeared, I turned to him inquiringly.

"Could you enlighten me as to whose ranch this is that we are now peragrating over?"

"This is still the King Ranch," he answered, "and will be for the next twenty or twenty-five miles."

"This seems to be a very large ranch," I answered. "Do you know how many acres there are in it?"

"Altogether the ranch comprises about a million and a quarter of acres," was the conductor's reply.

With that answer, I subsided. My own experience was so interesting that I concluded I would fathom how such figures affected others. I decided to try it on a friend,

305

for, after all, of what value are your friends if you cannot utilize them as a psychological study once in a while. This one was of the naturally sceptical type.

"I spent a day on a million-acre ranch down in Texas," I remarked to this friend, as I was relating to him some experiences in the Southwest.

"A million acres, is that all?" my friend replied with a rather incredulous smile.

"Well, it is all but about a hundred thousand acres or so. I used the term million just to express it in round numbers. It is about as difficult for the owner to measure her acres exactly as it is to round up all of her one hundred thousand cattle in the spring."

"One hundred thousand cattle!" said my friend with a gasp.

"Yes, so the superintendent informed me, as we were speeding over the prairie in an eighty-horse-power automobile at the rate of thirty-five miles an hour. We were then travelling across a fifty thousand acre field, and——"

"Fifty thousand acre field! That is almost inconceivable!"

"Yes, but the superintendent incidentally mentioned that there was another field of eighty thousand acres on the ranch."

"Is it all grazing land?"

"No, I saw five tractors at work overturning the pristine sod at the rate of sixty acres a day. With a night shift this amount can be doubled, for a tractor does not require any rest, and a headlight takes the place of daylight."

Now, where I live, back in good old Ohio, the farmer who possesses a half section, three hundred and twenty acres, of good land is considered very well-to-do indeed,

EXTERIOR VIEW OF SANTA GERTRUDIS

and the man who owns a quarter of a section of good land is looked upon as a very prosperous farmer. In round numbers, this ranch of a million acres plus is half again as extensive as the State of Rhode Island. It is pre-eminently a domain, if there is such a thing in our agriculture.

There have been greater land holdings in Texas, and in Mexico and Argentina to-day there are haciendas that surpass it in amplitude of horizontal surface, but none of them is developed or has the value of this. There is in Mexico, or was before the long revolution of 1910-15, a hacienda of seven million acres in the State of Chihuahua, but it was undeveloped land consisting of both hill and dale. It did not produce as much as the King Ranch. It seems almost inconceivable that such an immense tract of land should be the property of one family, and it is probably a fact that this is the largest ranch owned by an individual in the entire United States. But Texas is a land of big things, and there are many things in that commonwealth that are different from the rest of the United States.

Ranching in Texas is not without its romance. If one goes back into the incipient days of that industry, he will discover many incidents which are as truly romantic and fully as exciting as anything that can be found in our early history. The western part of Texas would be described by many as a great desert, and yet before the coming of the white man it was the peaceful abode of millions of buffalo, deer, antelope, and other game animals. The plains were carpeted with rich and nutritious grasses a large part of the year, and the hills were grown up to shrubs and trees. The grazing creatures ranged over a vast territory, migrating north in summer and ambling south in winter, always seeking the best feeding-grounds to which instinct infallibly directed them.

When the white man came upon the scene, his primary effort was directed to annihilating all of these animals whether they were needed for food or not. He slaughtered to the right and to the left. The Indians killed only for food, or raiment, and thus conserved their food supply. The buffalo yielded his hide to the Caucasian, which was made into a robe, while the carcass became repast for the vultures. He destroyed most of the deer and the antelope. He became more savage in some respects than the uncivilized red man—at least he had less consideration for others. The last buffalo of the great Southwestern herd disappeared about 1876, and it was not long afterwards that the Indians were hustled off to the reservations. There was no longer food left .on the plains for them.

There were many wild ponies on the plains of Texas. Mr. Duval, in his *Early Times in Texas,* says: "Once, too, at the distance of half a mile we saw a large drove of mustangs, but they were much wilder than the deer, for when several of us attempted to approach them, they circled around us out of range of our rifles, every now and then stopping a moment, stamping and snorting, until at last one of them that seemed to be the leader of the drove, started off at full speed, and the rest following, in a short time nothing but a cloud of dust indicated the direction they had taken. Some years subsequent to this, a company of rangers to which I belonged, when in pursuit of Indians in the country between the Nueces and Rio Grande Rivers, met with a drove of mustangs so large that it took us fully an hour to pass it, although they were travelling at a rapid rate in a direction nearly opposite to the one we were going. As far as the eye could

extend on a dead level prairie, nothing was visible except
a dense mass of horses, and the trampling of their hoofs
sounded like the roar of the surf on a rocky coast. Most
persons probably would be inclined to doubt this 'horse
story,' and to consider it one to be told to the 'horse
marines' alone; yet it is literally true, and many are still
living who were with me at the time, who can testify that
my statement is in no manner exaggerated."

Kimball writes of his experiences in the Panhandle
as follows: "At sundown a drove of mustangs, or
wild horses of the prairie, paid us a flying visit. They
were first seen ascending a hill at the distance of half a
mile, and as they were coming towards us were taken for
Indians. When seen on a distant hill, standing with
their raised heads toward a person, and forming a line
as is their custom, it is almost impossible to take them
for anything but mounted men. Having satisfied their
curiosity, they wheeled with almost the regularity of a
cavalry company and galloped off, their long thick manes
waving in the air and their tails nearly sweeping the
ground. They are beautiful animals, always in excellent
condition, and although smaller than our American
horses, are still very compact, and will bear much fatigue."

Soon after the vanishing of the buffalo came the cattlemen, who spread all over the plains from Dakota to
Texas. Texas proved to be one of the best sections of
this great grazing domain. It was indeed a golden land.
It seemed as if there was fodder enough for all the cattle
in the world. It was not long until vast herds of cattle
were roaming over the former stamping-ground of the
buffalo. They multiplied and spread like locusts, and
the cattlemen became rich. Even the horses were to be
had at that time for the catching. The cattlemen were

democratic in manner, warm-hearted, brave and free-handed. Sometimes they were hard drinking fellows—but always they were dead shots. It was, indeed, a condition of primitive society. There were no restrictions, save those set by a primitive conscience and a neighbour's six-shooter. Neither the land nor the grass cost the cattleman anything at this time, and he was king within his little principality, the boundaries of which were established by the precedent of prior occupation.

Free grass was one of the perquisites of the frontier, whether the domain belonged to individuals, to the school fund, or was part of the public domain. A man might possess one hundred thousand head of cattle, and not have the legal title to a square foot of land. His rights upon this range he enforced with blood and iron if necessary. Stories of sudden riches began to lure others into the cattle country, and finally the cattle became so numerous that conflicts arose. These newcomers were just as brave as their predecessors, and they were just as audacious. Some of them came from distant lands across the Atlantic. The building of the transcontinental railroads stimulated immigration. With immigration came the private ownership of land.

When the newcomers, who had secured a legal title to land, began to circumscribe it with wire fences, they came into collision with those free lances who had been occupying it for a decade or more. The squatter declared that there was not sufficient elbow room for all. Then came an era of wire cutting, and the result was often determined by the one who was the surest shot. Many men lay down in the burning sun never to rise again. This was because they disregarded absolutely the range boundaries that had been established by an honourable custom among the cattlemen. In the end, however, those men who had consulted learned lawyers, who, in turn, peered into bulky books with calfskin bindings, won out, and the free lance on the prairie was compelled to migrate farther toward the declining sun or go out of business. If Mr. Smith, the original pioneer, was killed, his son took up the fight, or a Mr. Brown, or some one else entered into the controversy with a paper which proved him to possess the legal title to this controverted land.

Thus it was that barbed wire had such an important part in the development of Texas. It first transformed the open country of the West into a series of pastures. Sometimes the only water holes in extensive arid areas were fenced in. School lands were enclosed as well as private property without the consent of the owners in the greediness of the cattle lords. The refusal of the cattle kings to "pay for the children's grass" aroused deep feeling. In West Texas, the entire country was divided between the free grass and the pasture men—the former representing free grass for the many and the latter free grass for the few. Outbreaks of violence were many, and a perfect mania for fence-cutting arose.

"I hold in my hand a map copied from one made by a grass commissioner of the land board, which shows twenty counties of the Panhandle in one block, wired in, every acre of them, in pastures built generally by corporations. Inside of those pastures are millions of acres of unrented and unsold school land, which are appropriated in defiance of law." These are the words of a speaker in 1886. In the end, wire fencing prevailed, but it was limited to lands actually owned or legally leased. The State was compelled to give its preference to the actual homesteader, who was granted from a quarter to an entire section, instead of leasing the public lands to the cattlemen. Such was the influence of public opinion. The construction of fences also had a potent influence on the development of the stock, for with it began the disappearance of the old Texan long-horn, which looks much better in a picture than the sleek white-faced Hereford.

Before the days of the railroads in Western Texas, cattle drives were important events. Regular trails were plainly visible across the prairie both east and west. To the east the cattle were driven to St. Louis or Kansas City, and to the west they trudged as far as California. It necessitated the employment of four or five men for every hundred of cattle. Some were old frontier men in the Western drives, and others were youths working their way to the coast. The cattle travelled slowly, as they were compelled to forage for their living, and it required from five to six months to reach the Pacific coast. A few wagons loaded with stores, cooking utensils, camp equipment, and ammunition followed the cattle. There were always losses on these trips, but the profit was ample. Hostile bands of Indians sometimes created havoc. But the drivers were equipped with a government rifle, and at least a couple of repeating revolvers for protection. The trails were always lined with the bleaching bones of cattle and horses that had perished by the way, and the graves of the drivers were not infrequent. Some of them died from natural causes, but by far the greater number met an untimely end.

There is as much change in the character of the cattle that one will see grazing upon the prairie as there is among the cattlemen themselves. A few years ago the long-horned steers, which are so well known, roamed over the prairie on an allowance of about ten acres to each animal. To-day you would have to make a strenuous search to find a single good specimen of the long-horn Texas steer. Year after year there has been a continual evolution. The ranchers have bred up their cattle, knowing that a steer of a better grade will consume no more of the grass than a long-horn, and will produce three or four times as much meat. One witnesses this in travelling across the broad ranges of Texas in the cattle that will be seen near the railroads; and again in the stockyards at Fort Worth, if one will glance over the cattle which may be seen in the pens. The cattle become fatter, heavier, slower, and more profitable year by year.

There is an association, with headquarters at Fort Worth, which is known as The Cattle Raisers' Association of Texas, to which all the leading cattlemen of Texas belong. This organization devotes its attention to everything that is needed by the cattle industry. It will fight the beef trust, contest with the railroads over rates, maintain a lobby at Washington if necessary, initiate measures to prevent the stealing of cattle, and accomplish everything it can to elevate the cattle industry to a loftier standard. It maintains inspectors at shipping and market points to insure that no man disposes of cattle bearing another man's brand.

In the former days the unit of area was the Spanish league of forty-four hundred acres, and a man always spoke of his possessions as so many leagues. This method will still be found in Argentina, Mexico and other countries of large ranches which have inherited the Spanish computation system. In Texas the English system of measurement has succeeded the old Spanish method. The largest ranch in Texas, and doubtless in the United States as well, was the one known as the X I T ranch, owned by the Farwell Brothers of Chicago. These

men and their associates undertook the contract to erect
the new capitol building in Austin and accept their compensation in land.   The three million acres were situated
in ten counties in the Panhandle, which suggested the
name X I T (ten in Texas) for the ranch. So much has
been disposed of that the X I T is no longer a significant
ranching proposition, for the remaining lands are in
scattered tracts.

One of the romantic ranches of the Staked Plain was
that of Colonel John Slaughter, who established and built
up the Slaughter Ranch of half a million acres.   He was
a native Texan, the son of a captain in General Houston's
army.   He entered the cattle business in the early '50s
by bringing less than one hundred head of Louisiana cattle into northwestern Texas and eventually became one
of the cattle kings and a millionaire.   But with his death
his ranch has dwindled.

The day of the imperial ranch seems to be passing
with the old-time ranchers themselves.   One feels like
heaving a sigh for it means the disappearance of a picturesque era.   The expansion of agriculture has absorbed
much of the former grazing lands and raised the value
of acreage to such an extent that the heirs are tempted
to break up their inheritance.   There are still a number of
ranches of two hundred thousand to a quarter of a million acres, and the motorist is reminded of boundaries
by the cattle guards in the highway, which are made by
placing old iron rails horizontally across the road, much
as railroads do. These do not interfere with motor
traffic and they do prevent cattle from straying off their
home preserves.   A number of these large ranches are
located in the "Big Bend" county of the Rio Grande.

In Armstrong County, in the Panhandle, and near the
Palo Duro Canyon, is the ranch established by the late

Charles Goodnight, another of the successful cattlemen of the old school. During his lifetime a part of his ranch presented the appearance of a zoo, for on it roamed the largest privately owned herd of bison in the world, about one hundred and sixty animals. He believed that he had solved the problem of this animal once threatened with extinction. Grazing on the fenced-in pastures could be seen a herd of strange-looking shaggy beeves. On the back of each was a noticeable hump, reminiscent of the buffalo that once wandered over those same plateaus in countless thousands. Some of them had white faces. These were neither buffalo nor were they cattle; they were hybrids developed from breeding together these two members of the great ox family, which includes the water buffalo, zebu and yak, and is closely related to the musk-ox. Upon these hybrids he bestowed the name cattalo. Those three-quarters buffalo strongly suggest the animal of the plains; those only one-fourth buffalo look more like domestic cattle. Although the animal in this last stage does not much resemble its wild ancestors, it does retain the desired characteristics, which are freedom from disease and ability to withstand the severe blizzards, and it will thrive on lean pastures where domestic cattle would starve.

Mr. Goodnight spent years in his efforts to develop his hobby and believed that he had solved the problem of cheap beef. He claimed that the cattalo retained the best qualities of both ancestors, for the flesh was equal to the best beef. An animal would provide one hundred and fifty pounds of meat more than the average steer. Because they required less food, less salt and less water, he believed they would flourish in arid regions where cattle find existence difficult. If this claim could be proved, the cattalo might prove a valuable development.

The history of the famous King Ranch near Corpus Christi is one of those tales that is stranger than fiction. It begins back in the time of the Mexican War. In the spring of 1846 General Zachary Taylor dispatched an aide up the Mississippi River to engage some practical steamboat men to assist him in transporting his troops to the Mexican border. Among those secured were Captain Mifflin Kennedy, commander of a river packet, and Richard King, a pilot. These two men, one as commander and the other as pilot, had charge of the transport which kept Taylor in touch with his base. After the war Mr. King for a time ran a small side-wheel steamer from Point Isabel to Brownsville and Matamoras, but business was not very prosperous. Deeply impressed by the future prospects of this remote region Kennedy and King acquired a wide stretch of mesquite and cactus land occupied only by a few Mexicans, who were not the most desirable citizens. It was part of the doubtful territory between the Rio Grande and Nueces rivers, on account of which, in part at least, the recent war was fought. On this prairie they laid out Santa Gertrudis Ranch. A steer for every ten acres was the best that could be maintained, and it was not long until they had their full quota.

When the two partners separated Mr. King retained Santa Gertrudis and Mr. Kennedy established La Parra Ranch adjoining. The holdings of the former associates stretched for a long distance along the Gulf Coast. La Parra is now included in Kennedy County, named after the founder, and stretches over some three hundred thousand acres. Although Mr. Kennedy died years ago and the land has been divided among the several heirs, La Parra is still operated as a unit and remains one of the important ranches of the Southwest.

Captain King, as he was generally called, was more than

a river navigator. The shipping business was uncertain and he visioned a great future for the cattle business. Land was very cheap. Sometimes two or three acres could be purchased for a single dollar. It was probably all the land was worth at that time, for transportation was so uncertain that the marketing of cattle when both animals and price were right was difficult. But Captain King was undaunted. He lived frugally and invested every spare dollar in more land. He saved money to buy more land to save more money to buy more land, and so on *ad infinitum*. When he died he owned almost a million and a half acres, which he left as a heritage to his widow.

The King Ranch is much smaller to-day than it was at its maximum. Eighty thousand acres were given to a railroad company to build its lines through the ranch, with the proviso that the company should establish its division headquarters and repair shops at the new town called Kingsville, only three miles from the ranch house. The town was laid out on a generous scale with wide streets and every modern improvement. The railroad company built repair shops and a splendid little hotel. Every deed contains a clause forbidding the sale of intoxicating liquors, which insures the sobriety of the citizens. The Texas College of Arts and Industries is located there, and some eight thousand people now have their homes in Kingsville. A couple of hundred thousand acres of the King Ranch have been sold to small ranchers and farmers. A new county was created, with Kingsville as the county seat, and named Kleberg County after Richard J. Kleberg, son-in-law of Richard King, who was for years the manager of the entire estate. But the King Ranch includes much more than Kleberg County, for it overflows into Nueces and Kennedy counties as well.

It was my privilege through a letter of introduction
to Mr. Kleberg to spend a day on Santa Gertrudis Ranch
and investigate an institution where farming and stock-
raising on a large scale have been reduced to a business.
There is as much system in the methods pursued here as
in the average manufacturing or mercantile enterprise.
Under the guidance of my host I was afforded every
opportunity to observe ranch life and see how such an
immense tract of land is administered. I did not see the
entire ranch, even though we travelled at high speed in a
high-powered car during the most of the day. The only
way one could view all the estate in one day would be
from an aeroplane, and the estate at that time did not
own one of those distance-killing contrivances. But the
main activities centre about the ranch house.

Hundreds of miles of barb wire were used in enclosing and partitioning the King Ranch. A field of a thousand acres is exceptional. Twenty, thirty and fifty
thousand acres is more common. Now a field of fifty
thousand acres, if perfectly square, would be almost nine
miles in each direction. The different species were segre-
gated. In one enclosure were Shorthorns, but Herefords
were most common. Their monotonous white faces
stared at you from every direction. There were hundreds
of Jerseys, which were used exclusively in the dairies.
In one field are kept calves (everything up to one year);
in another were two-year-olds. In addition there were
several thousand sheep and goats, as well as hundreds
of horses and mules, owned on the ranch. The weather
is so moderate that stock can run out all the year and
the salt breeze makes frequent salting unnecessary.

Santa Gertrudis was a beautiful sight that bright day
in April, and the picture remains vivid in memory. The
land, as level as a barn floor, was carpeted with a thick

setting of green grass, for most of it was virgin soil.
One's vision was limited only by the horizon. Daisies
and poppies, Texas bluebonnets and Indian blankets, yellow, purple and lavender flowers of species unknown to
me, dotted the ground in dense clusters. The result was
a variegated sheen of constantly changing colours. The
spring wild flowers were then in full bloom, and abundant
rains had brought them forth in unusual profusion.
Later on in the summer the prairie is sure to be sere and
brown. Windmills were outlined here and there on the
horizon, and herds of sleek cattle browsed contentedly
among the fragile flowers. A frightened rabbit was frequently aroused, and on a couple of occasions we saw a
sneaking coyote loping off in the distance. Coursing
after rabbits and coyotes, shooting quail and duck, hunting armadillos are among the diversions enjoyed on Santa
Gertrudis. The armoured armadillo is one of the curious
leftovers of a preceding age. It is protected as fully as
a land turtle. It is fully covered with a hard shell made
up of bony bucklers and polygonal plates into which it
withdraws its head and legs for protection. It is one of
the swiftest diggers among animals and is quite common
in portions of Texas. The shell is fashioned into various
articles.

The management of the King Ranch is constantly
endeavouring to intensify its value. They are always
studying how to improve the stock. Although the rainfall exceeds twenty inches annually, it is not evenly distributed throughout the year and there are times when
feeding is advantageous. Hence they have increased the
acreage under cultivation and erected dozens of great silos
as food reservoirs in which to keep the feed. These
loom up in groups of from three to five like the turrets
built for defense in medieval times. Thousands of acres

have been cleared of the mesquite, that low bush or tree which once covered almost the entire ranch. Mexicans are usually employed, and many of them were then engaged in this work.

"We have three hundred Mexicans at work here cleaning up the brush," said the superintendent. "They come to us half starved, having been driven out of Mexico by the political troubles. We could not see them starve and I never turned one away. If you have a loaf of bread it is your duty to share it. So I give them work here, and it is sometimes touching to see their gratitude. They work faithfully too, and I am glad to be able to give them something to do." Those that I saw looked happy and contented even though they lived in tents or improvised homes fashioned from the brush. They were happy no doubt that they had found a land where revolutions are unknown and there is no danger of conscription into the army.

A splendid mansion, worthy to be the abode of a prince, was built on the King Ranch a score of years ago before the family had separated. When the old ranch house burned it gave an opportunity for Mrs. Henrietta King, who survived her husband many years, to construct a palatial new home of which she had dreamed for years. Eminent architects were employed to draw the plans. Famous artists and decorators were called from distant cities. These men came out to these broad plains to design a home and decorations that would befit the setting. The predominating architectural effect is Spanish-Moorish, and indeed it is a magnificent home that was erected here on an elevation slightly above the general level of the land, which renders it conspicuous for many miles in every direction. At a distance it sometimes looks almost like a phantom castle floating in the glassy translucence of a mirage. On a nearer approach it loses much of this fairy resemblance because of the great size, but it is still glaringly white. In this great manor house hospitality is of the Southern type, broad and generous. The visitor is welcomed at the long family table. Remote as the ranch is the world comes to it, at least as much as the family cares for.

The instructions to the architects were to avoid elaborate ornamentation and gingerbread effects. On one side is a terrace one hundred feet long and on the others are great porches. There are eighteen bedrooms, each of which is connected with a bath. The reception rooms are massive, and the dining-room is large enough for a banquet hall. Every room in the house has a fireplace, a steam radiator and an inter-communicating telephone. There is an automatic electric elevator to reach the upper floors, as well as every electrical contrivance for cooking, dishwashing and laundering that inventive genius has been able to supply. Nothing has been omitted to provide comfort for the family and their guests and convenience for the help.

The day of the million-acre ranch has at last passed in Texas, for changes have recently come to the King Ranch. For ten years after the death of the widow a dozen years ago the entire holdings were operated as a unit under a trusteeship. At the end of that time two groups of heirs each received about two hundred thousand acres. The remainder, about eight hundred and fifty thousand acres, and including the mansion house, is under the control of the Kleberg family and incorporated as the King Ranch. But it is still a sizable farm, considerably larger than Little Rhody, where more than six hundred thousand people dwell. So there is plenty of room to work and play and enjoy yourself in general.

CHAPTER XIX

TEXAS COMES TO THE FRONT

THE one hundred years just ended witnessed a greater transformation in our mode of living than any equal period in the world's history. Especially is that true in the matter of communications and transportation, each of which has been wholly revolutionized. The telegraph and telephone came first, but to-day, by the use of the ether waves, we can span the earth with the human voice in a few seconds. A century ago the steam railroad was in its infancy and the mechanism exceedingly crude. The speed was slow and the coaches uncomfortable. The first railroad west of the Alleghanies was just being built with wooden rails. Although improvements have constantly been made until railroad travel has reached a high state of luxury, safety and convenience, the railroads are already facing a terrific competition from the gasoline-propelled vehicles, which paved highways have made possible.

The existence of petroleum has been known for many centuries through seepages of the oil in various places. Its value as an illuminant was realized and it was looked upon as a specific for many ills to which the human body is heir, being marketed as "seneca oil" and under other designations. But it was not until 1859 when a well was drilled in Oil City, Pennsylvania, which produced a few barrels of oil daily, that this foul-smelling liquid was discovered in sufficient quantities to be of any great com-

322

THE NEW INTERNATIONAL BRIDGE AT LAREDO

THE SKYLINE OF DALLAS

mercial value. Other wells followed and the petroleum industry began in a small way. Within a few years "coal oil" began to replace other illuminants because of its cheapness. The great Standard Oil Company was born and popularized its product. New uses were discovered for its by-product. The invention of the internal-combustion engine stimulated the demand until the Pennsylvania field proved entirely too small to supply it. Then began the search for new oil territory. In Ohio, West Virginia and Indiana oil pools were found and the hunt extended farther west. In Kansas and Oklahoma rich discoveries were made, and the prospectors finally turned their attention to the great state of Texas. Their hopes were not high, for Texas had never been regarded as a mineralized state. Soil and climate were considered its only assets.

As was their custom bands of Spanish adventurers had wended their weary way over the greater part of Texas in their futile search for

> "Gold! Gold! Gold! Gold!
> Bright and yellow! Hard and cold!"

The promising prospects of agriculture and homes in a new land had little appeal for the Castilian caballeros. They were unlike the Puritans and Cavaliers, who settled on the Atlantic Coast. They were unwilling to labour with their hands. They wanted only easy wealth with which they might return to their beloved Spain and build the castles of which they had dreamed. Although Spain held at least nominal possession of Texas for almost three hundred years, the total Spanish population at the time of the Mexican Revolution was only a few thousands. Mexico and Peru held far greater attraction, for here there were the coveted gold and silver and an unresisting native population who were easily enslaved and forced to perform the menial tasks. In Texas the natives generally remained hostile. They were unwilling to cultivate the soil for the invaders and made even life uncertain for them.

No one even dreamed that beneath the surface of Texas there was stored a mineral wealth far greater than the deposits of gold and silver in Mexico and Peru, so eagerly coveted by the grandees of Spain. The brief Mexican rule came and went, the Republic of Texas arose and disappeared and Uncle Sam had been in control for half a century before this fact was known. In any event this "black gold" would have had little value at an earlier date, certainly not in the seventeenth and eighteenth centuries. It was not until the increasing use of automobiles and the replacing of coal as fuel by crude oil in steam engines led to the frantic search for new sources of supply of this volatile mineral that the real wealth of Texas was discovered. Oil has been found in more than one-third of the two hundred and fifty-four counties. Houses are now heated, food cooked and factories operated as far away as Chicago, Detroit and Indianapolis by gas produced by the same wells or wells in the same districts. As a result wealth has poured into Texas as well as a constant stream of new citizens, who remain and increase the census taker's work. It already ranks fifth among the states in population.

It was not until 1896 that oil was discovered in paying quantity in Texas. This first successful well was located near Corsicana and was quickly followed by others, which brought prosperity to this little city. But these wells were not "gushers," so that the excitement aroused by the discovery quickly subsided. The world at large did not become greatly interested, although it did stimulate some prospecting.

In January, 1901, the famous Lucas Well, of the Spindle Top field near Beaumont, "blew in" with a roar that reverberated all over the United States and even beyond. Oil spouted forth at the rate of seventy thousand barrels every twenty-four hours, a production heretofore unheard of. Special trains carried thousands of the curious from remote points to see the unusual spectacle, and with them came speculators, swindlers and workers. The little town was filled to overflowing. A wild orgy of leasing and drilling now followed. A ring of dry holes proved that this pool was spread over an area of only about two hundred acres, and this small space was soon fairly covered with derricks, at least twelve hundred in all. Everyone wanted to drill there, and fancy prices were paid for space enough on which to locate a well. Millions of barrels of oil were marketed each year besides the large amount of wastage in the first few months. More than one hundred million barrels have been produced in Spindle Top and the end is not yet, for many of the wells are still pumped.

Texas was now definitely set down as promising oil territory, and prospectors began the unending search for new fields. Expert geologists, or those who classed themselves as such, travelled over much of the state looking for indications of geological strata that meant oil-bearing sands might be found beneath. Although they had some success, the results were not very satisfactory. The surface indications were generally disappointing. By far the most of the producing fields, and the largest of all, may be credited to that strange individual generally known as the "wildcatter." "Wildcatting" is a term generally applied to drilling in a section never before tested. The "wildcatter" is frequently more liberally endowed with that happy quality called hope than with scientific knowledge. He frequently possesses a persuasive tongue. He succeeds in interesting a few speculative friends or a community in some location, which to him appears promising, and then proceeds to sink down a hole into mother earth. The majority of these efforts result in failure, but every now and then some fortunate driller strikes a "gusher" and his own fortune, as well as that of his associates, is assured. It is not difficult as a rule to get sufficient backing from owners of land, who are generally willing to take a little chance on the prospect of reaping a rich reward. It proves that there is a little bit of the gambler in much of the human race.

The magic of oil has had more to do with the complete transformation and remarkable growth of the Lone Star State than any other one influence. The phenomenal development of one oil field is largely a duplication of the others. The "gold rushes" of earlier days were no comparison with the hectic conditions that immediately follow a newly discovered oil field to-day. The reasons are the quick dissemination of news and rapid transportation by railway, automobile and even aeroplane. Whereas a few hundred miners and adventurers might trickle into a new gold centre within several weeks or even months after the discovery, by horse and mule over the rough mountains and forbidding deserts, thousands will now gather at the scene of excitement within a few days. Among these will be speculators, operators, adventurers, builders, gamblers, drillers and men skilled in every phase of oil well operations. The men are generally eager, somewhat excited and more or less happy, but their women folks sometimes look anything else but cheerful. A town or even an embryo city will spring up like magic, for building materials are quickly assembled now even out on the treeless prairies of West Texas. The railroads and trucks see to that.

The development of the extensive oil field north and east of Amarillo is very typical of the excitement and rush following the discovery of the liquid mineral called petroleum, in a new location. The Panhandle was then an untried region, and the surface indications were not encouraging to the experts. But some hopeful "wild-catters" determined to put down a test well. When they reached the oil-bearing sands it proved to be a "gusher," making between two and three thousand barrels a day.

No sooner had the news spread to the outside world than the rush began by automobile, truck and wagon, for the nearest railroad was thirty miles away. This was in 1925. Borger immediately sprang into being. For a little while it was largely a tent city and many slept beneath blankets without other protection. Then all kinds of inharmonious and ramshackle buildings, frame stores, brick stores, corrugated iron storage houses and shacks of every description stretched out and became the two-mile-long main street. A hot-dog stand arose here and a chili parlour there. A drug store, a grocery, a hardware store, a bank, a barber shop, a beauty parlour occupied the store rooms as they were completed. A newspaper disseminated the news. The so-called hotels and rooming houses did a rushing business. The beds were occupied in relays of eight hours. The sheets were still warm from the last occupant when another weary body crept between them to secure some much-needed rest. Borger became a city of twenty-five thousand almost over night. Derricks arose in every direction. Two railroad companies engaged in a race to see which one could reach there first with the steel rails.

Borger passed through a "wild" period. Every disreputable element that followed the tide into the gold camps of Bret Harte's days found their way into the new oil town. Although prohibition was in effect, liquor was sold openly for a time. The thirsty one could rest his foot on a real brass rail. Some men carried guns openly in defiance of the law. Then followed the inevitable result, there were a few killings. The local authorities were either helpless or incompetent. A few rangers entered quietly and order was restored almost as quickly as disorder had arisen. The open saloon vanished, gambling houses were less conspicuous, the dance halls quieted down, and Borger became the law-and-order city that it is to-day. There may be fewer people, but they are a substantial citizenry.

A score of years ago the greatest oil activity in Texas centred about Ranger, Breckenridge, Caddo and Eastland, about one hundred miles west of Fort Worth. For a few years millions of barrels of the crude product were marketed annually. A few men became millionaires. Towns sprang up as if touched by Aladdin and his wonderful lamp. It was another of those chance discoveries which startle the world every now and then.

Although no petroleum of consequence had been encountered in this locality prior to 1917, a coal company operating there had come upon slight evidences of oil in its search for new veins of coal a few years earlier. When a test hole which they sank to a depth of one thousand feet flowed a few hundred barrels a day, considerable excitement immediately arose and the country was quickly overrun with men seeking leases. Derricks soon dotted the horizon. Most of the wells were "dusters," as a dry hole is termed. Only a few proved profitable and the field began to be looked upon as a failure.

The reason was that the first drillers did not go deep enough to reach the oil-bearing sands, which here are at a depth of thirty-five hundred feet or more from the surface. But when, early in 1917, a well "blew in" with an initial flow of seventeen hundred barrels in twenty-four hours, excitement reached fever heat. The little town of Ranger overflowed with a seething mob of restless humans estimated at forty thousand or more.

The coal company, which had shrewdly leased several thousand acres on most favourable terms, was able to sell more than half of its holdings at four thousand dollars an acre, thus reaping a tremendous fortune without the trouble of producing it. The purchasers were generally old established companies, whose managers knew values, and not greenhorns. The peak of production was reached in 1919, when more than twenty-two million barrels of oil were brought to the surface, an almost incredible quantity. Nine years later the production had dropped to two and a fourth millions, which is about the normal rate of decline. So many wells tap the same reservoir that the flow ceases and it is necessary to resort to pumping.

Every great oil discovery is interesting, with its tales of sudden wealth and the birth of new cities. Wichita Falls is one of them. The Wink rush in Winkler County is another, but only one other will be related. To the uninitiated it always seems strange that new oil fields are frequently found in territory that has been prospected over for years. It proves conclusively that scientific methods of locating oil deposits have not yet been perfected. An example of this is the opening of a richly producing area in East Texas less than a decade ago, and not far from earlier exploitations. This was in Rusk County, and the discovery was made by another "wildcatter," an Oklahoman by the name of Joiner. After purchasing some leases in this county from promoters his capital was so limited that it was several years before he was able to begin actual drilling operations. The large oil companies had not overlooked this field, but their experts had classed it as unpromising. Here it was difficult for Joiner to finance drilling operations, which are expensive when wells must be sunk to a depth of three thousand feet or more. One well in Texas is producing at nine thousand feet, the deepest in the state.

A second-hand outfit was finally assembled and actual drilling of the first well was begun in 1927. I say "first well," because success did not come until the third well had been completed. A "wildcatter" must be an optimist or his courage would fail him. The first well reached a depth of three thousand feet when the drill stuck and it was abandoned. The second well met with the same fate. Sometimes Mr. Joiner had not money enough to pay for necessary supplies or food for the workers. The lease expired, but he succeeded in renewing it. Two long, weary, trying years passed by. And then, just when everybody was beginning to lose faith, the miracle happened. Strange sounds were heard, which became a gurgle, and oil spurted forth. A new and rich field was recorded. Another millionaire joined the ranks of the super-rich.

The town of Joinerville arose. A forest of derricks sprang up. Pipe lines were brought in. The field expanded until it proved to be one of the largest in Texas. Numerous other towns were born. Existing towns became little cities. But Joinerville itself only flourished for a few years before the dwindling process began. Farmers once more turned their attention to the growing of cotton and corn, but the oil revenue had paid off their mortgages, built new homes for many and purchased fine automobiles. Their royalties gradually diminshed, but they were now independent and no longer feared the sheriff. The "black gold" still overflows from some wells and is pumped from hundreds of others in the rich East Texas field.

The opening of the great East Texas oil field, at a time when the market was already glutted with oil, almost demoralized the entire industry. The price dropped until it sold as low as twenty cents a barrel. Voluntary agreements for the curtailment of production proved impossible. New wells in this field were coming in at the rate of five hundred a month. Everyone wanted money. The Railroad Commission, which has control of oil production in Texas, issued a decree of prorating by which the output of each well was curtailed, but this only aroused the opposition of the producers, and did not prove effective. Governor Sterling finally established martial law and ordered the national guardsmen into the field in 1931, and it was kept under these rigid regulations for a year. Proration is still in effect, but the opposition is strong in some quarters and there is believed to be much evasion.

We have been so accustomed to look upon Texas exclusively as an agricultural and pastoral state that it is difficult to change our viewpoint. Cotton, which was for years king, is now secondary to oil in monetary value and, although it requires much more labour to produce a dollar's worth of cotton than oil, the latter industry probably gives employment to as many people, directly and indirectly, as cotton. Oil has also been responsible in a large measure for the rapid increase in population and material improvements. Sixty per cent of the exports from Texas ports are oil and oil products. The enormous taxes paid by the oil companies have benefited every political subdivision. What would the world have done without the three billion barrels of oil of forty-two gallons each which have been contributed by Texas? It leads all competitors, with California and Oklahoma falling far behind into second and third places respectively. Texas has yielded more than one-third of the total production of the United States and about one-quarter for the entire world.

Every section of Texas has responded to the stimulus of oil. Many of the smaller cities may be classed as purely oil towns, for their birth, growth and continued prosperity are due to the presence of this "liquid gold." Beaumont and Wichita Falls would come under this classification. Port Arthur and Corpus Christi largely owe their expansion as ports to this same magic influence. Even Houston, Dallas and Fort Worth and, in a lesser degree, San Antonio, must credit much of their affluence to oil. They became the home of the oil companies, refineries and other activities connected with the industry. And with oil must be associated natural gas, which is piped for hundreds of miles to consumers in distant cities, all of which brings dollars into the pockets of thrifty Texans. Carbon black, used by tire companies on the tread of tires to give them longer life, is made from gas in many places. Unfortunately much gas is wasted, but this strange commodity is produced by the billions of cubic feet, so that a little wastage is hardly noticed.

In no part of Texas is the predominance of oil so evident as around and between Port Arthur and Beaumont. Here and in the adjacent counties are a score of producing fields, and pipe lines bring the crude product from every other section of Texas. More than a half dozen of our very largest refineries are located here. Thousands of acres are covered with capacious steel storage tanks and are known as "tank farms." There are many factories for the manufacturing of everything that can be made from petroleum. And these products find their way to the remotest parts of the world. Great tankers will be seen at the docks in both ports loading up with crude oil and gasoline, to be transported to countries less fortunate than our own.

It is not only possible but very probable that general manufacturing will increase in Texas in the future. At the present time not over two per cent of the raw materials produced within the state are fabricated into usable form within its boundaries. When one sees the industrialization of such states as North Carolina and Georgia, he wonders why Texas has been overlooked. Cotton is here and the cheapest of all fuels, natural gas, is available everywhere in unlimited quantities. The population of approximately six millions are in themselves a large consuming public. An abundance of labour is available. These conditions lead one to believe that the next few decades will see a remarkable increase in industry.

Texas is still an agricultural empire. The rural population outnumbers the urban. What does the diversion of a few million acres mean in a state possessing almost one hundred and seventy millions of such units? The figures are staggering. The production of this vast surface can only be expressed in superlative terms. Up to a score of years ago Texas was essentially a one-crop state, since cotton accounted for about three-fourths of the total value of all crops. Now there is greater diversification. The wheat, corn and rice crops reach large figures also. But cotton still leads. Although it has been grown successfully in all but sixteen counties, the bulk of the cotton is produced in a comparatively few counties; in the "black belt"; the Panhandle and southern half of the Gulf Coast plains. It is the most valuable crop grown in any one state; as many as four to five million bales having been marketed in Texas in one year. To-day it produces from one-third to one-fourth of the cotton grown in the United States, and about one-fifth of the world's crop. Most of it is exported, very little of it being manufactured into fabrics within the State.

After oil and cotton the most important industry in Texas is the raising of live stock for food and traction. Although there will undoubtedly be a large increase in the acreage devoted to crops in the future, there are still many millions of acres that may be classed as non-plowable because of scanty rainfall, rough terrain or other unfavourable conditions, which are best suited to the raising of live stock in the simplest way; that is, leaving the animals largely dependent upon nature's bounty rather than feeding them harvested forage. This is true of Southwestern Texas, in the Big Bend and Davis Mountain region, the broken territory in North Texas east of Fort Worth and on the Edwards Plateau south of San Angelo. This may always remain a land of large ranches. This range stock will never have the value per animal of those constantly fed, as they are in Iowa and Illinois, but the cost of production is so much less that they are profitable. The winters are mild and the animals do not need to be sheltered.

Texas leads every other state in the union in the number of its live stock. It is only in swine that she lags, although one would naturally think the state well adapted to the raising of the porkers. There are more than six million cattle on the farms and ranches, which is just about one-tenth of the cattle population of the United States. Placed four abreast they would form a solid column reaching from New York to San Francisco. The white-faced Herefords predominate, but there are also many

Shorthorns and Jerseys. Some of the ranchers are experimenting with the hump-backed Brahmans by crossing them with the domestic stock, and they seem well pleased with the result. The Asiatic stock are freer from disease. Considering the number of cattle milk products have been neglected until recently, for the rancher has never paid any attention to this source of revenue. Calves run with their mothers as long as they wish. Of course, the milk production of a range cow would be small in comparison with a carefully selected dairy cow.

Texas sheep outnumber cattle by a few hundred thousand, which is about one-seventh of these woolly creatures belonging to Uncle Sam. The three million angora goats are several times as many as will be found in all the other states together. Hence the production of both wool and mohair is very large. One in twelve of American mules is Texas owned, or about one million of these long-eared stubborn animals in all. They outnumber horses by about four to three.

The State of the Lone Star did not really reach her stride until the beginning of the twentieth century, and ever since then she has been springing one surprise after another upon the rest of the country. The first great awakening was the discovery of oil in almost unlimited quantities and over a very wide area. The sinking of artesian wells transformed millions of acres, which had heretofore been deficient in water supply, into crop production. The development of dry farming methods opened up thousands of square miles of land to agriculture that were heretofore regarded as fit only for ranching. The expansion of irrigation on the lower Rio Grande, where a semi-tropical climate prevails, which introduced a dangerous rival to the citrus industry of California and Florida, is another of the unexpected and astonishing developments in this most surprising State.

What will be the next surprise that Texas has in store for us? Not being a prophet or the son of a prophet, this writer does not venture to predict. It is his belief, however, that the day of surprises is not yet over. The State is so immense in area, its resources are so stupendous, its climate and soil are so varied, the Texans are so aggressive and versatile, that the potentialities are practically unlimited. If those of this generation could come back one hundred years hence, when the Lone Star State will be celebrating her second centennial, they would probably be more astonished over her progress than we are now in this year of our Lord one thousand nine hundred and thirty-six.

THE END

BIBLIOGRAPHY

ALLEN, J. TAYLOR: Early Pioneer Days in Texas.
BANCROFT, H. H.: History of North Mexican States and Texas.
BARKER, EUGENE C.: The Austin Papers.
BARKER, EUGENE C.: Life of S. F. Austin.
BARKER, EUGENE C.: Mexico and Texas 1821 to 1835.
BENJAMIN, GILBERT: Germans in Texas.
BIGGRES, D. H.: German Pioneers in Texas.
BIZZELL, WM. B.: Rural Texas.
BLACKBURN, J. K. P.: Reminiscences of the Terry Texas Rangers.
BOLTON, HERBERT E.: Spanish Exploration in the Southwest.
BROWN, JOHN H.: History of Texas.
BROWN, JOHN H.: Life and Times of Henry Smith, the First American Governor of Texas.
BROWN, MARY M.: Condensed History of Texas.
BRYAN, GEORGE S.: Sam Houston.
CARTER, W. T. G.: Story of Texas.
CASTENEDA, CARLOS E.: The Mexican Side of the Texas Revolution.
CAVE, W. W.: Lone Star Ballads.
CLARK, JOSEPH L.: New History of Texas.
CRANE, WM. C.: Life of Sam Houston.
CREEL, GEORGE: Sam Houston Colossus in Buckskin.
DAVIS, M. E. M.: Under Six Flags.
DESHIELDS, J. T.: Border Wars of Texas.
DIXON, SAM H.: The Man Who Made Texas Free.
DUVAL, JOHN C.: Early Times in Texas.
EDWARDS, FRANK S.: A Campaign in New Mexico with Colonel Doniphan.
ELLIOTT, SARAH B.: Sam Houston.
FORREST, EARL B.: Missions and Pueblos of Old Southwest.
GAMBRELL, H. P.: Mirabeau B. Lamar.
GARRISON, GEORGE P.: Texas Diplomatic Correspondence.
GERALD, FLORENCE M.: The Days of the Republic.
GILLETT, JAMES B.: Six Years with the Texas Rangers.
GREEN, THOMAS G.: Journal of the Texas Expedition against Mier.
HALEY, J. E.: The X.I.T. Ranch of Texas.
HARTER, HARRY: East Texas Oil Parade.
JOHNSON, BARKER AND WINKLER: A History of Texas and Texans.
JONES, ANSON: Republic of Texas.
KENDALL, GEORGE W.: Narrative of the Santa Fé Expedition.
LLOYD, EVERETT: Law West of the Pecos.
MAILLARD, N. DORAN: History of Republic of Texas. (1842)
MORPHIS, J. M.: History of Texas.
OLMSTEAD, F. L.: Journey Through Texas. (1857)
PARKER, A. A.: A Trip to the West and Texas. (1835)
RAHT, C. G.: Romance of the Davis Mountains and Big Bend Country.
RAINES, C. W.: Six Decades of Texas. (1900)
RAMSDELL, CHARLES W.: Reconstruction in Texas.
TAYLOR, ALLEN S.: Early Pioneer Days in Texas.
THRALL, HOMER S.: History of Texas. (1876)
WEBB, WALTER P.: The Texas Rangers.
YOAKUM, H.: History of Texas.